STRONG BREW

STRONG BREW

One Man's Prelude to Change

Claude Saks

HEARTSFIRE BOOKS

AN IMPRINT OF HAMPTON ROADS PUBLISHING COMPANY

Cover design by Marjoram Productions

For information write:
Heartsfire Books
c/o Hampton Roads Publishing Company, Inc.
134 Burgess Lane
Charlottesville, VA 22902
Or call: (804)296-2772
FAX: (804)296-5096
e-mail: hrpc@mail.hamptonroadspub.com
Web site: http://www.hamptonroadspub.com

If you are unable to order this book from your local
bookseller, you may order directly from the publisher.
Quantity discounts for organizations are available.
Call 1-800-766-8009, toll-free.

ISBN 1-57174-050-3

10 9 8 7 6 5 4 3 2 1

Printed on acid-free paper in Canada

Dedication:
To all my relations

Contents

Acknowledgments and Disclaimers

This story is true to the best of my recollection; certain names have been left in code, which we used in our business, to keep the privacy of the individuals. Conversations have been reconstructed to give dynamism and reality to the story but cannot be interpreted as verbatim, as much time has elapsed and my memory can only paraphrase at best.

I acknowledge with thanks Commodity Trend Service for the use of the monthly coffee trading chart and the Chicago Board of Trade for the pictures of the trading pits, which appear on the back cover.

I would like to thank the various people who have helped with suggestions and edits—Iris Hawkins, Clark Kimball, Emer Featherstone, Karen Moye, and particularly Steven Nickeson and Kathy Grotz. I acknowledge with much appreciation Sara Held, my editor, who did such an outstanding job grasping the issues and denouements of my story and prodded me to expose them. And special thanks to Oliver Beaudette, who kept the manuscript in workable form through the many computer revisions.

Lastly, and most importantly, I acknowledge my wife Bette with great thanks for her patience and understanding and for having lived with all my turbulence.

Introduction

*"One must harbor chaos to give birth
to a dancing star."*

—Nietzsche

This story is a prequel to my previous book *Inescapable Journey* and, therefore, goes back to the energies of commerce, of power, of money, and of men in confrontation. You might say this tale is about the descendants of Martians that John Gray so eloquently talks about in his book *Men are from Mars and Women are from Venus*. My story is as much for women who are interested in understanding what drives the men in their lives as it is a mirror of change and hope for mankind. Before commodities, I was in engineering and construction. My favorite saying at that time was "If you're going to build something larger than an outhouse, you'd better put a decent foundation under it." My adventures here explore the heavy concrete foundations of men in a fast-paced commodity world where anything goes. Yet these high-voltage energies lead to change, to self-awareness and a search for a greater understanding of the connectedness of life.

This story is a play about man's relationships—father and son, partners, competitors, and co-workers, all intertwined with explosive emotional issues of ego and selflessness, fear and joy, envy and encouragement, winning and losing, as well as many others. This play of men's issues has the backdrop staging or props of business—

fast-moving, aggressive business in commodities staged from New York to Zaire, Burundi, Cameroon, Indonesia, Europe, and back to New York. My first two chapters give you, the reader, an understanding as to how I came to be what I was. I say "I was" because as the story moves forward you will see and experience how I tackled the world of business and eventually came to understand myself better and thereby changed my attitude toward relationships with other men and the world.

In retrospect, my successes then and later came because I "engaged the energy," as my spiritual teacher would say. The understanding that everything in life is energy, part of the life force, would form the basis for my subsequent spiritual search.

And so this book is about men's issues, particularly in business, and the prodding fingers of Spirit. My intention is to speak to all men and women who are prepared to look at themselves and their habits and are willing to venture into the realm of change and love.

1

Early History

Where do you live, son?

The beach in Amagansett, New York, was deserted at midweek, and the sun beat down on the sand as the waves rumbled in their rhythmic cadence of ebb and flow. A light southwest breeze left me cool while my emotions were definitely heated. I opened my father's diary.

Two and a half years had elapsed since my father's death in January of 1978, and, although I had started to understand myself, I was still struggling to understand our tumultuous relationship. His diary was written in French during the outbreak of World War II and perhaps would give me some clues to the start of my own journey. We had fought in offices, hotels, planes and jungles from New York to Kinshasa, Douala, Geneva, and back. I was still angry with him and could not speak about him without bitterness and malevolence. I had not resolved the turmoil of our lives together or its meaning for my own life and growth; my gnosis and spiritual search were only just starting.

Europe, 1940

The first entry in my father's diary, dated May 9, 1940, describes an evening of fun and family celebration in honor of moving to a nice apartment in downtown Brussels, Belgium. My father was 29, my mother 26, and I was two and a half. My father's coffee roasting factory was doing well, and he could now afford to rent this small apartment in a new building. He recorded that this intimate gathering, consisting of my mother's parents, Isidore (my father's father), and my father's sister Denise, who was 25, regrettably broke up at midnight. On May 10, he noted that he was awakened by *a bruit assourdisant*, a deafening noise, at four-thirty in the morning. As his mind cleared from sleep, he realized that the sound was the pounding of Belgian antiaircraft guns. At that moment, a bomb fell on the building across the street, *aneantissant* (literally "abolishing, wiping out") the structure and all its occupants. My father rushed my mother and me to the cellar, then rushed back up to turn on radio and gather clothes. Announcement: "Belgium is at war with Germany."

Between bombardments, my parents and I careened in my father's Citroen to the modern bomb shelter at my grandparents' home.

My father communicated with his father. A great discussion ensued. Grandfather Saks wanted to leave Belgium that same day. My father hesitated, as my mother's parents intended to remain. Isidore prevailed—this family was Jewish and the fact that my mother was Catholic would not have helped them if Belgium was overrun by the Nazis; and Isidore was the largest finished diamond dealer in Europe.

Isidore went to the bank and withdrew from the vault a hoard of diamonds and jewels. I subsequently learned that they were then hidden in the oil pan of his large Cadillac. My aunt Denise was to be his driver, as Isidore did not drive and did not want to be encumbered with the chauffeur. He lent my aunt's car, a Ford convertible coupe, to the general manager of his company, who was stuck in Brussels, and agreed that they would meet in Bordeaux, France, if feasible. After rushing all day—my mother packing clothes, my father giving power of attorney and saying goodbye to his factory managers—we headed for the French border in the two cars, Cadillac and Citroen. Isidore's and Denise's visas were in order, but my father's and mother's were not, and they were refused passage to France. Isidore and Denise decided to remain with Father and Mother to try and help them resolve the situation. Three days elapsed. The family watched convoys of French and English troops pour across the Belgium-French border. The Luftwaffe was continually strafing. My father related that for my protection I was pinned down under my mother in a ditch. I have vague recollections of her fear as she trembled over me and at the same time of being suffocated by her body pressing against my face.

At this point I put down the diary and went for a swim. I reflected on the tone of my father's diary. His words throughout were completely matter-of-fact and betrayed no sense of the terror he and the family must have experienced. I continued reading.

Everyone was exhausted. All the hotels had been requisitioned as hospitals, and my father noted that we were sleeping in the cars. He related that on the third day Denise found a friend who helped obtain the proper papers to pass into France. The family headed for Bordeaux and the home of our cousin, who was one of the senators in the French Assembly.

Again I reflected on my father's account as I bathed in the sun. I seldom heard him praise his own father while I was growing up, but I knew he considered Isidore a grand old-world gentleman who liked fine wines, food, and furniture. I remembered him always surrounded by beautiful things. A new light was being shed. My grandfather had been a very erudite man who spoke five languages and ran a large business; he also had great clarity of vision during the crucial moments at the outset of war. Here was a man who had an enormous amount to lose by leaving his business. I don't believe it was obvious in May of 1940 what atrocities the Nazis were about to perpetrate on the Jewish people and the world at large. My grandfather on my mother's side stayed in Belgium and survived, being Catholic, by keeping a low profile. I also reflected that in my father's diary there was little mention of me except for the fact that I was protected by my mother during the strafing. How did my parents handle a two-and-a-half-year-old under extreme conditions? The tenseness of the situation pervades my father's account, yet at the same time he elaborates on the decent meals he had along the way and the mannerisms and behavior of authorities as well as the many acquaintances he ran into, taking time to note their social position. I was getting a sense of his snootiness or his own lack of self-worth from these concerns. His feelings, and those of family and other people he encounters, are not expressed. His nervousness was obvious but he did not express anger, fear, or repulsion even while seeing truckloads of wounded French and English soldiers brought to the makeshift hotel hospitals. I read on.

The family temporarily settled in Bordeaux with our cousins. My aunt Denise reconnected with the people who borrowed her car and took it back. The decision was made to put my grandfather's Cadillac in a garage for safekeeping after retrieving the diamonds and jewelry; it was never to be seen again. Denise's Ford used less gas, and she had joined the Belgian Red Cross before the invasion and therefore had a special Red Cross emblem on her car's grille. During these tense times the French government bureaucracy was disorganized, with directions and orders being continually changed and countermanded; her Red Cross emblem permitted them, many times, to move more freely without question.

My father noted the 28th of May as the most memorable and unforgettable day of the war. (Needless to say, he had no idea what was to follow.) This was the day the king of Belgium surrendered with the entire Belgian army to the Germans. In one fell swoop, a wide corridor was split open between the French and English armies, and the Hun rushed in. This day was to remain fixed in my father's memory. He was unable to understand this most inappropriate gesture, "Ce geste si mal approprié," by the king. I was curious about the formalities of his language.

By the 1st of June, the British evacuated 350,000 men out of Dunkirk, leaving all their matériel behind. Belgians and Belgian cars were personae non grata in France, and we became the target of many insults and experienced more than our share of difficulties. My father recommended that the family obtain visas for Portugal or the U.S.A. and leave France. Isidore and the French senator called him a defeatist and insisted that the French Army would hold. Father noted that on June 4 I came down with a major asthma attack and my temperature went up to 101 degrees. A doctor was called and hot chest poultices were applied, as it appeared that bronchitis was present as well. My father brought mechanical toys from town and the family spoiled me while I was sick. This was the first tender entry in my father's diary.

June 5: The German army continued to advance and the radio became more pessimistic.

June 8: My father had an asthma attack and got a shot to calm him down. My mother nursed both of us.

June 16: Father noted that my temperature was now 102, and they were continuing the hot poultices.

June 17: The radio announced that General Pètin was the new President of France and that he was asking for an armistice with Germany. Father couldn't believe the news. Finally the entire family decided to leave France.

June 18: My grandfather wanted to eat a proper meal at a hotel in Bordeaux; since he didn't drive, Denise went with him. He reprimanded her because her car was dirty and insisted that it be washed. There was a garage next to the hotel, so the car could be washed while they had lunch. Afterwards they went back to pick up the car and by coincidence met Mr. Fernando de Cunha, an old friend of grandfather's, a Portuguese who had lived most of his life in Belgium. He insisted that everyone should leave France immediately. Isidore explained that it was impossible to get a Portuguese visa, or any other for that matter. De Cunha reassured them that he knew everyone at the consulate and could arrange the visas. The only problem was that his car was also in the garage to be fixed, and the prospects didn't look good.

Denise and my grandfather took him in the clean Ford to the Portuguese consulate, and within forty-eight hours visas were obtained for the entire family. Fernando crossed the borders of Spain and Portugal with grandfather and Denise in the Ford and my parents and me following in the Citroen. By the 26th of June, the family had installed itself in a small hotel in Estoril, not far from Lisbon.

Grandfather made a few diamond trades to obtain the local currency, the *escudo*. While depositing the jewels in a Lisbon bank vault, he made his introduction to the bank president, who informed him that many diamond shipments that were destined for France had been redirected to his bank for safekeeping until the end of hostilities. He showed my grandfather the shipments, and Isidore recognized several as his own that had been lost in transit. He reclaimed them and advised Lloyds of London of the status of the other shipments. Lloyds asked him to sell them for their account and paid him a 10% commission. The family continued to be financially secure.

Grandfather and Father appealed to the American Embassy in the hope of obtaining emigration visas to the U.S.A. They were informed it was not possible. The decision was then made to try to go to the Union of South Africa, where Grandfather had a partner in the diamond business; but, again, it was impossible to get visas. The partner recommended that we move to Lorenzo Marques in Mozambique, thus facilitating the paperwork.

Interspersed throughout the account are notes about my continued asthma attacks and the various hot poultices applied to my chest. Father's diary also described at great length the various Belgian expatriates they met and the wonderful dinner parties they had. In reading, I found the descriptions of the various charming and elegant people they met through their travels at odds with the tensions and problems continually facing them. The diary recorded few emotions and no clue to my father's relationship to my mother, no concerns for her or tenderness toward her. The only mentions of me as "Claude" referred to attacks of bronchitis and asthma. There were just a few entries which stated that either Denise or Papa (grandfather) kept an eye on *le gosse*, the kid. My father's writing was always very precise and descriptive. As I sat on the beach, I just couldn't believe that he reported no emotional exchange between family members.

I read that letters from my mother's parents arrived and that they were well. This was to be the case throughout the war. Precise descriptions were given of the many days spent gathering visas and getting passports. Detailed references were also made of visits to my father's tailor, where he and Grandfather had tropical suits made for Africa. Finally, on Saturday the 13th of July, the entire family boarded the *S.S. Monzinho*, destination Lorenzo Marques, via the west coast of Africa and around the Cape of Good Hope. My father noted here that Grandfather made a package of all the Cadillac's tools and the family's gas masks and sent it off to the garage in France. A thought went through my mind that perhaps this was Grandfather's subconscious ritual of closure in farewell to the Cadillac and Europe.

The first day out to sea, Father noted that there were 85 Belgians on board, all refugees headed for the Belgian Congo for the duration of the war. He indicated that he made many friends and organized many *concours*, competitions, of bridge, ping-pong, Mah Jong, and chess. I sensed his competitiveness. During the day he read; at night he went to dancing parties. He mentioned that each time the sea was rough the ladies did not come up for lunch or dinner. My family said goodbye on July 28, when most of the Belgians got off in Matadi, Belgian Congo. In one of the few emotional notes, my father commented that another piece of Belgium left his heart as the passengers disembarked.

Father's diary expressed no hint of the emotional tantrums that would pervade our lives in the coming years.

I read on and noted that on August 4 I coughed all night and my mother became *folle d'enervement*, crazy with nervousness, each time *le gosse* was sick. Again, I was struck by his reference to me as "the kid." I felt a distance, a lack of attachment. I continued to cough and developed asthma. For three days my mother did not leave my side, insisting that all meals should be brought down to the cabin. My temperature kept climbing. The ship's doctor was called, and again hot poultices of flour and mustard were applied to my chest. My temperature reached 104 and my mother was beside herself. I was given a shot of I don't know what and more hot poultices. Finally, on August 8, I was well again and allowed to go up on deck for fresh air.

Sunday, August 11: Arrived in Lorenzo Marques. Many details of baggage, passports, and forms. A special note was made about the very nice port captain, who was well educated and spoke many languages and who became a close friend. This friendship proved crucial. After waiting for a month to be allowed to enter South Africa, we were refused and the port captain extended our visas for another three months—just in time. He was made governor of Macâo in China and left immediately afterwards.

During the wait, Father became ill with dysentery and phlebitis in his right leg. At the age of thirteen he had spent a winter vacation in St. Moritz, Switzerland, where he and a friend took an illegal bob-sled run. They crashed, and he broke his right leg in three places. It did not mend properly and had to be re-broken to be set normally. This stay in Africa marked the start of his circulation and phlebitis problem, possibly related to that early injury. I again came down with bronchitis and asthma, and again hot poultices were applied. No mention was made in the diary of my screaming when the poultices were applied; but I have a scar two inches in diameter on the left side of my chest as a reminder that, somewhere along the way, a poultice was too hot.

Father decided to try once again to obtain immigration visas to the U.S.A. The consul in Lorenzo Marques was much nicer and more helpful than the one in Lisbon. By early October the family received advice that we could enter the U.S.A. under the November quota. Now the difficulty was to obtain temporary visas for South Africa, as the only ships bound for the U.S.A. stopped in Capetown. Another month of heat, sickness, and waiting transpired before the family obtained transit visas and confirmed cabins aboard the *U.S.S. President Polk*, leaving Capetown on November 9.

Father again recorded life on board, but this time more briefly, with fewer references to bridge games, dancing, and parties with friends. I was curious to see that there was a brief entry on November 17 about seeing a movie on board, but there is no entry on the 18th, my birthday, when I turned three years old. There was another brief entry on the 19th about a bridge tournament. Father continued his short notes to the diary until November 26, which was blank.

Here I was in 1980, bathing in sunshine, at the height of my material success—driving a Maserati, owning a house at the shore and a racer-cruiser sailboat, yet I was still a prisoner of my feelings toward Father. God had already knocked at my door, and, although I had started my spiritual search, my feelings, ego, and personality were still split and I could not accept or feel compassion toward his journey.

I knew from family stories that we entered New York Harbor sometime in the first half of December 1940, and that my sister Marianne was born a year later at New York Hospital on December 3, 1941, four days before Pearl Harbor. The family subsequently moved to Great Neck, Long Island, where my own memory continues the story.

Great Neck, Long Island, 1943

During the war I was switched from a private kindergarten to first grade in a public school. At the end of my first day all the children were let out of class to ride the familiar yellow buses home. I recognized my bus, Number 19, as the one I rode that morning when my father dropped me off at the corner. I got on with all the other kids; everyone was talking and joking, happy to be out of school and planning their fun for the afternoon. I was a bit quieter, because I had a problem. I did not know where to get off, so I watched carefully at each stop for my mother. The bus lumbered along; and I sat anxiously on the smelly, sticky, black seat on this warm September day. At each corner the smiling mothers would hug their children as they got off the bus. The bus was now three-quarters empty and I had not recognized any streets. The trees were lush, full and dark green, the color just before autumn. Finally I was the only student left. The bus driver, an old grey-haired Negro man, turned. "Where do you live, son?"

"142 Overlook Avenue."

"Oh! We passed that corner a long time ago."

"My mom wasn't there. I don't know which corner."

"Alright, alright. I'll drive you back to the corner so you will know next time. Then I'll drop you in front of your house."

"Thank you."

And so I learned the corner and my home. I entered the house. Mother was sitting dreamily smoking a cigarette. She was a large-boned woman with bleached blonde hair and soft, big brown eyes.

"Hello Claudy, did you have a nice day at school?"

I felt like crying out, "Why weren't you there? Why weren't you at the bus stop? I needed you!" But I said nothing. I just looked at her, needing so much to be embraced. I did not understand why she was not taking care of me and why all arrangements were made by my father, who seemed so distant. I remember Father planning meals and then getting angry when she did not follow the program and instead spent ration coupons and money on the black market for butter and better cuts of meat. He expected my mother to complete the tasks—tasks that she seemed unwilling or unable to perform. I was six years old and did not understand her feelings of loneliness and abandonment, what it was like to be so far away from her home, her family, and her country, which was under military occupation. What I did understand was that for the rest of my life I would always have to take care of myself.

Shortly after the end of the war, telephone communication was re-established with Belgium, and, through a long procedure and wait, my mother was finally able to talk to her parents. I remember her many tears and great joy she had in knowing that her parents and two younger sisters were all right. The emotion was so great and the elapsed time so great that it was hard for them to speak. My father got on the phone to say hello and so did I, but I did not remember the people I was saying hello to, who spoke to me in a foreign language. My mother got back on the phone and just cried, unable to say anything. My father became angry at the length of the conversation and kept motioning to Maman, as I called my mother, to get off because of the tremendous cost. Maman kept crying and trying to find something to say. Father started to scream about the cost of the call and grabbed a vase full of flowers and water and slammed it to the floor. Maman hung up, crying and screaming at my father. I was crying also. I grabbed my father's favorite pipe and broke it in half, throwing it at him and screaming through my tears that I did not want to see him anymore. Suddenly the entire scene quieted down and my father stormed out of the room.

This was the pattern that shaped my relationship with my parents. Even though in my early years I didn't understand that her mind was beginning to fail her, I felt I needed to protect my mother. I accepted without anger her inability to handle many situations and expected little from her. It was my father who made the decisions that affected our lives, and it was from him that I expected so much. It was from him that I in vain sought validation of who I was.

Shortly thereafter, we moved back to Belgium.

With my sister Marianne and my mother, in 1945.

2

The Die is Cast.

I'll disinherit you.

Brussels, Belgium, 1945–1950

We moved back to Belgium when I was eight. We lived at my maternal grandparents' house for six months before my parents bought a house on the outskirts of Brussels. My grandfather Isidore and my aunt Denise had stayed in New York. I was enrolled in a small private school and had a tutor to help me get my French back up to speed. My favorite time was the summer at my grandparents' country house in the Ardennes. This was a special time. My grandparents were formal with meals served at specific hours, which were to be attended on time, clean and with proper attire, which included slacks for the evening meals. There were a gardener, a chauffeur, and a house person in attendance at all times. Outside of this limited structure, to which I quickly adapted, I could do as I pleased. My father was there only on weekends to relax and had no interest as to what my sister and I were doing. So every summer, for nearly three months, I was a free spirit. Next door to my grandparents lived two brothers: Alain, one year older than I, and Yves, one year younger. We "three musketeers" were known throughout the small village of Bomal as the ultimate pranksters. One of our favorite tricks was to throw a small pebble high up in the air from a cliff overlooking the river bank. The pebble would land in the water, making a small *two-*

tak sound like a trout. The local trout fishermen would cast their flies in that direction. We would laugh hysterically and throw another pebble after a few minutes. The episode would always end with the fishermen figuring out what was going on and chasing us up the cliff out of our hiding place. Sunday mornings were less fun because I had to attend mass with the whole family, except my father. My two friends came from a strict Catholic family, who did not allow us to have spitball fights in church.

During the rest of the year I attended a private school. I was for the most part left alone; I learned in retrospect that my father could not relate to young children until they reached twelve years of age and he could then have a more mature conversation with them. My mother was always pleasant and Father would interfere and show his wrath, by spanking, only when my grades were poor, which they were on many occasions. I had the ability to multiply and divide correctly two three-digit numbers in my head but was unable to do so by the standard system, on paper, as required by the school. My father was exasperated with me and I felt that he considered me mentally slow. As I grew older, the spanking became slaps in the face.

When I was twelve, my mother decided I should get a more serious religious grounding. I was enrolled in catechism class at the local parish church in Brussels.

At the time I was a typical European kid. I was pudgy with brown hair drooping to one side and wore short pants and high knee socks. I took my religious education quite seriously and felt a direct connection to the Most High, to the spirit of Christ.

My father was very ill at this time, and he considered me to be a lucky charm, perhaps because whenever I was sick or in a difficult situation I always seemed to pull out of trouble. He told me that if I prayed really hard and his life was spared, he would convert to Catholicism and give up his Jewish faith. In fact, although he was Jewish, he was non-practicing and would attend church from time to time with my mother, my sister, and me, as my mother did not drive. Although my father had been Barmitzvahed, he was ambivalent about his religion. He had been influenced by his mother, who was embarrassed by all the Jewish diamond dealers and had insisted that

With my father, in Brussels in 1949.

my grandfather Isidore live in Brussels and commute to his business in Antwerp. Family history has it that when my grandmother died, and a service was held in the synagogue, my father refused to attend. This caused a rift between my father and my grandfather. Isidore, therefore, did not attend my baptism. This does not seem to have affected our relationship; in later years we enjoyed each other's company, and after he moved back to Europe I visited him in Paris and Geneva.

At the time my father made his proposal to me to convert to Catholicism he was in bed, quite white and weak, with none of his aggressive determination. His eyes were watery and pleading. As best I could understand, he had ulcers, possibly with a ruptured appendix, further complicated by an extreme allergy to penicillin. I watched as he scratched his red swollen welts with a comb.

I prayed for his life as hard as my young soul could. The time was late spring, and I would go behind the house in the open field to pray. I had learned all about the martyrs and saints. They had all sacrificed themselves for a higher good.

The field I prayed in was full of a European weed called *Ortille*, a type of nettle, which grew to a height of two feet. The leaves and stems had minuscule barbs which appeared soft but were terribly stinging. If I grabbed them firmly, the barbs would crush and cause no harm. But if I brushed against them lightly the barbs would raise great itchy welts which would remain for several hours.

The sun was warm on my sparsely clad body and the colors of late spring were surreal. My sacrifice to the higher spirit was to grab the *Ortille* by the base of the stems and lightly brush the leaves against my bare legs, torso, and arms. I would break out into massive itching hives. I would fall to my knees and, without scratching, pray for my father's life and health. Tears of pain would stream down my cheeks. In one such incident, I was transported beyond space and time with no consciousness of the itching mass of my body. I knew my father would be well.

The Belgian doctors operated on my father, cleaned up his abdomen as best they could, then closed him up, stating he was beyond their help. He survived, and one month after my confirmation into Catholicism we moved back to the United States. Once again Father underwent an operation. He stayed in the New York Hospital for nine months, after which he came home—emaciated but alive. He converted to Catholicism.

During my father's convalescence I did whatever I pleased, as Mother rarely reprimanded me and intuitively I knew Father would recover. I had been advanced a grade in junior high school, except for English, because my test scores were higher than normal. I rarely did homework and spent much time in front of the television, fascinated by all the old westerns of the time.

My mother's parents had died and left her a tidy inheritance. She had spent it all to pay for my father's operations and hospitalizations.

Soon after my father recovered, he suddenly seemed to take a more serious view of my academic studies. My grades were lackluster and a tutor was hired, particularly for English, so that I could double up that course and have all my classes on the same level. I had always been physical and so was involved with various sports. My parents, particularly my father, felt sports were unimportant relative to my academics and therefore gave me no encouragement or support. Despite this lack I was rated a first starter in the 120-yard low hurdle. By the age of sixteen I was six feet and was building my independence. I was becoming more sure of myself and cocky. I remember an argument with Father, although I don't remember the substance, when he lunged to slap me in the face. I ducked, picking up a chair, and told him that if he tried again I would break the chair over his head. That was the last time he was physical with me; instead, his control became totally psychological. I spent much time alone in the attic painting and drawing, enraging my father, who considered these activities unmanly and non-beneficial for advancement in life. His tone toward me was accusatory and intimated my inadequacy in academics and life's purpose in general. He always pushed engineering, in which my mother's father had been engaged, and business, which was his activity. The ironic part was that although he talked a tough and impressive presentation about business, his personal business was not doing well. My mother, although artistically inclined, would not contradict my father about the direction of my career and life. The more my father pushed me toward math and business, the more insecure I felt; these were not my interests, and my self-esteem suffered because I believed I could not succeed in these subjects.

St. Lawrence University, Winter 1958

When I went off to college I had great questions about God and the meaning of religion. During high school I had joined the Knights of Columbus' Squires, and through that organization the Nocturnal Adoration Society. This society was dedicated to going to church one hour each Saturday to Sunday to pray and commune with God. The hours would start at nine the first Saturday, then ten the next Saturday, and sequentially until six in the morning on Sunday many weeks later; then the sequence would start again. During these waiting times I learned to play poker with my fellow Squires, as well as drink beer and revel. I was grateful to learn all those "man" things, but found that by the time devotion in church came around I was not too well connected to spirit. The situation got out of hand,

and eventually the parish assigned a young priest to supervise our activities more closely and give us guidance.

The priest was a Harvard graduate who had joined the priesthood after his fiancé had died in a car accident. He was to be influential in my thinking because he advocated following the teachings of Christ and not to be concerned about the Church's dogma and rules. I started to understand that the experience in the field in Belgium and some of my dreams were of a more mystical nature and that eating fish on Friday or going to church on Sunday were not that crucial.

My spiritual search further deepened in February 1958, when Canton, New York, experienced one of the coldest spells in its history. Pipes froze and broke all over the campus. I decided to stay in bed for the duration and beyond. The only classes I would attend were "Religions of Man" and "Studio painting." I won first prize in an art contest for a painting of the crucifixion and I decided I would become a painter. My roommate was also taking this class and had won second prize. During my isolation in the cold spell I became totally self-analytical. I kept a notepad by my bed, and as soon as I became conscious in a dream I would wake up, make notes, then analyze it. I started to dissect all conversations with my friends, searching for ultimate meaning. At times, I felt I was going crazy; at others, I felt I had an understanding and deeper knowledge of the secrets of existence.

In a painting class I was attending, a very attractive sophomore woman was posing for a portrait. My roommate was painting an exquisite rendition of this dark-haired, dark-eyed beauty, but I could not connect to the energy of this woman. My tendency was to paint more exuberantly, more in the style of the impressionists or even the Fauves. My brush strokes would not come together, and in exasperation I blanked out her face and painted instead veins and arteries coming out of her neck with blood gushing and her vertebrae mangled. She was decapitated in a car accident a week later. Her parents bought my roommate's painting.

Father came up to school to "talk" to me about my decision to become a painter. This was our first major man-to-man confrontation on the issue of my life's direction. I thought I was ready for anything. I had reached my full height of over six feet and was muscularly toned from participating in soccer, track, and swimming. Although I considered myself "grown up," my only security in life came from Father. My mother's mind had slowly continued its decline. When I was in my teens, I realized I could not get rational decisions from her and needed to turn more and more to my father for guidance and help. The full extent of my mother's condition became apparent when in my senior year of high school she started hearing the voices of friends lost during the war. At that time, I had not connected to my spiritual teachings and did not believe in reincarnation. I went along with my father's decisions, which eventually led to my mother being heavily sedated with Thorazine.

My father drove up to St. Lawrence to see if he could get me back on track, his track. We sat in my room and he became very serious. "Claude, what is happening to you? The dean tells me that if you don't improve your grades substantially, you will have to repeat the entire year!" He stated that I had the world in front of me. He insisted that I finish my math degree at St. Lawrence, then go on to engineering at Columbia University. "Then you will be in a position to get into Maman's family's engineering business in Brussels," he concluded.

I hung my head. My heart was not in it. Math and engineering were too dry, too mechanical. I needed to be creative, I needed to express myself. I said, "I want to paint! I'm inspired by Van Gogh and all the Impressionists. I'm so excited that sometimes I feel like exploding!"

"Stop this nonsense!" he retorted. "You can paint as a hobby, for leisure. Art is not serious. Look what happened to Van Gogh. He died broke! Don't throw your whole future away. I know you can be a good engineer. I have great confidence in you. You have always been good at math." The thought ran through my mind that he himself had flunked out of engineering school in Brussels.

I was stubborn. "I don't care if I am good at math. It's not what I want to do!"

"Look, if you persist in this ridiculous obsession you can do it on your own. When you get out of school, you'll be on your own. I'll cut you off! I'll disinherit you! You'll be no son of mine!"

I was devastated. My entire support system was my father. Maman was already in her dream world and would smile and acquiesce to anything my father said. I was beaten, trapped, cornered. I felt inadequate in the world of engineering and business into which he was pushing me. I didn't know where to turn and I was too insecure and shy to forge ahead on my own.

Then my father expressed his love for me. When we had an emotional conflict, the battle always ended with his hugging me tenderly. He knew I would yield to his will. My father was all I had, and he knew it. Although his hug was physically comforting, I sensed that somehow I had lost my masculinity. I felt like an adolescent dog, beaten by the bully of the pack. I acquiesced. I agreed to toe the line.

His victory complete, my father cast a discriminating eye about my room. "What you need is a desk!" he declared. He then went out and bought the largest desk the fraternity had ever seen. He was convinced the desk would give me the proper working environment to succeed. Then Father left.

The desk was too large to fit through the fraternity door. I had to saw three inches off the legs. This was the only humor in a situation which had left me frustrated and deeply angry. I left, then, my world of dream time and creativity. I turned my focus to becoming successful in the material world. I quit painting and distanced myself from all non-concrete objects or situations, including religion. I still felt connected to a higher intelligence in the universe, but put the feeling aside to concentrate on the details of earthly life. I realized that I had been manipulated and that my father had given me a loving hug only because he was once again in control. He controlled me through conditional love. I had to become my own man, independent, and take him on nose to nose, toe to toe. Seething with anger, I vowed to become more successful than Father in the material world.

New York, New York, 1960

The only softness in my life occurred shortly after the incident with Father in 1958. I was looking through the freshman handbook when I came across the picture of a long-necked, blue-eyed redhead, and I was struck by lightning. I knew that this woman, Bette

With Bette, at my graduation from St. Lawrence in 1960.

Germann, would become my wife. One of my fraternity brothers was dating one of her sorority sisters, and a blind date was arranged. I fell head over heels in love and decided to remain one more year at St. Lawrence to complete my math degree, instead of doing the three-two program with Columbia University engineering. This was a program that would yield a math degree from St. Lawrence and an engineering degree from Columbia in a total of five years. This decision caused a confrontation with Father, but I was adamant. I would do his program but take a year longer, because I wanted to be with Bette. He sensed my resolve and yielded. I graduated from St.

Lawrence and Bette and I were married. We moved to New York while I was in engineering school. We were fortunate to get a small apartment near Washington Square which belonged to a friend of the family who had moved to Europe and gave us a cheap rental. I tutored high school kids in math and French during the school year and worked in construction during the summer to meet expenses. My father was going through major financial reversals in business, so my schooling was all on loans from Columbia. The family fortune had been depleted due to my father's long illnesses. To compound the situation my mother was diagnosed as schizophrenic and put on heavy doses of Thorazine. She smiled pleasantly throughout the day but was unable to make decisions or run the household. Father took over all responsibility.

Our first son, Eric, was born in 1961, and in 1962 I graduated and joined Rust Engineering in Covington, Virginia, as a field engineer. In 1963 I was transferred to their headquarters in Pittsburgh.

Pittsburgh, Pennsylvania, 1963–1967

I was working as a design engineer when I hit a stumbling block which propelled my career forward. I worked in a room with more than a hundred engineers and draftsmen divided into three sections: civil, mechanical, and electrical. I worked in the civil section. I was called to the chief engineer's office and told that my work was unacceptable. I was taken aback, as I thought all my structural calculations and designs were perfect. He shook his head and said, "No complaints on your abilities, but your handwriting is so bad that the checkers prefer to re-do the calculations rather than follow your work. When they are finished they come out with the same answers as yours, but we can't afford to have the work done twice because the engineer can't decipher your work." I had started my master's degree in business at Duquesne University, and I could not stand the daily repetitive math work. I wanted out. I told the chief engineer that I would produce the best he ever saw, but eventually wanted to transfer out of the design department. He told me to produce, then we'd see. Indeed I produced some of the best work.

Steel mill, Pittsburgh, PA, 1966.

Then one day I was asked to check one of the best engineer's work before it went to steel manufacturing, as the man was going to the hospital for surgery. It was supposed to be a perfunctory check of a small administration building in an oil plant on the Gulf of Mexico. I soon realized that the design of the building had not taken into consideration the heavy wind loads from the Gulf. The man was already in the hospital so I could not go back to him. I took the work to the chief engineer and told him it was unacceptable and asked if I should redesign the structure. He yelled at me, "This is my best engineer! How dare you question his work!" I just threw all the designs and calculations on the chief's desk, walked back to my drafting board, picked up my briefcase, and walked out. The next day the chief called me back. "You're an arrogant son of a bitch, Saks, but OK, you're right. I had the work checked and it needs to be redesigned. Do it." And I did.

The chief then sent me to Naheola, Alabama, with a draftsman to solve some design problems; after I successfully did so, he warmed to the idea that I was turning out to be one of his better engineers. He then gave me the problem of designing foundations for a turbine and compressor connection which had two different resonant frequencies. The easy solution was to pour so much concrete that nothing would break. Instead, I went to the newly formed computer department. The department was looking for projects, since no one trusted them yet. I gave them all the input and the computer spat out a solution that cut the cost of concrete in half. The chief was beside himself and decided to have one of his Ph.D.s check it by hand. He called me back in his office again. "Saks, good work. I want to promote you to squad boss." A squad boss had two to three engineers and three to four draftsmen reporting to him. I told the chief I had no interest and wanted out of his department within a month.

Somehow the gods smiled on me and I was transferred to the purchasing department. I was known as a maverick in never accepting the status quo, but always looking for new ways to do things and succeeding. I initiated new procedures. Within a year, two more engineers were brought into purchasing and I was promoted, to become the youngest assistant project manager in the company.

I worked in that capacity for a year, overseeing the construction of paper and steel mills. I was embroiled in a "man's world" of heavy construction, rough language, and no-nonsense decisions. I had just finished my M.B.A. at night school. I was cocky and confident, both from my swift move up the corporate ladder and my success in graduate school. I had proved to my father, and more importantly to myself, that I could succeed even in a career I did not like and be a man to be reckoned with. I felt strong and the time had come for major changes.

I decided to go into the coffee business with my father, where I could unleash my business creativity and really find out who Father was—and take him on. More importantly, I had to find out if I could handle business, make money, and really find out who I was.

Bette encouraged me: "If commodities are calling you, go ahead; I will follow you anywhere."

Bette had a soft exterior and a strong interior that would continually be tested in the future as I careened through business, family, and health problems. Bette was expecting our third child, Claire, who would turn out to be a pretty, blue-eyed blonde little girl. Our oldest son, Eric, who was then six, had my brown eyes and Bette's curly hair. He had our common strong chin, as did all our children, and was already showing artistic creativity in his school artwork. Marc, three, a blue-eyed towhead, was full of mischief. He had the uncanny grace, fun, and joy that allowed him to get away with his many pranks. I was about to move them all to a new environment near the financial center of the coffee world, New York City, in the pressure cooker of the commodity world, and in the process would distance myself from my children. Ten years would pass before I would come to a brutal awakening.

3

A Rage to Succeed

The business will never work.

I joined Father's small coffee brokerage firm in July 1967. For months, I had been having a vivid, recurring dream. I was in a Roman chariot pulled by four strong brown steeds, running at full gallop down an open grassy plain, as one would find in Africa. The sky was bright blue. The sun was beating down and heat waves shimmered on the horizon. The terrain was rough and treacherous. I careened across this savannah with red leather reins in my hands, controlling the fastest, most powerful team of horses imaginable. I was in an exhilarated state, continually on the edge of disaster. I was on top of the world. I had a rage to succeed. I wanted—needed—to be on the fast track. I wanted to make large sums of money.

A college friend, Howard Silver, had worked for my father for three years before I joined. He was operating a specialty food brokerage from Belgium, under my father's tutelage, which had no relation to coffee. He convinced Father that my technical and organizational background along with my M.B.A. would be of tremendous help to an emerging brokerage firm which had the eventual goal of becoming a dealer.

Howard, at twenty-eight, was short and stocky, had thick hair and sparkling blue eyes, and was a year and a half my junior. He was as tenacious as a bulldog, a streetwise native of the Bronx. We had met as undergraduates at St. Lawrence University, where he had started a business, eventually controlling all the Coke machines on campus. Howard wanted to join my fraternity. He was such a great storyteller that many of the fraternity brothers thought he was a braggart, and there was opposition to his joining. Fraternity meetings were my first lessons in group dynamics, politics, people, and control. I had garnered my penchant to manipulate people and situations at the feet of my father. I always had the innate ability to see the crux of the situation and the inner state of the people involved. But, because whenever I decided what I wanted I was reprimanded by Father, I learned to operate behind the scenes.

Our fraternity meetings were held in the living room with all the chairs and sofas pushed to the sides so as to form a circle. The president monitored the discussions. I learned to develop my own agenda and plant supporters at key locations around the room to interject at crucial moments of the discussion. Getting Howard accepted at the membership voting meeting took an hour and a half and all my skill. I had even gone as far as starting on the side of the opposition, and then, with a prearranged supportive speech for Howard by a friend, I switched sides and convinced the opposing brothers to vote affirmatively. The fraternity was a testing ground for my future role as a deal maker.

Howard and I became close friends and business confidants, although we were of opposite worlds, he being streetwise from the Bronx and I brought up in Europe. As I felt my way into the coffee business, he gave me every encouragement.

One late afternoon after the staff of two and my father and his partner had left, Howard and I had our feet up on our desks talking about the future. The surroundings were pleasant. My father's office was located on one of the higher floors of a lower Wall Street building, overlooking the East River. The main office was oak-paneled in the style of an old English law firm. Howard was leaning back and puffing on a cigar.

I confided in Howard. "If I last five years with my father, it'll be a great accomplishment." I told him that Father was a castrating son of a bitch, but a brilliant innovator with great imagination. I wanted to learn commodities, specifically coffee, and I couldn't think of a better teacher.

"How can you feel that way?" Howard said. "He's your father. And he's surrogate father to me. He's taught this Bronx kid the way of the world. He's taken me to Europe for negotiations, taught me manners—even how to smoke and hold a cigar. There isn't a detail that he hasn't helped me with."

I shook my head. "Howard, that may be true, but he also extracts his pound of flesh from you. You travel all over the country and are at his beck and call every hour of the day and night." I stopped short of telling him he was underpaid and manipulated. I expressed hope that my father and I could work together. If we did, it would be because of Howard's support. I told him that Father wanted me to be an engineer because he flunked out of engineering school in Belgium, that I became an engineer to satisfy his ego, and that he was healing his failure through my success. I did him one better: I went to Columbia Engineering, one of the toughest schools in the country, and obtained a position of power in a very short period of time.

I told Howard my most intimate thoughts. "I want to build a large international coffee firm and be more successful than Father."

Howard thought about this, then challenged me. "So you want to learn from him then go into competition with him?"

"No, but I want to take this small brokerage firm and turn it into a market-maker, a company to be reckoned with. He will know I did it, and that's enough."

"If this is your attitude," Howard said, "the business will never work."

I told him Father was a manipulator but that I was a better long-term strategist, and that I would give my father the benefit of the doubt and work extremely hard for success. The other side of the coin was that I wanted to please Father because I want him to be proud of me.

I confided in Howard further. "I tell you all this as my best friend and as a forewarning of any difficulties."

G.M. Saks, Inc., or G.M., as my father's company was known, brokered coffee, arranging contracts between buyers and sellers and taking a small percentage from the middle. Our aim was to become a dealer, to buy for the company's own account and risk. This would take a lot of money and strong bank financing and included taking the downside risks of poor quality, delivery default, late shipment, rejections from customers, food and drug hazards, and all the other vagaries associated with the business. Brokerage was safer because the risks and financing were for the buyer's account; but the returns were minimal.

Father had started to put creative deals together for some of his European friends and was being compensated at a higher-than-usual percentage. He was itching to become a dealer. I felt that he just needed encouragement. Someone—I—had to hold his hand as he moved forward.

It is only in retrospect, after reading his diary, that I understood his innate insecurities and need to build the business slowly and carefully. These insecurities were compounded by his very difficult experiences: the loss of his business at the onset of the war, his serious illnesses, the loss of my mother's inheritance during his hospitalization, my mother being sedated and ineffectual, and his near-bankruptcy while I was at Columbia. But I felt strong and confident. I was going to make a fortune. I did not understand at the time that my attitude was my own reaction to my war experience and to Father bullying me when I was in college.

Father's partner, Herman, was afraid of the risks and wanted to avoid all exposure. Within three weeks of my joining, he declared that one Saks was difficult enough, but two would be impossible. He quit and withdrew all his funds. His withdrawal put a crimp in our plans. We would have to bide our time until we were financially strong enough to take the plunge and become dealers. With Father's partner's quitting, I propelled my apprenticeship into high gear.

I was fortunate enough to have several excellent mentors to feed me the information I needed. The first was a small, friendly competitor, Abba, whose business had been in New York for two generations. He taught me the "cupping" of coffee. This term refers to the process, after the roasting and grinding, in which the cupper tastes and spits out five and ten cups of coffee. Abba was a far better teacher for me than Father; there were no personality clashes over our opinions of the various coffees. The situation was similar to a sixteen-year-old learning to drive from an impartial instructor rather than from a nervous and hypercritical parent. Abba was fifteen years my senior. He was from the old school of coffee brokers and would sell each lot with an involved story as to the coffee's merit. Unknown to either of us at the time was the fact that Abba would one day work for me.

My second mentor owned a small roasting operation to whom Father had sold a lot of specialty coffees. He taught me what an end-user looked for in coffee: yield, color, acidity, or, for a filler, blandness. He also made me aware of the marketing problems and supermarket attitudes toward price changes: how to gauge whether coffee was moving on the shelf, customer resistance to sales, and how much the supermarket had in stock.

My third mentor was a heavyset, balding, wild-eyed maverick trader named Ed Cameleri. Camel, as he was known, was born of Italian parents but was brought up in Lebanon and had emigrated to Brazil at the onset of World War II. He spoke Italian, French, English, and Portuguese fluently and had a good smattering of Arabic, all of which he spoke with a heavy Brazilian-Portuguese accent. He was a true dealer, a one-man show. Camel concentrated 90 percent of his trading out of Angola, which, at that time, was the largest producer of robustas, the low-grade coffees needed for instants, fillers, and vending machines. His favorite saying was, "Don't geeve me dis jhazz, geeve me di coffee."

I lived in Montclair, New Jersey. He lived in the next town and often drove me home. On the way, he would discuss his ideas, strategies, opinions, and deals. I was like a sponge, absorbing all the information and the fine tonalities of the market.

"Claude," he said one day, "I've been checking around and I don't see any robustas on di docks. I sink di big guy, General Foods, eez running out of coffee. Does your Dad see many offers nearby, afloat on di ships or on di docks?"

"No, everything seems to be offered from the country of origin. There's very little afloat."

"Good, dat's what I tought. I sink tomorrow, first ting, I buy all di loose robustas on di docks, and everysing afloat, and squeeze di market. I'll make a foortune. I'll bet you a sousand tons cleans up di market!"

My eyeballs popped when he mentioned such large quantities. Our company was lucky when we brokered a tenth of that in a day.

Similarly, he would not hesitate to go short markets. "I'm checking di warehouses," he would say. "Dey're all full. Coffee is being unloaded on di docks daily. I'm telling you, eet's time to sell di hell out of di market. Maybe sell 500 tons a month, January–February-March short. What you sink?"

The man had great balls. He could make the big decisions and take great risks. I too wanted to become a wheeler-dealer.

Slowly, I learned to evaluate the market and give my opinion. I was fired up to get into the big leagues, and after six months I felt I understood the dynamics of the market.

My ultimate mentor was my father. He had the style of a European gentleman. He stood six foot two, taller than I, and always very erect, although his stomach protruded due to various operations on his ulcers. He had a slight duck-like motion to his walk, because his right toe had been rotted away by severe phlebitis in his legs. Mixed in with all my other confused motives for succeeding in this business, his courage in light of his ailments bred in me a need to excel on his behalf. He had a well-formed round head with thick, dark, brilliantined hair, a sharp part on the left side, a strong, thin, and slightly hooked nose, and inquisitive blue eyes. In contrast, I had dark eyes which ranged from grey to green to nearly black, depending on my moods. I had his strong chin, and, much to my consternation, a receding hair line.

During one of my first sales, I had made a pitch on a good quality coffee and sold it to the roaster. I then proceeded to offer the customer, at a lesser price, a cheaper quality of similar coffee from another origin. After listening, the roaster canceled the first deal and took the cheaper coffee. I was stunned.

Father angrily reprimanded. "Never, ever, do that! Make your pitch. Ask for the order. Close the deal. Then say thank you and hang up the phone. Wait half an hour, then call him back and offer the next quality. Two separate deals and he can't back out. Got it?"

I got it. I felt like a stupid child unable to grasp the subtleties of big business.

Father insisted that the key to the business was buying and controlling sources of supply. In 1968, international phone calls were an extravagance, but he believed in using the phone as if they were local calls. Instantaneous information and developing a web of suppliers and informants were the keys to success. I listened in on all his European calls, as ideas and the formation of deals were volleyed over the lines.

I attended every meeting, lunch, and dinner with Father where business was discussed. Afterwards, he would review with me the various players and the subtle intricacies of the conversations and negotiations. The trade people knew manners, wines, art, music, and politics. They behaved as refined gentlemen, yet would not hesitate to cut your gizzard out or squeeze your balls if they could get the slightest advantage. Father would always bring back the finest silk ties, from Hermes-Paris, for Howard and me, so that we would develop a hunger for the best and make more money. I loved the game, the intensity, because I could see through it all and get what I wanted. I lived, breathed, and dreamed the business.

While I devoted my body and soul to coffee, Bette was holding the family together. She was not particularly fond of my father and his controlling, manipulative ways; and she was concerned about what was happening to me and to our family.

"Sweetheart," she would say, "you get home at seven, too late for the kids' supper. Then you are right back on the phone with your father, talking business. You're under too much stress. You need some quiet time for yourself, and I'd like to have more time together—a little more loving and a little less business adrenaline."

I told her that I needed to understand the business thoroughly, to be the best, and to build financial security for our family. She understood, but didn't want me to become like my father and devote my entire life to business. She wanted me to spend more time with our kids and have a good relationship with them. She wanted me to stop going to New York on weekends to meet with my father. She was concerned that I would be affected both emotionally and physically by the extreme stress. I kept repeating, "As soon as I fully know the business and develop my own niche, I promise to slow down." But external forces would have to intervene to make me keep that promise.

I started developing my own contacts and was creating business, particularly with the roasters instead of the dealers. When Father and I had differences of opinion on the market or positions to be taken, I would prevail in the shouting match and we would take my course of action. Father would show his disapproval by not talking to me. His lips stretched along his teeth into a thin line of displeasure. This grimace was particularly accentuated when the outcome of my opinion was successful. I didn't give in to him, but rather let the anger and resentment build within me until I wanted to scream. One of our first opportunities to be an importer involved a deal for 500 bags of coffee, thirty tons of "Kivu-7," which came from the eastern province of Zaire. Father wanted to sell it as a broker. I wanted to import it as a dealer and sell it to a roaster, because I knew we had the financing to handle the deal.

"What is the price on the coffee?" my father asked in an accusatory and deprecating way.

"The shipper is asking forty-five cents, but I want to bid thirty-five."

"You're crazy! You're going to lose the shipper."

"Let me try. I can always be blamed as the young novice bad guy and you can save the day."

He agreed with much apprehension, coughing, gagging, and spitting all the while. It was his "CGS" routine, as I called it, a nervous habit when he was under pressure, which he kept up until the position was safely delivered to the end user.

The shipper consented at thirty-seven, and we made a handsome profit on a small quantity. Father made no comment about my success in handling this deal. Instead, his lips stretched along his teeth in that thin line of displeasure.

With my aggressive strategies, I evolved into the role of a bad guy, the black hat, to push new ideas, methods, and deals. It was a role I loved. And, if the situation didn't work out, Father could always come in, as the good guy, and save the day. What I did not understand at the time was that my talent was in game playing and situational confrontation, but that I was a total failure at emotional encounters with my father. Intuitively, I knew I had to become an expert in the business, and financially independent, before taking on my father emotionally. Still, our arrangement gave me the room I needed to experiment.

Father was very creative, and he could obtain great supplies of coffee. But he had an innate fear of doing deals by himself; he always wanted a partner, and I was hopeful that he would rely on me for that role. After some successes, we did other deals together, often doubling and tripling the quantities. We convinced our bank that we were ready to expand as a small dealer, and obtained the necessary financing. The profit picture was improving, and I finalized an arrangement with Father whereby I would get a small survival salary and 25 percent of any net profits on business I developed. Due to his health, he was not traveling to Africa, his main source of supply, and was relying more and more on European, colonial brokerage houses for coffees. I pushed him to let me travel to the source, to Africa, going direct and controlling our own supplies. I had to be very diplomatic. "Since you are covering mainly west Africa," I said, "perhaps I could try east Africa, where, if I made mistakes, it would be less damaging."

He considered the proposal, then said, to my surprise, "Yes, I think it's time you cut your teeth at source. You could visit a man named Jack Fisher in Tanzania and see what he's up to. He's a clever fellow who might come up with large quantities of good coffee. Then you should visit our usual supplier, Mr. Vohora at Coffee Exporters, and follow up by trying to make some new contacts of your own."

I wondered about my father's easy acceptance of my proposal. Was he finally recognizing my talents and trusting me, or was he setting me up for failure?

4

East Africa

I vowed to become an expert.

When the airplane door opened on the Dar Es Salaam tarmac, I was overwhelmed by the heat, pressure, and the heaviness in the air. There was a strange, acrid smell, smoky, like a slow, slow smoldering fire. Later, as I traveled into the little villages and out of the cities, I realized that the smoke came from burning banana leaves or other types of tropical vegetation that was used in the huts for cooking or warming up from the chill of the night air.

I went through Tanzanian customs when all the symbols of the British Empire were still in place: stiff khaki shorts, high knee socks, and mandatory uniform caps. The ambiance was officious.

Once through customs, I was met by Mr. Fisher, a short man with thinning blonde hair; he was very suave and unctuous. I instantly disliked him, despite Father's belief that we should do business with him. I felt him creeping into my inner space, and I automatically put up a psychic barrier to his tentacles. The sensation may have been exacerbated by Dar Es Salaam's general atmosphere. Dar was heavy with humidity, a body-drenching, dust-sticking, shirt-clinging dankness. The buildings were old British colonial structures, very drab and run-down. Many appeared to be empty. We drove through the city, where the streets were rather deserted, even though this was 1968, and Julius Nyere had not yet forced his Marxist ideas on Tanzania. Besides the heaviness, one could feel the uneasiness in the air, the suspicion, the tenseness of the people in the street. There were few cars and little traffic. I was whisked to Fisher's house on the outskirts of the city and was given a room downstairs with a full complement of mosquito netting around the bed. It reminded me of all the old movies about Africa. Later, I found out Fisher was upstairs with air-conditioning. I was downstairs, no air-conditioning, out of town and out of touch. Humidity and a smoky smell filtered in through the window, and I developed a slight asthmatic wheeze during the night.

The next morning, over a breakfast of toast and coffee, I told Fisher that I intended to move to the Intercontinental Hotel downtown. He made a scene about the lack of room availability at the hotel and claimed his residence was the most comfortable. Looking at him I realized that Father was always impressed by people who made a good presentation, whether in Europe or Africa, but I usually wanted to probe beneath the veneer. I was developing a distrust for Fisher and stood my ground, insisting he drop me off at the Intercontinental. He said he would call. He later told me that by some miracle there was a room available because of his connections. I did not believe a word of it.

Once at the hotel, I began to meet with some of the shipping companies, learning who were the important shippers from Tanzania and what was happening at the port. One of my key contacts turned out to be the general manager of Belbase. The case of Belbase was typical of what happens in Africa.

Belbase was part of the Belgian Line facility, but was also a diplomatic territory within the port, a property of the Belgian Government and off-limits to individuals without proper passes. It was the most efficient loading facility in the Dar Es Salaam port. A ship could wait in Dar for two weeks to two months, waiting to be loaded, but in Belbase it would be loaded and turned around in two to five days. Belbase was the key storage area for Burundi coffees which came down through Lake Tanganyika and Tanzania.

In discussions with Fisher, I learned that, through his friendship with the Minister of Agriculture, Fisher had a special purchasing arrangement with the Tanzanian coffee board that gave him a major advantage over other buyers.

Fisher had decided to do business only through our company in the U.S. and another firm in Europe. This arrangement gave us the ability to obtain quantities in multiples of 1,000 bags, which amounted to sixty tons. At that time, this was a real advantage, as most coffees coming out of east Africa were offered in small, odd lots that were more difficult to market. I negotiated with Belbase to handle Fisher's coffees, which made for an even more efficient operation. Our contracts with him were very profitable and Father took credit for the connection.

Our relationship was to be short-lived, however, lasting only eighteen months. I started to hear rumors that Fisher was late in paying his shipping bills, and questions were being raised as to whether he was paying his Tanzanian export tax. We cut back on buying, and shortly thereafter he defaulted on his last shipment, which luckily was only sixty tons. This incident was part of my education in the machinations and uncertainties of the coffee business. I was losing my naiveté. And the fact that my intuition about Fisher proved correct strengthened my judgment when on my own.

After finishing in Dar, I took a small plane, a Fokker Friendship, up to Arusha to see our usual shipper, Mr. Vohora at Coffee Exporters.

I was met by Mr. Vohora, an elderly, grand Indian gentleman, garbed in his white linen suit and tie, standing erect. In those relatively early days of democratic Africa, formality was already being shed, particularly in smaller towns. But Vohora stood for the old guard.

Arusha was a small town but was considered an important center. The contrast to Dar was amazing. Arusha is on a high plateau with day temperatures around eighty-five to ninety degrees, little humidity, a beautiful blue sky and, at night, cool enough temperatures to use a fireplace.

As he drove to the hotel, Vohora began explaining his various business interests. "Mr. Saks, I'm so pleased you are here. I have been doing business with your father for many years. Unfortunately, he has not come to visit Tanzania for quite some time, which I think is the reason your volume has declined."

I got the message real quick. You have to stay in touch with your sources—relationships are everything. I vowed to become an expert in East Africa. I made some excuse about my father's health and assured him I would be in touch.

At this point we arrived at the hotel. The Arusha Hotel was a charming place in the old English-African style, with varnished wood paneling, tile floors, and many cottage-type leaded windows for cross ventilation. There was a big fireplace in the main salon. I soon experienced the quick and refreshing temperature drop which occurred each evening, slept with the window open as the air was delightful, and became accustomed to the night sounds of Africa.

Next morning we drove down to visit the Tanzania Coffee Marketing Board in Moshi, which is south and east of Arusha. As we left the Arusha plateau and came down the plain to go to Moshi, in the distance I saw a huge mountain rising out of the flat, flat savannah which stretched as far as the eye could see. The plain was a sea of brown and yellow grasses with heat waves shimmering above it. I was reminded of my dream about the chariot and galloping horses. Out of this plain rose Mount Kilimanjaro, the colors changing from brown to green to white on top. The vastness and power of Africa exceeded my preconceived ideas. This was a truly spiritual mountain.

The main road between Arusha and Moshi was dirt, sprayed in places with black oil. But in Africa things are not always maintained, so parts of the road were extremely dry, and we created dust storms as we traveled along. The dust got into every nook and cranny of our suitcases, the car was covered, and our skins were encrusted. By the time we arrived in Moshi, we had an orange-brown-maroon glow. The town, compared to Arusha, appeared abandoned. Our hotel, the only one, was dilapidated, with musty walls and crumbling paint and was barely clean.

Moshi sits at the bottom of the Kilimanjaro plain in an armpit of humidity and blazing sun. The town's only claim to fame was the Tanzanian Coffee Works. It not only auctioned off all the coffee exports from Tanzania, but also did quality grading, curing (blowing the dust from and drying the coffees), bagging, and some shipping.

We arrived at the curing works and met the chairman of the marketing board. Afterwards I went into the cupping room and spent a whole day tasting one coffee after another. I learned about different grades, what each meant, and how these coffees came to market. The board had numerous small lots, which took an extensive amount of cupping. From my perspective, this was a waste of time. The exporters, then the dealers, and eventually the roasters had to repeat the procedure.

By the next day, I had come up with a new approach and explained it to Vohora. My idea was to create types of coffees. I suggested that, through our cupping, we develop standard types for the whole year that could be matched from each auction. I proposed three grades: a high grade, a medium grade and a lower grade. I asked Vohora if he could do that.

Vohora raised his eyebrows in mild surprise.

"Yes, my staff could do that. We then could send you a very large sample at the beginning of the year and you could register it with each one of your buyers."

"Yes, that's exactly it."

This was the start of a new concept in the coffee business and I was the innovator. It gave me the confidence that I could think quickly on my feet, be imaginative and, therefore, was the equal of my father.

When I came back from the trip and explained my decisions, my customers decided to give the system a try. Just about that time, several of the larger coffee roasters had begun to computerize their products and required standardized coffee lots. They agreed to run with the standards, computerize them, and add them to their blends. Although our company did well with the types, we were too small to capitalize on them. Our larger competitors, who figured out the system within six to nine months, really did well. Over the next three years, most of the industry changed to buying standardized types out of East Africa.

I flew to Kenya. Arriving in Nairobi, I was struck with its difference. There was no doubt I was in a capitalist country. There were many cars and fast traffic, customs was efficient, the streets were clean, and people seemed busy and content.

Nairobi is about 5,000 feet in altitude. It is similar to Arusha, with its cool evenings and pleasant days. The tenseness of Tanzania left my body as I enjoyed the streets lined with flowers, jacaranda trees, and hibiscus bushes. This was just the beginning of Nairobi's development, before all the high-rise buildings were erected and the hotels built. Expectation was in the air and business was the energy of the day. I stayed in a beautiful gardened home, guest of the Farrell Lines representative.

I covered Nairobi, met with some of the shippers, discussed business with Farrell Lines, and used their excellent communication system to contact New York. After visiting the coffee works and the auction system, I realized the real business came out of Mombasa. Early next morning, I flew off in another Fokker Friendship.

Mombasa and Nairobi, although in the same country, share no other similarities. Mombasa, with its large, efficient harbor, was really the commercial heartbeat of the country. In the old port, Arab dhows, trading for coffee and sisal, still arrived with their colorful, odd-shaped sails. They were filled with spices and multicolored carpets, emanating pungent and exotic odors, with sugared tea, perhaps, being served on the poop deck. Mombasa is also the place to meet the Kenyan exporters, the people who really make it happen, who keep the crop moving out. Most of the shippers at that time were Indian.

There I met Panju, a small shipper, who was dynamic, imaginative, and eager to show me his facilities.

He had two small buildings. The first one housed clerical staff, a cupping room and a very small roasting operation. The other was a warehouse, or *godown*, where they mixed and stored the coffee.

At this time the coffee world was operating under the International Coffee Agreement, or ICA, on a strict quota system. There was an excess of coffee, and to prevent a dramatic fall in world prices, the ICA put in place quotas that restricted imports into the consuming signatory countries, meaning the industrialized nations. Prices were thereby held at artificially high levels. The excess coffee was sold to the "new market," non-quota countries, which included the Iron Curtain, Middle East, and Asian countries.

The International Coffee Organization, or ICO, located in Berners Street, London, controlled the ICA with a stamp system. The stamps, much like postage stamps, were issued to each country with its code numbers printed on the face. The exporting countries would then export all their better coffees at higher prices, with quota stamps, to the importing members of the ICA. The remaining coffee was sold at tremendous discounts to the new market countries.

Since Kenya auctioned all its better coffees for quota markets at high prices and its lower qualities went cheaply for new market countries, there was a game to be played. Panju had developed customers in the Middle East, a "new market," who required fine acid coffees and were willing to pay high prices, even higher than quota prices, as they had difficulty obtaining good coffee due to the quota system's unnatural selectivity. Panju simply solved the problem by buying high-quality, medium-quality, and some low grade, free from defects, at auction. He received his quota for the high qualities and part of the medium qualities, and then switched the coffees, re-bagging the high quality for the new markets and mixed the others for quota markets.

The re-bagging was to be my first encounter with the manipulations and the internal re-application of the ICA's quota. This is how Panju supplied us consistently with acceptable coffees at a reasonable price. Unfortunately, he was not well-financed and consequently could not handle large quantities. Since we were also a small company and unprepared to advance large amounts of money in the Kenya interior, our business with Panju remained limited.

After finishing my business in Mombasa, I flew to Kampala, Uganda. It sits in a beautiful location, high up on a plateau, with temperatures as pleasant as in Nairobi. The town had mainly dirt roads and old dilapidated colonial buildings.

I spent a brief time with the coffee board, learning that their marketing was done through their New York and London offices. Their main crops were robustas, the lower grade coffees, versus Kenya's and Tanzania's fine arabicas.

This was the end of my first African adventure, and I flew back to New York.

I came to understand that the entire ICA system was a political morass, whereby the citizens, consumers, of the signatory countries were paying inflated prices to support overproduction. The price of the inferior and new market coffees would range from 30 to 50 percent cheaper than quota coffee. Instead of governmental aid it was the coffee consumer of the developed nations that supported the developing countries. Nature was not taking its course, and Panju's method was only a small example of how the system was being circumvented. I did not feel any moral or ethical guilt because the customer was being rewarded.

The trip was significant for me because, as in engineering, I had made my bones. I could think on my feet, be creative, and develop very profitable business. Although Father was anxious about the increased quantities and how to finance them, for the first time I had a sense that he trusted me and was pleased with the outcome of the trip.

5

An Opening to the Far East

Our deals were bantered, bartered, and bargained.

In the midst of my need to succeed and conquer the world, my family was growing and changing. I was a difficult father, very demanding. I believed that success in the material world was the answer to my existence. My standards were high. I expected no less from my kids than I did from myself. Eric was now an active eight-year-old, Marc was a tall five-year-old, and Claire was in her terrible twos. I wanted my kids to excel in school and in sports. I wanted all three to have the same interests as I had. My issue at home, as in business, was control. I did not know how to really love my family, which, in a way, was like loving a bird. Loving a bird requires an open palm so that it can fly away. If the bird loves you, it will come back to the open palm. It was a lesson that would be forced on me in later years. In some respects, I had the very traits which so disturbed me in my father, but which I believed I needed to be successful. Although I was not at home much of the time, the saving grace through all these intense expectations was my equally intense love for my children. Unfortunately, at the time, I did not know how to express my deep feelings of love and wanting to protect them from the outer world.

Bette was a loving Earth Mother, absorbing these high electrical charges bouncing through our home. Bette and I agreed that, because of my traveling and long working hours, we should spend our vacations together as a family. The first few years were spent at my parents' house at the shore. Bette and I would go walking down the beach as the sun set and splash through the surf as it came up on the sand. We would embrace and sneak off into the dunes to make love. The dunes were always reminiscent of our earlier lovemaking in the sand traps of our college golf course. I went body surfing in the waves with Eric and Marc, or built sandcastles with Claire. The friction between Father and me was not apparent to the children, and they loved to fish with him and have him read bedtime stories. My mother was the favorite, for she had no rules and loved the children no matter what they did. If they did something dangerous, she would say in her thick French accent, "Zat is not a good idee! You might hurt yourself!" And they usually stopped as she sat quietly smiling at them through her haze of Thorazine.

Woven into the vacations were ongoing business discussions with my father. And again, Bette would spend more time with the children than I would, because I was engrossed in the world of coffee. Bette came from a family that never showed their emotions or discussed their feelings. By contrast, my family had continual flareups and screaming matches, complete with my father throwing dishes across the room. My mother, heavily sedated because of her mental illness, did not react to these outbreaks, which further infuriated my father. Shortly after Eric's birth I had a similar tantrum, when we were living in my parents' apartment in New York, and I broke the chandelier. Bette had just turned twenty and was unable to cope with such behavior. She therefore took a very quiet approach to directing my energy away from business and having vacations with my parents. She was right.

One summer we rented a home in Maine, to avoid aggravating the mounting conflict between my father and me. Maine provided sailing, which I had always loved, and clamming in the mud flats at low tide.

We loved clamming. We dug our feet and toes down into the cold mud, while the sun warmed our backs, and when we felt a hard object we would reach down and pull out a clam. We had mud all over us as we dropped each clam in the bucket. The kids loved this wonderful opportunity to get filthy on purpose.

We beachcombed, and one day we even had dinner from the bounty of the sea and the land. The clams were fine, but as Eric exclaimed, "These wild beach peas are like eating stone pebbles. They taste like grass!"

I enjoyed the whole experience, just "being" both with my family and myself. But I was more concerned that the phone system did not work, that I could not be hooked up to international calls. We were on a party line, and I could not discuss deals. I was missing the action.

Because of my travels through East Africa, our company began to expand and become better known in the coffee world. We became known as reliable dealers who could find suitable qualities and quantities. As we made these inroads, we recognized that our food brokerage was stagnating. Howard was anxious to get into the action with coffee, and Father was unwilling to commit funds to the food division's development. After some discussion, Howard joined the coffee side of the business, and the food brokerage was closed down two months later.

Howard was a salesman. He had the ability to lead the fish down the river, avoid other peoples' traps and nets, and guide them into his own private preserve and close a deal. I enjoyed the buying. I always felt that if you could get the right coffee at the right price, there would be no problem in selling. However, if the ability to market well was included, a handsome profit would be made. Howard attacked the marketing with a vengeance and enrolled in an M.B.A. night program. I accepted his intensity as beneficial: we were two partners moving in the same direction. I did not understand at the time that a competition was developing between us. Howard wanted to be my equal, not only in education, but in other respects as well— perhaps even to surpass my success. For my part, I was still insecure and unsure about business, and turned to him for support with my issues with Father.

Coffee sales immediately picked up, and the pressure was on Father and me to keep up supplies. Howard retained his salary, which was the same as mine, so I agreed to split my 25 percent in half, and we agreed to be partners. I figured that even though this would initially greatly reduce my income, the loss would be more than made up by the volume increase and my not having to worry about marketing strategy. In retrospect, my willingness to give away such amounts came from my need to have my back watched while I was off in the bush cutting deals. I trusted Howard more than Father.

Father's deals with his European and West African connections brought in coffees from Guinea, Zaire, Madagascar, Cameroons, Ivory Coast, and other countries. Howard would narrow down the clients and sell the coffees. We began taking larger positions in the coffee commodity markets, both long and short, and Father was getting very nervous at the risk and exposure. He would go into his CGS routine (cough, gag and spit) as his tension mounted.

Father's early experience of loss at the onset of war and his near-bankruptcy while I was at Columbia made him hyper about any loss. Being a coffee dealer implied calculated risks and speculation, meaning that certain losses had to be expected over the year. Father, I felt, was irrationally fearful of losses, and therefore Howard and I had great difficulty in getting him to try big deals on his own. Howard and I would try to keep him calm as we pushed to expand. I wanted to obtain new sources of supply. We all felt we were not ready, or sufficiently well-financed, to lock horns with the bigger dealers in Central and South America. We needed another source, outside of Africa, to increase our volume and competitiveness, without overexposing ourselves.

One day Father walked into the office and said, "Indonesia! That's it! Claude, go out to the Far East and sniff around. There are very few dealers handling Indonesian coffees. Let's see if we can make an impact."

We knew nothing about the Far East. It was a great chance to test my abilities and push myself. I looked up all the shipping lines handling traffic in the area, their routes and whose cargo they carried. I quickly found out that Singapore handled most Indonesian coffees.

I have always been very lucky in my life, in the sense that things come to me when I need them, but as Howard used to say, "Luck is a residue of design." I have come to believe that when fully committed one's own energy draws the energy of other people or events that are needed.

I was going to Singapore cold, knowing no one, with only a few names given to me by the shipping lines. Shortly before I left, Bette decided to have a neighborhood cocktail party. She knew the wives through one function or another, but I did not know the husbands. During the party, I chatted with different people. One was a Dutchman. He worked for a large Dutch conglomerate, Hagemeyer N.V., who marketed products all through the world. When I learned they had a major presence in Singapore in electronic equipment, I told him I was going there to purchase coffee. Hagemeyer apparently had a subsidiary in Holland, Multitrade, that dealt in coffee. Multitrade in turn had a representative office in Jakarta, Multicontinental, which purchased Indonesian coffees for their account.

The energy of the trip was coming together. I was on track. I took all the phone numbers and the contacts for Multicontinental in Jakarta.

In the spring of 1969, I left New York, destined for Singapore via San Francisco, Tokyo, and Hong Kong. On landing in Singapore, I was overwhelmed by the efficiency and cleanliness of the airport. This was before Singapore became a city state of high-rise buildings. The streets were still busy with rickshaws and Chinese in gray or blue traditional dress. Low sprawling buildings dating back to British Colonial times dotted the landscape. The old inner harbor still existed, where Chinese junks arrived daily. I set off to keep my appointments with the shippers. The first appointment was at the inner harbor, where barges and sampans of all sizes and shapes were tied up to the stone quays. These large, fat barges were so overloaded with rice that the flat crossboards on their bows nearly touched the water, leaving barely two inches of breathing room to the gunnels.

I watched in awe. The planks crossing from gunnels to quay bent and strained under the shoulder loads of rubber and coffee. The Chinese laborers in tattered shorts showed betel-nut-red gums and missing teeth. They scurried ant-like, carrying loads twice their slight-boned body weight across their shoulders. Yellow-brown bodies glistened with sweat-caked dirt, eyes bulging under oppressive loads

Singapore Market, 1969

of tapioca, and cracked bare feet performed balancing acts on the narrow planks. My nostrils were attacked with pungent peanut satay air, mingled with the odor of feces running in the open sewers. At the outdoor markets on the quay, customers bargained for fly-covered hanging meats, the sellers shooing away the flies. Chickens cackled from their wooden crates while vendors hawked their wares of green and red peppers and tropical fruits of brown rombutons and yellow-green streaked duriams. I was surrounded by a cacophony of sounds which melded with pungent aromas engulfing me in the heat and humidity. The inner harbor was surrounded by a row of buildings which were stained, soiled, and aged. The walls of my appointment building were red-brown with mud fingerprints that guided me up the narrow, rickety, tilted stairs, out of the bright sunlight and into the shaded inner sanctum. The oppressive heat departed with my last step off the stairs and through the sign-painted, creaking, glass and wood office door. Inside I was greeted by a blast of frigid air.

In the back office I met a small man, wearing a white short-sleeved, open shirt, pin-striped trousers, wing-tip shoes and no socks. One very cold winter, three years later, when he visited New York and we went to some of the finest restaurants in the Big Apple—still no socks! As soon as I saw him, his eyes all a-twinkling, I knew we were going to do great business together. He had a round, well-defined head, jet black hair, and relatively large ears. Lin Min Che, or Mighty Mouse, as we code-named him, had entered my life. "Ah, nice to meet you, Mr. Saks," he said. "Please sit down. I finish phone conversation."

We shook hands. I smiled and sat down while he carried on an excited conversation in Chinese and his small fingers flew back and forth on an abacus. I noted that Mighty Mouse calculated faster with his abacus than I did with a slide rule or adding machine. He hung up the phone.

"Welcome to Singapore. What can we do for you?"

"My firm is now mainly in African coffees, but we are looking to expand into Indonesian coffees. I know very little, but one must start somewhere, and you are the first person I have visited."

"You have come to the right place. We are most active in Indonesians. I am happy to show you around."

With that, he took me into the sample room and explained the various coffees. Our deals were bantered, bartered, and bargained. Later, joined by his entire entourage, we dickered at a freezing restaurant. The lazy susans on tables turned, filled with spicy condiments, steaming colored meats, and pungent vegetables. All demanded to be eaten and I gorged myself. Waitresses scurried about, replenishing and responding to our every need. Shots of cognac were downed to boisterous toasts of *Yam sings*, good health, then replenished immediately. Chopsticks left telltale trails on the white tablecloth, forming spokes fanning out from the revolving lazy susan. Lichie, kumquats, and iced melon balls refreshed my palate. We finished with the rounds of hand-shaking and bowing rituals which concluded a deal, followed by my belly-bulging taxi ride to an antiseptic and boring American hotel.

I met with other shippers but did not greatly add to my knowledge except for odd details here and there. My main task now was to make contacts in Jakarta, specifically Multicontinental.

In the midst of the throng at the Jakarta airport, a tall, thin, white-haired, balding, blue-eyed Dutchman waved at me. I was the only American-looking man among the Chinese, Indonesians, and the few Dutch getting off the plane.

I was met with a wonderful warm smile by Mr. Tijsseling, Tijss, or the Reichmeister, as he was called. Even with this help of the Reich-meister who spoke the local dialect, the process took at least an hour.

Arriving in Jakarta within a year of Sukarno's overthrow and at the inception of Suharto's rule was a shock to the senses. People had just lived through a very bloody revolution, and the atmosphere of fear and hatred of the communist regime had not yet dissipated. There was little sense of optimism that a better life would come from a free democratic system.

Leaving the airport, we wove our way down the crowded streets and boulevards, and I noted the many boarded shops. Our Indonesian chauffeur continually leaned on the horn. Most Indonesians are short in stature and dark in complexion, resembling a mix of Filipino and Thai. Pedestrians, bicycles, and petchaks scurried out of the way. At that time, petchaks, which were three-wheeled bicycles, were still the main means of conveyance. A seat in front for passengers was covered by an awning to protect them from the sun or the torrential rains. Taxis did not exist, and buses were rare. The buses looked like sardine cans set on their sides with wheels, with groups

Loading local trading vessel in Jakarta Harbor, 1969.

of people clinging to the apertures. Few cars were seen except for vehicles belonging to foreigners and official cars of one sort or another.

The Reichmeister apologized for not getting me into the Hotel Indonesia, which was relatively new and booked months in advance by foreigners. My hotel was small, with minimal facilities, which meant running but not hot water. The toilet was complete with seat, which I later found out was quite a luxury, particularly if you traveled the back country. The hotel was clean and, most importantly, air-conditioned. The humidity in Jakarta seemed to average about 95 percent, with corresponding temperatures.

I left my hotel to meet the Reichmeister and his wife at the Hotel Indonesia. There was no taxi and no one spoke English, so I decided to skip the petchak and walk to the hotel, several blocks away. This was a mistake. The humidity, mixed with my perspiration and the dust, made for an interesting sight as I made my grand entrance into the frigid lobby of the Hotel Indonesia. There I was met by the Reichmeister and his wife Annette.

I found out Tijsseling and Annette had met at the end of the war in Indonesia and that Reichmeister meant "ring master"; Tijsseling had been a cavalry captain.

The Reichmeister believed Indonesia would explode developmentally under the new political leadership, and that would mean much greater coffee exports. He felt that the U.S. market would be a natural expansion for the low-grade Indonesian coffees, and that they would be perfect for vending, instants, and fillers in coffee blends.

I was excited at the prospect of opening a major new market, but concerned about quality control and financing the long shipping time to the U.S. Tijss told me that our agreements would have to be cleared with Multitrade in Amsterdam because Multicontinental, Jakarta operated only as an agent.

The deal rested in Amsterdam. I flew back to New York via Paris and called Multitrade to review the business. I spoke to "Penguin," which would become our code name for the director of Multitrade. He suggested I write him. After reviewing my letter with his Board, he would be in contact with me. Penguin was very prim and proper, a little bit too stiff-collared. But I figured "Okay, this is Europe," and so I complied.

Three weeks later, I had a response from Penguin. Multitrade did not have any presence in the United States in commodities and wanted to know if I could come to Holland to discuss mutual interests.

Here we were, in the modern age of phones and telexes, which worked well when dealing with Europe, and yet this gentleman was writing letters. The commodity business was a very fast-moving world, even back in 1969. Penguin's use of the mail reflected his character and made me wonder how successful the company was in its marketing practices.

To find out more about Indonesian coffees, I ran a complete survey of our roaster friends. The consensus was that Indonesian coffees were risky due to poor quality, meaning mustiness in the cup, which could be compared to the aroma of shoes left in the closet too long in very humid weather. There was also the problem of weevil holes (more than 10 percent), which caused rejection by the U.S. Food and Drug Administration. The FDA was concerned by the excrement the weevils could leave in these pin holes. Europeans did not care, because any contaminants were burned up in the roasting process. But to us, an FDA rejection meant re-exporting the coffee to Europe with all the associated costs, and the U.S. roaster would be left in a panic to fill out his blend. Finally, there was the problem with the unions in the large roasting plants. Indonesian coffees were shipped in 80-kilo bags, compared to the standard 60-kilo bags for most of the world, and 70-kilo bags for Colombia and Central America. The unions would not handle more than 100 tons of 80-kilo bags, which meant limited sales.

Armed with all this information, I phoned Penguin. I proceeded to give him a report of my findings and expressed the possibility of developing a large business if we could resolve the problems. He concurred and suggested I travel to Indonesia again. I responded, "Have passport, will travel!"

Within a week, we had made an appointment to go to Indonesia. I first flew to Holland, to meet Multitrade's staff. Penguin was the head man in the office, and reported to a division chief within the Hagemeyer conglomerate. Multitrade was simply the produce arm of the organization. Penguin looked about forty, had a pink, cherubic complexion, and was on the pudgy side. He had light blue eyes and thinning blond hair. He wore steel-rimmed glasses and favored blue blazers and grey flannel trousers. Penguin's most distinguishing feature was his walk: short-stepped with toes out, pudgy body shifting from side to side; hence his code name in our organization.

Multitrade imported spices of different types and teas from Indonesia, as well as from India, Ceylon, Turkey, and Russia. Ninety percent of their coffee imports were Indonesians.

Penguin invited me to lunch, with the Hagemeyer divisional director, whom we code-named "Aristocrat." Aristocrat was a tall, elegant man in his early fifties. I soon learned that he was very proud, having come up the ladder in Hagemeyer through the school of hard knocks. He had joined in his teens with no college education and was sent to Africa. I subsequently learned that much of Hagemeyer's management personnel had been horse traders in the underdeveloped countries and had been promoted in the same way.

Privately, I was thinking that they were missing half the equation. It was great to have learned in the bush, but in this modern world they needed knowledge of computers and management techniques. I wondered how well this company could compete in the world of the future.

The Reichmeister met us in Jakarta. Even in the few months since my last visit, modernization was evident. There were more cars, more motorcycles, and more people in the streets. There were fewer boarded-up shops, and the streets appeared in better condition.

The Reichmeister had arranged a tour, and we traveled through Bali, Java, Sumatra, and into the ports of Medan, Telukbetung, and Palembang—unheard-of destinations for the average person.

Indonesia is a volcanic land with huge, mountains rising out of the Pacific. It was green, green, and more green. The hillsides were terraced with rice fields, one after another, after another. When the rice was first planted, the fields, or terraces, were under water, like shimmering blue and silver lakes among the green mature fields and vegetation. The fields were planted in rotation, so some were bare. The countryside was a patchwork of green rice fields, silver water, and rich brown earth: an incredibly lush, wealthy country.

In contrast to the heat and humidity of the countryside, the Chinese restaurants were huge and freezing cold, with air conditioning going full blast. On entering, we were handed a hot towel to wipe

Indonesian farmer looking over his fields, 1969.

away the grime and perspiration. I generally let the Reichmeister order, as I did not understand the menu, which was written in Indonesian or Chinese. The food was scrumptiously tasty, at times very hot and spicy. Once, while dining, I looked across the room, and there was a huge rat, perhaps a foot and a half long, walking along the floor. This animal looked like the original monster of horror movies. I pointed to the rat and said, "My God, Look at that!"

"He's a lucky beast," The Reichmeister replied. "He hasn't been caught yet, or you would be eating him right now!"

"Come on, you're joking!"

"No, I'm not joking. Rat probably wouldn't be served in this restaurant because of its high quality, but in many other places, rats are cut up and dumped into the frying pan."

For a few seconds the thought stopped me from picking up the next morsel. Then I decided there was no way to find out the true identity of what I was eating, so I might as well sit back and enjoy.

Since large sections of Indonesia were very undeveloped, many problems surfaced. In those early years, all business was funneled through Jakarta. Production in the interior was primitive. Coffee literally has the texture and look of a cherry, not fully round, but red when ripe. The part used for the drink is the pit, roasted and ground. The question arises as to how the pulp is removed. In the early years, the farmers had no machines for this task, so they spread all the tiny fruits on the dirt road. As carts and cars went by, the tires crushed the pulp. After a day or two, all the pits would be picked up and stacked at the side of the road to dry. The pits were usually moist and swollen from the meat of the fruit.

In East Africa, the pulp is removed mechanically, and blowers or elevated screens are used to dry the coffee. But in Indonesia, some of the beans were dried right there in the dirt, then mixed with good lots, ruining the whole batch. Mildew and other problems occurred. In extreme cases, because of the mud, the coffee beans grew a fuzzy mold. There was nothing wrong with the beans. The coffee was great, but terribly mishandled. After further investigation, I found that the better coffees had been dried on concrete slabs. I specified that for all our shipments, the beans had to come from farmers who dried on the slabs. This method became the standard for the industry.

The problems were many, and it took us two days of negotiation to iron them out. I obtained the concession that all shipment coffees

Indonesian coffee sorters, 1969.

Coffee drying on concrete slab, 1971.

Negotiating with Indonesian exporter, 1969.

would have a minimal moisture content and low defect count. Our company would pay a minimal fee to have the Reichmeister's office inspect all coffees before shipment and get the shippers to load the coffee in 60-kilo bags. Furthermore, we would take the payment risk of the customers, but they would finance all coffees until thirty days from port, with us paying our portion of the interest costs, before we paid on the documents. We would convince the U.S. customers of our better quality by marking the export bags with the Multitrade imprint.

Under this type of arrangement, I could talk to the banks to extend our line of credit. Financing was needed to cover only the short period of time from docking to delivery to roasters and payment to us, so the banks would be more likely to extend credit. Penguin agreed to these terms, which meant that, at minimal cost to us, a large company was going to finance large trades and take all the shipping and quality risks. I was ecstatic.

I returned to New York to set up this business with the roasters. In a very short time, we began to do 200 tons per month and quickly climbed to 800 tons. As this growth occurred, G.M. Saks Inc. began to be considered an important player in the marketplace because we had the West African product, handled by my father, the East African product, which I had developed, and now we had the Indonesian product. The latter became an important calling card for us. We were to become king of the robustas, the low grades. I felt my personal power growing at its source, in the industry, and in the company.

My father *had* to recognize my abilities.

6

Zaire

*A scraggly youth in a khaki uniform stuck
the point of his rifle in my ear.*

My father was reluctant to admit that the projects I undertook
worked out well and were profitable. Nonetheless, since he did not
want to travel to West Africa anymore because of the heat and its ill
effects on his health, he decided to take me on a trip to see if I could
handle his area of expertise as well.

We flew Sabena Airlines from Belgium to Zaire. Kinshasa was a
new adventure—hot and tropical, the surroundings dripping with
humidity and the familiar smoldering smell of smoke in the air. The
health, currency, and passport controls turned out to be the worst I
had ever encountered. The officials at the airport moved at a snail's
pace, as baleful agents checked every aspect of our documents, suitcases, and money. As Father and I proceeded through the labyrinth of
officialdom, I became uneasy; the bureaucrats were brusque and pro-
jected a hate-the-white-man attitude. Fear has a certain odor, and the
Europeans going through the controls were sweating fear. The Zairians were like predators smelling their prey. I observed that certain passengers were met by local representatives and were able to move ahead
of the other passengers through more relaxed controls. I made a mental note that next time I would have such a system in place.

By the time we got to Passport Control, the official there had
shunted eight people aside for visa irregularities, meaning he was

looking for a payoff. We decided we would not let him know that we spoke or understood French. After some comments to Father and me, about which we expressed a lack of understanding, we were finally allowed through.

Kinshasa sprawled indolently on a big curve of the Zaire river which flowed—or crawled—along, a massive, muddy bulk, deeply choked with algae. Kinshasa consisted of two towns: one was the European section, with large, colonial buildings and expansive palm-lined streets; the other was *la cité*, where most Zairians lived. There, small, makeshift shacks with corrugated rooftops lay baking in the sun. Along the twisted dirt roads were many small businesses: bicycle repair shops, hair cutting establishments, and sewing machine shops. Throngs of people milled about in bare feet and tattered clothes. Radios blared from every shanty. Within *la cité* there were a few compounds where the well-connected citizens lived. Mobutu Seseco ruled as emperor of the country, which seemed to lumber forward on a system of political connections and *Pot o Pot*, a sort of payoff.

Father and I were staying in a decent hotel about fifteen miles out of town. The oppressive heat was not agreeing with Father's health, and his ulcers and the phlebitis in his legs were flaring up. The first two days were spent mainly in taxis, getting our bearings and visiting various Belgian colonial shippers with whom Father had done business through their Antwerp and Brussels representatives.

I kept getting a feeling of disquiet from those old, pompous colonial shippers, a sense of unraveling, and a fear for their future. Their management expressed displeasure with some of the new small shippers, which were better connected politically: the Pakistanis, Portuguese, and even, heaven forbid, Zairians. I came to understand that the old quality control system of the *Office National de Caffe* (ONC) was defunct. The ONC operated in name only. Their machinery had broken down or worked only part-time due to lack of parts. Quality certificates were issued to most anyone willing to pay a "dash of oil," as the British would say.

To me, this made for exciting times. Whenever there is chaos and disorganization, that is the time to make money. It was just a matter of being clear as to my own objectives. Once I knew where my "meatball" was, I would let the system's "sauce and spaghetti" confuse appearances, so that I could operate and get exactly what I wanted with little interference from the outside.

Father's health worsened. He was just not in condition to run all around Kinshasa, commuting back and forth from the hotel. He decided he would stay at the hotel and I would report to him every evening. Two days later, he pulled one of his typical surprises. "Fred Matter arrives this afternoon," he announced, "and he'll give you a hand covering Kinshasa."

"What the hell do you mean he'll give me a hand covering Kinshasa?" I retorted. "I don't need him. I can develop this business without a large Swiss firm holding my hand. Why didn't you tell me he was joining us?"

"I knew you would be upset, because you always want to do business by yourself. But Walter Matter & Company has been very helpful to me over the years in financing several large deals in Europe. I don't have that type of capital, so I make alliances."

Fred and I were the same age. He was a little more reserved, of medium height, with thinning brown hair. He was extremely knowledgeable about Central American arabicas, and his father's company was one of the largest importing houses in Europe.

"Making alliances for financing is fine, but Matter & Company takes advantage of you. You do most of the creative thinking and set things up, then they take two-thirds of the profit. On top of that, you give away all your connections in Africa free of charge. You're crazy!"

"Don't you call your father crazy! I think you're too short-sighted. You and Fred are the same generation, and Walter and I are about the same age. We could develop a perfect match. Think ahead. We could market for North America, and their company could cover Europe."

"Come on, you're dreaming," I said. "Matter is an established firm with traditional roots. They're not about to give anything away. They'll never share. That company is an old stuffed shirt. If it weren't for your innovative thinking, they'd be on the decline. It's only because of your introductions and what you've taught Fred that the company is being revitalized."

Once again, Father thought he needed a larger partner to hold his hand. I was faced with a *fait accompli;* I had to share my thinking, my new connections, and my work with Fred. And for what?

Father started to hack and dry-heave, as he usually did when nervous, particularly in confrontations with me. I had no choice; he was not feeling well, and I needed to make the best of the situation.

Fred himself did not annoy me. Although conservative compared to me, he had a similar perspective about business and life. What annoyed me was Father treating Fred as if he knew more than I did. He did have expertise in Central and South American coffees, but no more than I did about other coffees or business in general. Father kowtowed to Fred to obtain financing and to make himself look like the grand old gentleman of great African and deal-making knowledge. I was envious of Fred's receiving Father's preferential treatment and acknowledgment while I was treated like the new kid on the block. I decided to get as much information as possible before Fred arrived.

I left Father in the hotel and headed down to the *Agence Maritime Internationale Zairoise* (AMIZA), which was the old arm of Belgium Shipping Lines. There, I had a meeting with the governor, as the president of the Agency was called, in a large, high-ceilinged office with wood paneling, a leftover from the old colonial days. The meeting immediately revealed the governor's concerns regarding future changes—the Zairization of the major plantations, private enterprise, export, and quality control. There were rumors that all foreign companies would have to take in Zairian partners or be nationalized outright. He felt that, as an outsider, I could get the most information, and he proposed to treat me to a wonderful dinner if I could keep him informed. I thought: what a cheap bribe! I gratefully but politely declined and asked instead that he get me an appointment with the Minister of Agriculture, and I would keep him posted. He warmed to the prospect, and with one phone call set up the appointment for later that day.

From the governor's office, I went to see the traffic director. He was a typical beer-drinking Belgian, red-nosed, pot-bellied, and very charming. He explained that coffee was moving very slowly in the interior due to the disrepair of equipment and bribes proffered in all directions. I invited him to lunch and was able to arrange for a clearance person to help me with customs whenever I would travel to or from Zaire.

I left the pub and arrived punctually at the Ministry of Agriculture for the appointed two-thirty meeting. The ministry had been dutifully painted the national color, light puke-green, inside and out. I made my way up the old grand colonial staircase with its sweating and badly soiled walls and entered the Minister's antechamber. A droopy-eyed secretary took my name and informed me the Minister was expecting me; in the meantime, would I be seated, and she would call me. I joined the other four supplicants on the plush velour couches, which, when sat upon, made a squashing sound from the absorbed humidity. I noted the smudge marks on the walls, at head level, which blended nicely into the famous green. Several hours passed and finally I got in to see the Minister, who turned out to be a very bright and erudite man. He did not fit in with my preconceived picture of the typical civil servant.

I explained who G.M. Saks, Inc. was, as a company, and our interest in buying directly from Zaire large quantities of robustas for the United States. He was pleased at our interest because he knew that the old colonial houses had developed a monopoly and he intended to break the market open. He further told me that the ONC was going to be properly reactivated under the direction of a Frenchman whom the Ministry had retained. The Frenchman would train a new Zairian elite to take over in ten years. The Minister then called in his Deputy Assistant, who was in charge of the entire project. I invited them both for lunch the next day, to the best restaurant in town. The Minister declined, but the deputy accepted and suggested inviting the newly appointed head of the ONC.

I was jubilant. I was on an inside track, and I smelled business.

Returning to the hotel, I found Fred with Father. What a damper to my enthusiasm; I knew I had to reveal all my detective work and arrangements. I was peeved to have to give up such information so easily. But as we proceeded to dinner, I slowly warmed to the idea that perhaps Fred and I could develop into a good combination at origins, he covering the European marketing and G.M. Saks, Inc. covering North America. I invited him to join me for lunch the next day with the Deputy Minister of Agriculture. He accepted, and would join me after he visited the old traditional Belgian exporters whom Father and I had seen the previous days. This left the morning free for me to visit new, upcoming shippers, evaluate their prospects, and see if I could connect with a future wheeler-dealer.

After several dead ends, I met André, a young Belgian in charge of a small, Portuguese import-export business. He was two years my junior but seemed older, being prematurely bald with a full black beard. We were immediately on a first-name basis. We talked about the poor state of Zaire and its overvalued currency. He offered to change all the currency I wanted at the black market rate. We then talked about coffee and proceeded to negotiate a contract for better coffees, but marked as low grades. He had worked out a deal with the ONC to avoid the higher tax.

We closed our first deal for seventy-five tons, which worked out fine. We talked about the upcoming changes in the ONC. "I'm having lunch with the Deputy Minister on the subject," I told him.

"I know," he said. "You will be joined by the new *Directeur Général* of the ONC, a Frenchman, and the Assistant Director General (ADG), a Zairian political nominee. I suggest you keep an eye on the ADG, as he is an upcoming man with the right tribal connections, and could eventually replace the Frenchman." Obviously, he was well informed, and tight with the ADG—great! I had connected with one of the new insiders, and future prospects looked like fun and profit.

At 1:30, accompanied by Fred, I joined the Deputy Minister of Agriculture at The Brussels, the most elegant of the remaining European-run restaurants. As predicted by André, the Deputy Minister had brought along not only the newly designated French D.G. of the ONC, but also his assistant. I arranged the table seating so that I sat between the Deputy Minister, to my right, as protocol called for, and the ADG to my left, with the new D.G. in front of me and with Fred between the Deputy Minister and the D.G. I liked this positioning because the Deputy Minister, a political appointee, would probably not be the person who arranged the contracts, beyond giving his blessing to future large deals. The Frenchman was a quick, nervous type, a cigarette continually dangling from his lips. "My friends," he said, "wait and see what I'm going to do with the ONC. That old facility will become a model for Africa. In addition to handling coffee for shippers, we will start purchasing coffees in the interior, process the coffee, and market it directly to the international markets."

Privately, I thought he would be lucky to accomplish 50 percent of his goals, but that would be enough to get things rolling. I wanted to be on the bandwagon. I gave him every encouragement, and the Deputy Minister kept up the political banter about how Zaire would become the leading African coffee producer, with the best qualities, all handled and controlled by Zairian nationals. In my mind, I wondered about the longevity of the Frenchman under such conditions and decided I had better probe and develop a relationship with the ADG.

Meanwhile, the waiters bustled about us with the finest imported foods, and the champagne flowed. The ADG to my left sat stolidly in his chair and said little. He was on the portly side, big, bulging eyes with lids half closed. He was to be code named "Hippo." He was biding his time, knowing he would take over as soon as the mess was cleaned up. I wanted to be his North American friend and confidante. We struck up a conversation. "This development with the ONC is very exciting. How did you come to be nominated ADG?"

"There are not that many educated Zairians," he said. "Particularly those with an economics and marketing education from Louvain."

Louvain is a Jesuit University in Belgium, one of the toughest and finest schools in Europe. He continued: "Being well educated was the prime requirement. The other is that since Zaire is populated by many different tribes, there must be a balance of power in positions of responsibility. I was fortunate to be at the right place at the right time."

I explained that I wanted to support the ONC development and that our company was very interested in importing large quantities to the U.S. I asked him about the old European houses.

"Some will survive because of politics," he answered. "For the most part, we will be the exporters, and we will support new and upcoming aggressive firms, particularly if they have any Zairian participation."

I thought of André. I knew he was already in discussions regarding taking in a Zairian partner.

The Assistant Director General then astonished me. "I'm very interested in pursuing our talks, perhaps in a different setting. I would like to get to know you better. Have you ever been to *la cité*? Or had a typical Zairian meal?"

"No, I've done neither, but would very much like to do so."

"Good! Join me tonight without your friend, and I will show you the real Kinshasa. A friend of mine will be joining us. André—you met him this morning. I will ask him to pick you up at your hotel."

I accepted with great enthusiasm. The "meatball" was presenting itself, while "spaghetti and sauce" were being flung around me. Fred was still in the middle of a political and economic conversation on the future of Zaire with the deputy and the D.G. Their eyes glowed at the prospect of a large Swiss importer with lots of money. But I was pleased to have developed my personal contact with the ADG.

During the rest of the meal, Fred and I presented a common front for purchasing coffee worldwide and supplying technical expertise. The meal eventually broke up at 3:30. We stepped out into the real world of downtown Kinshasa, stunned by the brightness and the overwhelming heat. The cost of the meal had been twice New York's, at the official exchange rate. Thank God for André's black-market rate.

All of our guests drove off in their air-conditioned cars, as Fred and I got into our waiting, baking taxi. All windows open, we shed our jackets and ties and headed for the hotel.

That evening, André picked me up at 8:00. We met the ADG in the heart of *la cité*. The sun had set. It was cooler, and crowds were out on the street. Music blared, joyful that the day was done. There was little electricity and no street lights. André and I were the only white faces, and I was tense.

"Loosen up!" André urged. "The ADG is a bigwig, and everything will be smooth as long as we're with him."

We went to one of the local restaurants and had a typical Zairian meal of *capitaine*, a local fish, with hot *pilipili* sauce; manioc, a root vegetable with no taste whatever and the texture of rough strained potatoes—but an absolute must to absorb the heat from the *pilipili*; some carrots; and, of course, lots of beer to wash it all down. Sweets and coffee followed. Well-wishers kept popping by to shake the ADG's hand during dinner, which took two and a half hours.

Leaving the restaurant, we ambled to a local night spot that was just getting into the swing of things, with rock and roll and American pop, but mainly African music. We drank a lot of scotch and beer.

Finally, at 2:30 A.M., we called it a night. We weaved to the car, and found our way out of *la cité*. André, feeling no pain, sat tall-shouldered, hands tense on the wheel, with his black-bearded chin jutting forward, as the car careened, all windows open, down the deserted Boulevard Du Cinque Juillet. There was not a soul on the streets; it was pitch black. Blurred lights flashed by, illuminating old colonial buildings that vaguely registering on my inebriated brain.

Suddenly, the car screeched to a halt in front of a military checkpoint. A scraggly youth in khaki uniform stuck the point of his rifle in my ear. His finger rested lazily on the trigger. "Passport?" he casually inquired.

My head not budging, nose straight forward, eyes slammed right, I tried to watch his every move. My right hand moved slowly, reaching backward to my hip pocket for the little blue book with an eagle on the cover. Very slowly it was passed from white hand to black hand. The barrel point receded six inches. Seconds ticked by as fingers flipped pages, searching for the leopard-head stamp of Zairian Visa Control. My mind became conscious that André had stepped out of the car and was involved in a screaming match with the sergeant in charge.

My guard mumbled, "Your visa is not in order." My thumping head wanted to screech at him that he was fucking full of shit, because he could not read, and he was holding my passport upside down.

"Really, Citoyen, I'm astonished! My visa was issued by your Embassy in Washington."

At that moment, André kicked the car fender and started yelling at the top of his lungs. The sergeant motioned my guard to come over and join him on the other side of the car. My passport was returned, and the rifle barrel receded from my window. I quickly became aware that André did not have his passport or driver's license or registration or his Zairian working papers or any other papers or identification.

The sergeant was yelling. "I'm going to throw you and your American buddy in the clink, and I assure you it'll be a month before they find you!"

"Look, Sergeant," André said, "I have no pockets except my hip pocket where I keep my money. I live here in Kinshasa, and there's no need for all this."

"What do you mean, no need? The law is clear! The two of you are probably conspiring against the Zairian state. I should have you shot on the spot."

I became cold sober, with fear fluttering in my abdominal cavity. The sergeant continued to harangue André for another forty-five minutes. Then, suddenly, I saw André take the sergeant by the arm and walk off out of earshot, partially concealed by the bushes. The private stayed behind, guarding me and the vehicle. My mind raced, thinking of the condition of Zairian jails: filth, bugs, rats, heat, contaminated water, survival food, and dangerous criminals. I was panicked in my solitude.

Another half hour passed. By now, it was 4:00 in the morning, and I was drenched with sweat. Finally, André walked back, got into the car, started the engine and moved through the checkpoint with the sergeant telling him he let us off lightly. We pulled away.

I yelled at André. "What the fuck was that all about? Why the hell don't you carry papers?"

"Relax, just a lot of bull," André said. "I gave him thirty Z's and that's the end of it. At the black market rate, that's not even fifteen dollars."

"Jesus Christ," I exclaimed. "Why didn't you pay him off in the first place, instead of scaring the shit out of me and leaving me sweating here for over two hours?"

He shook his big head in disbelief. "What, are you crazy? You can't do that. You've got to give them their little pleasures. They've got nothing else to do at this hour of the night."

"Then why not carry your papers and get on with it?"

"You don't understand," André said. "I could carry all the papers in the world and they would still find something wrong, so they can collect their thirty Z's. In fact, I'm astonished they didn't do that with you."

"My guard started to, but he was short-circuited by the sergeant calling him over to your side."

"Just remember for future reference: anywhere in this country, always let them give you a hard time, and make sure you appear very annoyed. Not only does it fill their time, but one of their greatest pleasures is the humiliation of a white man. Then, and only then, can you pay them off. And, it's got to be the right amount. If too much, they might fleece you or turn even nastier, and if too little, they could lock you up for twenty-four to forty-eight hours before a friend gets you out. The bribe is to be proffered with respect, and humility, so that he can reluctantly accept and overlook all your supposed transgressions."

"Jesus Christ, is that what business is all about in Zaire?"

"Here's your hotel. Yes, it is. Well worth it though, because there is little competition, and most people can't handle Zaire. Goodnight Claude, sleep fast."

"Goodnight, André. Thanks for the lesson."

7

Cameroon

*We are a small firm, and you are frittering
away our money by chasing windmills.*

Next morning, Father, Fred, and I caught a plane to Douala,
Cameroon. On the way, Father took an aggressive tone and reprimanded me. "Claude, what you are doing is very dangerous. It will
take Zaire at least two or three years to take over coffee production,
assuming they ever succeed. You are putting me in an embarrassing
position with the large European shippers. You will ruin what little
business we have in Zaire."

I stood my ground. "Look, you wanted me to establish direct contacts in West Africa and not work through the mother houses in
Europe as you do. You know you can't keep traveling in the heat and
humidity. If I'm going to start taking over West Africa, then I'll do
it my way. Zairization of the coffee industry will happen. I'm not
ruining anything. I'm talking to the best-connected people in the
system. Maybe the change will take two years, but I intend to be
there when it happens. Right now, it's just talk, so no harm is being
done to your precious European shippers. When the change does
occur, the Europeans will fall like stones."

Father was getting agitated. "You underestimate the power of the
colonial shippers. Your concept will backfire. The Europeans could
blackball our business. And André—who the hell is he? Just a young
upstart from nowhere. He does some small tricky business, but no big

deals. How do you know you can rely on his quality? At least, with my large European connections I can rely on quality and performance."

I raised my voice. "Cut the bravado. The deals with André will be fine. Of course, I'm keeping the business small for the time being, so I can check his performance. All we get from the Europeans is a small commission, so nothing to rejoice about. If the old colonial houses question you, just blame the new business on Howard and me, your 'kindergarten,' as you like to call us. Just relax. We can play both sides, until we jump onto the winning team. I'll make a wager it will be the ONC. In the meantime, my business with André has a greater profit margin than your offers from Europe."

"I think you're wasting your time and effort, not to mention my money. So I will stay in close contact with my connections and I will watch how you make your deals develop."

I was frustrated by what I considered to be his arrogant, know-it-all attitude, especially since he had never succeeded in Zaire.

The plane's wheels touched the tarmac in Doula, Cameroon. The runway was built up on a promontory, with jungle vegetation steaming on three sides. The familiar blast of heat and humidity hit us as the door opened. Douala was the armpit of West Africa, both geographically and atmospherically. The airport was yellow-brown with age, and musty smells permeated the air. But, although passport and health control lines were lengthy, the customs officials were cheerful and smiling, in contrast to those in Zaire.

Fortunately, Father had contacted Socopao S.A., a subsidiary of a large French freight forwarding company. One of their reps came to handle airport clearance for us. What a godsend! We waited for our luggage, jackets in hand, while he processed the paperwork.

The whole process took forty minutes, a record time. Socopao's car was waiting, and we drove off for the Hotel Cocotier, passing through the slums of Douala with their colorful shops, noises, and smells. It was very similar to the Kinshasa *la cité*, but downtown Douala was more integrated. At one point, a palm frond was sticking out of the middle of the road. The driver explained that when heavy rains came, parts of the road would cave in, so people would put a palm frond there to warn oncoming cars.

We finally arrived at the Cocotier, a typical old colonial African hotel. The lobby had no doors and few walls. What breeze existed would float through and keep the temperatures bearable, relative to the outside. We registered, then proceeded to our rooms to take quick showers. The motor of the window air conditioner continuously battled to complete each revolution. The walls were heavily varnished dark mahogany, covered with mildew. In the bathroom, the mildew was compounded by the lack of a shower curtain or enclosure. The shower stall, if you could call it that, consisted of a porcelain square at floor level with a hand-held shower hose. When I showered, the entire bathroom was sprayed with water. The sewer lines were not vented; gases backed up through the sink and shower drains. I could readily understand why, with Father's advancing age and deteriorating health, he wanted me to take over Africa.

We met in the lobby, Father, Fred and I, and proceeded to call on Jean-Claude Filastre, the director of Socopao S.A. Father was guiding Fred and giving him pointers as if he were another son. I was fuming, perhaps out of jealousy, but certainly because information and connections were the real capital of G.M., and Father was again giving it all away for free. Jean-Claude was a friendly, solid, dark, Mediterranean type of Frenchman, who was well-informed and sparkled with brightness and imagination. He addressed my father as elder statesman of the group. "Monsieur Saks, I think you have arrived at an important time for the Cameroons. The coffee industry is going though some major changes. The *Caisse de Stabilization* is flexing its muscle and appears to have the political authority to control our export prices. The Cameroons is a democracy, so it will not nationalize the production facilities. I believe the *Caisse* will market the coffee, and the shippers, who are mainly French, will receive a percentage of their processing and production costs. The main profits will be retained by the *Caisse*."

My Father responded with a knowledgeable air. "I am very aware of the changes in Africa. We have just come from Zaire where we are witnessing similar occurrences."

I felt like screaming. After the argument on the plane and his discounting all my work, now he was taking credit for everything I had learned.

The *Caisse* in the future would market the coffee and assign quotas to the shippers who had the best performance, or the best political connections. The head of sales at the *Caisse* had a very powerful position.

It happened that Jean-Claude had a tight connection with the *Caisse*. His company, which was the largest freight forwarder and warehouser, cleaned, dried, and bagged coffee for export as a representative of many shippers. It also represented most of the large steamship lines calling on the port of Douala.

At Father's insistence, we spent the next twenty-four hours visiting several shippers. I was impatient. I felt we were wasting important time. The shippers would become dinosaurs when the *Caisse* controlled the price and export quota.

Finally we called on the *Caisse*. Mr. N'Dongo was head of sales, and I took an immediate liking to him. He was a strong, dark man, wore an open, short-sleeved shirt, and had one lazy eye which slowly roved the room from left to right and back again, as the other eye held us in its glance. During our meeting, he explained the system that Jean-Claude had already delineated. "I am pleased with the business that G.M. has done with the shippers," he concluded. "Now it is time to do business directly with the *Caisse*."

Father responded, "It will be with pleasure. The difficulty that we have had in the past is that most of your coffees are sold to Europe. Furthermore, your sales are in French francs, which makes it more difficult in the U.S."

I thought to myself, "That's a lot of bull, Father. You are just afraid to take on the positions." I was sure I could work out advantageous French franc conversions with the bank. I kept quiet. I would bide my time.

Fred got into the conversation. "Well, Mr. N'Dongo, this is the reason I came down with Messrs. Saks. My company is located in Switzerland, giving us the advantage to distribute throughout Europe. Regarding currencies, we deal with them all day long. I look forward to starting a solid business with the *Caisse*."

"I'm sure that will be possible, as your firm comes highly recommended by Mr. Saks, Senior."

I was going crazy! Father had set up Fred perfectly to take advantage of our contacts. I felt like the bastard child.

Father asked N'Dongo to dinner, and he accepted provided Fred and I joined him afterwards to go night clubbing.

Nightclubbing with N'Dongo was fun and informative. He seemed to know all the local beauties, and we were always surrounded by beautiful women. The nightclub was typical with its blaring music, frigid air-conditioning and very sparse lighting. Over the band music and the giggling of the girls, I gathered that N'Dongo was the first Cameroonian to hold the job of marketing manager for the *Caisse*. Previously, it had always been a French technical advisor. His coming to power signaled the Cameroons' intention to market the crop directly.

I asked if he had the freedom to initiate sales at his discretion, without the shippers' approval.

"Not yet. That final decision needs to come from the *Ministry du Plan*. But I assure you, it is imminent. I will then be marketing more than 90 percent of the Cameroon robustas."

Fred and Father were planning to fly to Europe the next afternoon, but I decided, in the midst of nightclub smoke and noise, that I would go up to the capital, Yaounde, and meet with the *Ministry du Plan*.

The next morning, over breakfast, Father told me, "You're wasting your time going to Yaounde. There's nothing but bureaucrats who cannot give you contracts. We are a small firm, and you are frittering away our money by chasing windmills."

My annoyance started to show. "I couldn't disagree more. Changes are occurring here, and I need to take advantage of them. Staying for three more days will more than pay for itself in the long run. In fact, I think you should come with me."

Father started his CGS routine. "I'm not feeling well, and I want you to accompany me to visit my connections in Europe. I want to introduce you and to solidify our relationships in the areas where our real business comes from."

"I can meet your connections some other time. I intend to dig up all information I can while I'm here in the Cameroons."

"Have it your way."

And I did.

Parting after breakfast was a bit tense, but I had no time to mull over the situation. I had to find a way to arrange an appointment with the minister of "the Plan." I went to see Jean-Claude, who encouraged me and arranged an appointment with Mr. Hayatou, the assistant minister. Jean-Claude told me that the assistant minister made all the important decisions and the Minister, a political appointee, just rubber-stamped them.

I decided to pay a quick visit to N'Dongo to inform him of my intentions and to cement further the friendship which was developing. I told him I did not want to leave the impression I was going over his head. To the contrary, he supported sales to the U.S. market to enhance his own position.

I loved it. We were becoming co-conspirators. He needed our market for his bid to power, and I needed him to get quantity and to bypass the shippers. I pushed further. "We would like to see you develop the market, provided you do it through us. We are the only firm that can communicate with you in French, and we have the knowledge of the robusta market."

"Yes, of course, through you. If you can convince Hayatou, I assure you we will do great business."

Yaounde, in early 1970, was still developing as the capital. It had only one paved road down the center of town. All the others were red clay that left a red hue on all the buildings and passing cars. I checked into the Sheraton, which literally had been finished the week before.

The following morning I met Mr. Hayatou, the Assistant Minister du Plan, who kept me waiting a relatively short time, as African customs go. He was a tall, lean, dark, handsome man from the Chad border in the northern Cameroons. He was a member of the Philibe tribe and a Moslem. He had a University of Paris education and was extremely poised and erudite. He went to great lengths to explain to me that he was giving more power to the *Caisse* so that Cameroon coffees would be represented globally, especially to the U.S. market, which had been neglected by the shippers. The meeting lasted until late morning, so I invited him to lunch.

Cameroon market, 1970.

During lunch we got into African politics and he gave me his analysis of the Cameroon scene.

I thanked him for giving me the background. "I always find the information helpful in doing business," I told him. "Do you come from a large family?"

"Yes, we are thirty-four brothers and sisters."

"Thirty-four!"

"Yes. Are you shocked by African marriages, Mr. Saks?"

"No, why?"

"When someone tells you a large number, you should always ask 'if from the same belly.' In my case, not. My father was the chief of our village, and so had eight wives." He laughed, casually, with his white teeth flashing in the sun.

Before he returned to his office, he said, "I have decided to give the *Caisse* the go-ahead to sell to you directly for U.S.A. destinations only."

I was jubilant. I felt the power flow through my arteries. I wanted to jump up and hug him. He had validated my decision to come to Youande and further strengthened my position with Father.

I thanked him, reassuring him we would do a great job for the Cameroons. I headed back to Douala and connected to Paris.

In Paris, I stayed only long enough to visit one of Father's old cronies. He headed up the French operation of a Dutch trading house, and all his deals with Father had a twist I did not care for: he always insisted on a side commission for himself. Eventually, the Dutch headquarters got suspicious of his business practices. To monitor his activities, the Dutch brought a young Frenchman, Bernard, to Paris, from their African operations. Unknown to either of us at that time, Bernard was to be a major help in our mutual business careers.

Father's friend treated me as a young apprentice and went out of his way to explain to me his "great" knowledge about the Ivory Coast, Republic of Central Africa, and the Cameroons. I took the information in and flew off to New York.

My accomplishment in the Cameroons caused a furor with Father. The potential increase in quantities, direct with the *Caisse*, called for additional lines of credit. Father went into his CGS routine and immediately looked for security.

"The only way we will be able to finance these additional quantities is to turn to Fred. I will explain to him what you have set up, and in return he will finance. He will probably want a third of the profits above his usual interest rates, but we will work it out."

I was enraged. "Bullshit! Bullshit and bullshit! We don't need Fred. I don't want to tell him what I set up, and I don't want to give away my hard-earned information or profit. Let him discover it for himself. His interest rates are above the market, and you want to give him a profit besides? Let's set up a meeting with the bank and see how the loan officer reacts to this new business. Your financials are very good, and there's no reason the bank should not increase our line of credit."

He responded, "Even if I could make an arrangement with the bank, we still would have the problem of covering the French franc exposure. On top of that, when my French shipper friends find out that we are doing business directly with the *Caisse*, we will no longer get offers from them. Claude, life is an evolution, not a revolution. You're turning the business upside down, and you'll ruin my reputation!"

I could feel my temples pulsing. "Bullshit again! I'm going where the trend is developing. I'm going with the action. As far as your shipper friends are concerned, we do 500 tons, maybe, a year. So the risk of loss is minimal. I think I can more than double that in the first six months. And there is no French franc problem. The foreign exchange department at the bank told me the franc is trading at a one percent discount to the dollar on three months forward and two percent on six months forward. By covering our French franc forward against the spot rate, we can pick up another one to two percent profit, depending on the shipment."

Father was indignant that I had covered all the bases. "How dare you go behind my back to the bank! I am still head of this company, and I will keep the contacts with the bank." I was damned if I did or didn't.

I said in disgust, "Cut the crap. I didn't go behind your back. I didn't talk to the account officer. If we're supposed to be a team, let's act like one. All I did was obtain all the answers to the objections I knew you'd raise. I also anticipated that, from time to time, we'll be buying more coffee than we can sell right away, so I checked into hedging on the London futures market. Your broker friend there agreed to let us operate against original margin only."

Father's lips tightened across his mouth as he spoke. "You're making this business much too complicated. I used to make a very nice living just doing brokerage and helping some of my European friends on deals."

I did not let him get away with it. "That's a lot of horseshit. I've looked at the old financials and you were not doing well. In fact, I recall one year, when I was at Columbia University, when you almost went broke and I had to finance my education, so don't give me that. You wanted to become a dealer and that's why I joined the company," I said. "Stop worrying. I'll take care of the details, but I need you for the overview and the bank. Let's work together on this or let's close it all down."

He calmed down and decided to give my suggestion a try. I

needed Father to help make a presentation at the bank. He was the symbolic strength of the company. Our account officer placed implicit trust in my father, a grand European gentleman. Howard and I were considered young, aggressive upstarts.

Our meeting went well. I laid out how the operation would work, our future reliability and growth record. The banker was convinced not so much by the numbers, but by Father's assurances that he had a complete grip on the company.

The following year we consolidated our sources and marketed successfully to the roasters. Our Cameroon business expanded from 500 tons per year to 6,000 tons, as a result of my close coordination with N'Dongo and Hayatou's blessing. I became very involved with trading French francs and the British pound, hedging our positions, doing the transactions inter-bank, as the U.S. currency futures market had not yet developed. Howard, meanwhile, was developing an important following in the roaster community.

But Father could not keep a secret, and as always wanted to show off how much he knew: he told Fred of my successes. Fred went down to Youande to cut a similar deal for Switzerland and eventually Europe. Fred and Hayatou became close friends.

8

Nest Egg

The king must die.

By mid 1971, we were the largest dealers in Indonesians and second largest in Africans. Howard and I were running the entire business. Father became involved only when large deals were in question. He spent much of his time either at his seashore house or in Europe. Our communications usually occurred at crazy hours. His calls were generally nervous, apprehensive, and critical of any positions, long or short, we had taken. The business had expanded to the point where we needed another trader to handle the daily functions. Father refused to spend money for a knowledgeable coffee man, for which we were grateful, because we wanted to train him ourselves. We placed ads in *The New York Times* and were fortunate to find an American currency trader, Steve, at one of the foreign banks. He spoke good French and some Spanish and German. Steve became a great back-up in the trading room.

Howard and I, after some major fights with Father, got a substantial raise in salary and an agreement giving us 25 percent of the profits on *all* business before taxes, not just what we generated, to be split between us. The increase in our remuneration was heavily paid for. Our every decision was a source of harassment from Father. His deep-in-the-night calls from Europe to check on us became incessant. Howard developed a bad case of colitis, and I developed asthma, which I had not had since I was a child. We were working fourteen to sixteen hours a day, covering all points of the globe.

I found out that Father had developed an intimate relationship with a woman, Margot, from Belgium. This explained his increased traveling and I believe she had an influence on him which made him more belligerent toward us. Every time he returned from a trip he would emphasize how ungrateful we were for everything he did for us.

Four years had gone by since I had joined Father and I was prodding him to give us a chance to buy into the company, but he refused. As his only son, I was incredulous at his egotistical attitude, his attempt to hang on to power. After every fight, Father would leave for his seashore house or Europe, leaving Howard and me steaming. My anger with Father was close to the surface. When it threatened to erupt, I would release the tension, and accept my shadowside in retrospect, by sitting at my desk and mock machine-gunning our competitors, situations, and Father's attitudes. But even this physical ritual was not enough.

The impasse with Father was a powder keg waiting to explode. Then, in late July, a deal came up which was to change all our lives. Jean-Claude telephoned, asking that Father and I come to Douala immediately. He insisted that Father come with me; the elder-statesman father-figure was very important in African negotiations. I was a bit peeved, but excited. Jean-Claude told me that the deal involved the U.S. "basket quota," and that I would have to come to Douala to learn the rest. Father had not traveled to Africa for over a year and it would definitely not be good for his ulcer or his phlebitis. After two days of fighting with me, he finally agreed to go, warning me that, if he got ill, it would be my fault, and my greed would be on my head forever.

The "basket quota" was a system set up by the ICO for all small, non-signatory countries, producers of under 200,000 bags a year. Since these producers were non-signatories to the international coffee agreement, the ICO out of London had no way of controlling their exports by stamp allocation. Therefore, the ICO had to rely on all the importing countries to play by the rules and limit the import of non-member coffee. The U.S., at that time, could import a total of a 280,000-bag "basket."

Basket deals were delicious, because the coffees were bought from small producer countries at substantial discounts, occasionally up to 60 percent off the regular market, and then sold at only a one-to-two percent discount to the full market. The difficulty was to establish contact with these remote countries' coffee producers, find a reliable counterpart to do a deal, and have a guaranteed quality and delivery time. Delivery time was crucial. The basket quota opened on October 1 of each year, and as soon as filled, on a first-come first-served basis, it would close. Theoretically, this meant the quota could be open for a full year or only one day, depending on the players.

The deal which awaited Father and me in Douala was bound to be large. It was the end of July 1971, with the new basket opening on October 1. Time was of the essence. We arrived in Douala and were met by Jean-Claude in person—this had to be important! En route, in a bumpy car, Jean-Claude briefed us. We stopped at the Cocotier, musty as ever, registered, showered, and were in Jean-Claude's office within the hour. Father was tired, and I could tell that the heat was bothering him. He kept scratching the open drain for his ulcer, where layers of gauze bandages bulged under his shirt.

Jean-Claude explained that the Cameroons had offered help to Equatorial Guinea, the small country next door to the Cameroons, which had run into financial difficulties and needed food staples, particularly meat and sugar. In exchange, Equatorial Guinea offered to barter their coffee. I interrupted. "That's crazy," I said. "The Cameroons have more coffee than their quota."

"That's true, Claude, but this is where you and your father come in. The Cameroon government wants to sell it to you for the basket quota, in hard currency."

I asked, "Will the Cameroon government be the official sellers?"
"Yes."

I laid out our requirements, while Father sat scratching his abdomen. The Cameroon government needed to substantiate proof of origin, markings on bags, bills of lading from origins, Chamber of Commerce certificates of origin, and any other documents needed for entry into the United States.

Jean-Claude assured me he could meet our requirements. "You must understand, though, that Equatorial Guinea's shipping port is quite shallow, and only small steamers can negotiate the entrance sandbar. So, movement may have to be by overland truck. As far as a Chamber of Commerce certificates of origin are concerned, there is no such thing."

"I'm not too wild about that," I answered. "I would rather have connecting bills of lading with some sort of Equatorial Guinea official certificate of origin. In other words, I need the entire transaction duplicated on paper for U.S. Customs and the ICO."

"I think you're being too demanding. You only need the U.S.-bound ship to show transhipment from Equatorial Guinea."

"I just want the requirements to be cricket," I replied. "But most importantly, what's the quality, price, and quantity?"

Jean-Claude leaned forward, elbows on his desk, and said: "The price is totally between you and the Cameroon government. They may use their own interior production costs as a basis, which is twenty-five cents per pound, making it twenty-three cents below the world price in New York. The quantity is between forty and fifty thousand bags."

"Wow, I don't know if we can handle that much for the U.S. basket, especially since it is now the end of July. It doesn't give us much time before the October 1 opening."

Father continued to scratch his abdomen. Jean-Claude said, "Add to that our two weeks to work on the coffee."

Jean-Claude's firm would grade the coffee down to the standard sizes, ones, twos and threes, then give the beans a final blowing before shipping, and re-bag them with proper markings.

"Listen," I said. "You don't have to grade the coffees for us. If they are similar to the Cameroons coffees, we can sell them in bulk in the U.S., provided the beans are clean. And, without your work, our costs will be lower."

"We could do that for the twos and threes," he said, "but we need to sort out the bigger beans, the ones, for Europe. The *Caisse* and the ministry assumed you would take the twos and threes. The government would sell the remainder to Fred's company, for the European basket."

I thought I was going to have a fit. Once again, Fred was profiting from our information, and we were not getting a penny out of it. Father was getting tired. We agreed to adjourn and continue our negotiation over lunch.

It turned out the only thing left to do was to negotiate a price with the *Caisse*.

"Actually, you will have to do it up in Yaounde," Jean-Claude told us, "with Hayatou and N'Dongo in attendance. I've booked you both on a flight for tomorrow morning."

We finished lunch, and Father went back to the Cocotier for a rest, while I tidied the remaining details with Jean-Claude. He informed me that the turnaround costs of re-bagging, cleaning, grading, warehousing, financing, and insuring, including an estimated one-percent loss in weight, would come to about six cents a pound. The time involved in finding a small steamer to pick up the coffee in Equatorial Guinea and do three trips to complete the transfer would take three weeks. Adding two weeks for Jean-Claude's work put us into the first week of September.

Now we had a real problem: making sure we had, at that specific time, an outgoing steamer from Douala, which would then take three weeks to sail to New York. The shipment would arrive in the first week of October, and there was an outside chance the basket would not be open.

We were cutting it close. Father and I went over all the details. He agreed with nearly everything but had a major problem with the delivery time to New York.

"The schedule is too tight," he said. "You need to get Socopao to ship at least one week earlier."

"I agree, but logistically it can't be done. There's no reason to believe the basket will fill up the first day or even the first month." After further argument, Father agreed, stipulating that the final decision would be based on the price.

The following morning, on the plane for Yaounde, Father said, "We should offer twenty-five cents per pound, the Cameroon cost of production."

I shook my head in disbelief. "But these are not their coffees—they didn't produce them," I answered. "Twenty-five cents a pound already includes the *Caisse's* percentage. In light of the time risk, I think we should be real ballsy and bid seventeen cents a pound. If you figure six cents for Jean-Claude's work, and another seven cents for cost from Douala to New York, that would leave us an eighteen-cent profit on the basis of the current market."

Father felt I was pushing it, but he warmed to the profit prospect. He was tired and not feeling well, so he capitulated. We arrived at the *Ministry Du Plan* just in time for our 11:00 A.M. appointment, and were led in immediately to see Hayatou—most unusual. As predicted by Jean-Claude, N'Dongo was in attendance. We sat through some preliminary pleasantries, and then Hayatou laid out the scenario exactly as Jean-Claude had forecast. Jean-Claude was obviously well-connected. Father and I sat quietly for the hour of explanations, raising the appropriate questions and receiving appropriate assurances. The result was a 30,000-bag deal of Equatorial Guinea coffees equal to the samples they showed us. The samples appeared to be a mixture of Cameroon twos and threes. Shipment was to be from Douala, no later than September 5. All that remained was the price. I suggested a price of seventeen cents a pound, and the two Africans were visibly shaken. Hayatou regained his composure and suggested to N'Dongo that the two of them consult for a few minutes, and asked if we would mind waiting in the antechamber. We retired to the small room between the secretariate and Hayatou's office.

Father let me have it. "Did you see their faces? You've ruined our relationship with the Cameroons forever! I should never have let you bid seventeen cents!" His ulcer problems were forgotten as his old aggressiveness erupted.

"Relax!" I told him. "If my bid was so obnoxious, Hayatou would have turned it down immediately. Obviously, they weren't happy with it, but they'll make us a counter. It's no loss to them. It's Equatorial Guinea's problem as to how much produce it gets."

Father said, "I'm not convinced these coffees are really Equatorial Guinea's, so you should accept their counter."

I wasn't ready to give up so easily. "Let's see what Hayatou counters before we accept. On any price over twenty-five cents, we should pass. A price in between is probably workable. As far as the true origins of these coffees, I insisted with Jean-Claude that I wanted a bill of lading from Equatorial Guinea to Douala, with Cameroon customs stamps for entry and exit."

Father had obviously thought this one out. "You know as well as I do Cameroon customs will do what the ministry tells them to do."

I stuck to the procedure. "Maybe so. As far as Cameroon customs goes, who knows. I can't do any more. All the paperwork is correct, and I assure you it will stand up to U.S. Customs, and the Cameroon government will back us. I can't go personally and check on every bean. Stop being so negative."

Father backed off. "I'm not negative, only cautious. Fishy deals to Europe, I don't care, I don't live there. But the U.S. is different. I want to stay clean."

"The deal is as clean as deals get, so we're clear."

At this point, the door opened, and Hayatou invited us back into his office.

"N'Dongo and I have reviewed your proposition, and based on the presentation that Equatorial Guinea made to us, the best that we could do is twenty-five cents a pound."

I could see, out of the corner of my eye, that Father was itching to accept, and I hoped he would sit still long enough to let the heaviness of the air sink in. I wanted to probe, to see if this was really their final price. But Father and I had worked together on deals before, and he read my intention perfectly. All four of us just sat quietly for at least a full minute, without a word or motion.

Hayatou was a good poker player. He did not budge. N'Dongo's lazy eye was sweeping the room faster than normal. He could not handle the silence and broke. "The only thing we could possibly do is call Equatorial Guinea, and see if we could obtain some concessions from them, but this might take some time."

I knew I had them.

"Good, that might be worthwhile. At twenty-five cents, the timing and market risk are too great. In these types of deals, we remain exposed, because we are unable to sell until cleared by all U.S. authorities. The best we could do is twenty cents a pound. How long do you think it would take to get through to Equatorial Guinea?"

"Well, we have government priority lines. Within fifteen minutes we could get an answer. Why don't you and your father wait in the antechamber while we try and make the connection."

Hayatou did not budge. What a great game.

"That'll be fine."

Father and I once again retired to the antechamber, and he again reprimanded me. "Did you see Hayatou's face? I'm not sure he is going to give us any concessions. You're upsetting him! I'm concerned about the market moving against us, in addition to the time factor for the basket quota."

"I don't understand you," I said. "You want to accept their price on the one hand, but you worry about the market risk on the other. The market risk is the reason we need to fight for every penny we can get. And notice, nobody is running away."

Father and I waited for another twenty minutes before the door opened again and N'Dongo invited us back in. Hayatou sat behind his desk, stern and unmoving. N'Dongo carried the conversation. "After talking to responsible parties in Equatorial Guinea, the final price is twenty-two cents a pound. I urge you to accept."

I slid a glance at Hayatou. His face was expressionless. Father looked at me with that knowing look. It was his turn to accept graciously and close the deal. I blinked in acknowledgment.

"My son and I reviewed the possibilities while you were on the phone, and it is with pleasure that we close this important deal with the Cameroons at twenty-two cents a pound."

Hayatou smiled for the first time in an hour, got up, shook our hands, and invited us to lunch. Details were ironed out, and we would have a contract before we left.

The next evening, back in Douala, Father and I met for dinner at the roof restaurant of the Cocotier. As I sat down, I could tell he had been ruminating in his room, and dinner would not be pleasant.

"Claude, I've been thinking, and I've come to the conclusion that we should cancel the deal."

I was flabbergasted. "What do you mean? That would really ruin our relationship in the Cameroons, which you were so worried about. After all the negotiations we've been through, you can't. Why the hell would you want to cancel such a sweet deal?"

"The risks are too great. The market could move against us and wipe out our margin. On top of that, we could be closed out of the basket and have to reship to non-quota countries, costing us a fortune."

"In the first place, on a cost basis, the market would have to drop by over 35 percent before we would be exposed. And as far as the basket is concerned, historically it has never shut down within a few days. Even now, with heavier shipments by dealers, the basket is still open, and we're coming up to the new year."

"It's not your money that's at risk. I've had to struggle for every penny I've got. Now that we've made a few dollars, you're acting like a know-it-all. You dragged me down here in this heat when I'm not well. And for what? I'm financially comfortable. I don't need this risk. Cancel the deal. Tomorrow, I'm flying to Geneva. You stay here and work out of it."

I couldn't believe this.

"You can't be serious. We've been negotiating for three days, and everything's in place. If you want to cancel, you tell them. But you just can't cancel! It's committing commercial suicide."

He was fuming, hacking. He was totally unable to handle a big deal on his own without Fred or someone else holding his hand. Then came the big surprise.

"You and your buddy Howard are such big shots, why don't *you* do it?" he said. "Why don't you put up your houses as collateral and take half the risk?"

"Do you mean that?"

"Sure, big shot. I'll go fifty-fifty with you. Put your money where your mouth is."

"All right, it's fine with me, but I need to check with Howard. Getting through on the phone is very difficult. It may take some time."

"Well, you have until tomorrow at 8:30, breakfast time. My flight is at 11:00. Let me know. And by the way I want a letter from you and Howard guaranteeing your share of the risk as a pledge."

I could not believe my own father was doing this to me. I was reaching the end of my rope with him. But I vowed to myself that I would make a lot of money out of this deal.

At 3:00 A.M., the local operator was able to connect me with Howard. In cryptic, couched language, I laid out the deal. I was concerned about those listening in on our conversation. He got the gist—my main concern was arrival in time for the basket. He agreed to fifty-fifty, said he wanted to check the status of basket imports and would be back to me. I told him the phone was difficult, and I had to give an answer to Father by 8:30 A.M. If need be, he would have to get back to the office at 1:30 A.M. his time, and send a telex to Jean-Claude's office, which opened at 7:30 A.M. my time. I would check in before having breakfast. I reset the alarm for 6:45 A.M. and bolted out of bed when it went off a few hours later.

No call had come. I found a taxi and sped down to Jean-Claude's office. At 7:45, I looked at the telex. There it was: "Everything as best can be this side. Go ahead. You have my pledge. Signed, Howard/partner."

I was jubilant. I dashed back, just in time to meet Father for breakfast.

"All right," I said, breathing hard from the run to the restaurant. "I spoke to Howard, and he agrees to go fifty-fifty partners with you and pledge his equity."

"Well, I've been rethinking, and you're right. I can't back out on the Cameroons. Maybe Fred would go partners with us."

"Bullshit! Howard and I have been up all night and we've agreed to do it."

"Well, what's your equity? I want it in writing."

"I have it on telex with time and code number from Jean-Claude's telex!" I yelled. "I'll countersign it with whatever equity Howard and I have in our houses."

"Don't scream. I'll abide by what I said. We'll be partners. But be assured: I will not hesitate to collect if it turns sour, son or no son. You'd better be sure you're prepared to take the risk."

"We are. You've got a deal. End of conversation."

I got what I wanted, and now I needed to get him out of my hair. We turned to pleasantries until he left for the airport. I stayed another day, making doubly sure all arrangements were complete.

The whole operation was as smooth as silk, and our shipments entered the basket quota with room to spare. In the end, two hitches occurred. First, the market had turned down by three cents, which was no big deal. Second, which outraged me, was that Father now wanted to charge Howard's and my joint account for overhead and additional financing.

"You can't do that. That wasn't part of your original agreement. I put together the most profitable deal of your life, and you turn around and screw your own son!"

"I'm not screwing anybody. Overhead is part of any business. And the financing costs of this deal tied up my credit lines at the bank. I was unable to do other business while this went on."

I was beside myself. "This is absolute horse cock! This deal alone represents more than 20 percent of your profits for the year, and it tied up the financing for only three weeks. You have no balls when it comes to big risks, but you sure trot them out to fuck your own family!" With that I kicked his mahogany desk so hard I put a hole in it.

"You're an ungrateful son, considering everything I do for you!" he screamed. "There's nowhere else you'd make as much money." He swung his hand across the metal sample boxes on the shelf, knocking their contents to the floor. In the process, he caught his thumb on one of the sharp edges, and gashed it open. Blood spurted in all directions. He half fainted. He looked very tired and ashen; we ended up calling the paramedics to take him to the emergency room and stitch him up. I refused to go with him.

The next day, Howard and I sat at our desks doing nothing, refusing to work until paid. Father was visibly shaken, but insisted on charging the financing. We finally settled matters.

Howard and I had cleared a nice profit for a nest egg, which we resolved to keep as a reserve for the day when we would leave and start our own company. For me, this episode was the last straw. I decided that my major thinking and energy would go into a strategy of fighting Father to the death in one form or another.

In retrospect I look at this as a Greek tragedy of warriors and kings fighting not only for the kingdom but for their egos and self-preservation. The king must die.

9

Getting Support

All I can do is point out what I think is an unfair split.

Howard was extremely upset with the hassle it took to collect our share of the profits and especially with the discount Father forced on us for additional financing.

Howard was the one to push me over the edge to a decision. "I want to look for another job," he told me. "I have to quit, Claude." His colitis was acting up, and his pleasure in the business was spoiled by my father's constant criticisms and demands.

My own rage was like a pressure cooker about to blow. My asthma was getting worse, and my blood pressure had begun to rise above normal. "I agree, but I feel strongly we can make it on our own. It would be silly to leave in a huff and go looking for a job. We need time to prepare for our independence. We need to make sure the suppliers will go with us."

I was convinced that East Africa and Multitrade would follow me. I had set both of them up from scratch, and even though both might perceive G.M. as having the financing, I was the one who came up with the ideas and the process, while Howard dealt with the sales. West Africa was my big concern, because I was betting on the governments and the native shippers. The transition from the old colonial houses was not yet complete, giving Father a possible advantage. In the Cameroons, I knew I was fairly well implanted, except that, all over Africa, the male father figure was of utmost importance. They would ask how a son could leave an older, wiser, sick father and go into competition with him.

Furthermore, Father had so well introduced Fred that his company was a major factor in the European market, and my father was Fred's surrogate father. If Fred's company sided with Father in Africa, then we would have great difficulties. I told Howard a lot of work had to be done, and I needed to get Fred and his company to take a neutral stance: to do business with us as well as with Father, and especially not to side with Father in Africa. To put all my resources in place, I needed three to six months, during which Howard would consolidate his position with the roasters.

Howard was impatient to get on with it. I was clear we needed time, particularly for the Boca Raton Coffee Convention, in the first week of February 1972, when we could see the trade and sound out some friendly bankers. Even with all our good sources, sales, and ideas, the business could not start without financial backing. We needed a bank, and obviously not the same one as Father's. Furthermore, once all the other factors were in place, we would need to make one final pitch to Father about buying into the company. Howard was not so sanguine about that, feeling he would prefer to start off much smaller on our own, rather than be partners with my father. But when all was said and done, blood weaves thick ties, and I was not prepared to leave until we made one last pitch. We agreed to gear up, get prepared, and then make a decision.

I set up a trip throughout Europe to touch base with old acquaintances and especially to stop in Geneva to see Fred. My aim at this time was not to tell him what I was planning, but rather feel him out and guide him to a neutral position. Father had always brought Fred's wife and children elaborate gifts, to solidify his relationship. I refused to play the game, and when I was invited to his home for dinner, I sent an appropriately large and beautiful bouquet, but no more. Fred and I talked as friends of similar age, comparing the changing market and musing on the future. I explained to him in great detail the deal I had set up for the "basket" out of Equatorial Guinea, knowing full well he had already used all my systems gained from my father and Jean-Claude, and asked him how his deal had worked out.

"Great. Everything went smoothly. Thank you for setting it up. I followed all your parameters." He asked after my father's health. I told him my father was doing fine, adding, "I think our trip together was the last time he plans to be in Africa."

"When's your next scheduled visit?"

The conversation led to plans for a trip together, to Zaire and the Cameroons in January.

I was elated. By that time we would know if Zaire had implemented their plan to nationalize the coffee production apparatus, and we would be in a position to solidify our relationship with the ONC. I would also have a good idea by then where Multitrade stood and, with that knowledge, could consolidate my relationship with Fred and tell him of our plans. Furthermore, our traveling together would set a mental stage for the D.G. and Hippo in Zaire, as well as N'Dongo and Hayatou in the Cameroons. Momentum was building.

The next day I flew to Amsterdam and met with Penguin and his staff. The operation no longer gave the impression of the slow, fuddy-duddy office of old. Instead, phones were ringing off the hook, and a brisk trading atmosphere was reflected everywhere. Penguin had learned quickly, becoming an aggressive moneymaker. Even his waddling walk seemed more fluid and faster.

Penguin and I flew on KLM to Jakarta, first class. I used the twenty-three hours on the plane with my captive audience to approach him with a new idea, and then tell him about Howard's and my plans to leave G.M. The idea was to set up Multicontinental as an independent profit center using the disparity between the interior prices and the export prices. The margins were great enough for Multicontinental to become an exporter and amortize all the capital equipment. He liked the idea, but what did I want out of it? I told him I would help them set up and in return I wanted the shipments to be higher quality and I wanted the elimination of the premium we were paying for their inspection of all our shipments. He agreed. I took this moment to lead into my changing plans.

"Actually, I really need your help for Howard and me."

"What do you mean? You boys in some sort of difficulty? You know I would do anything in my power to help. What's going on?"

"Well, as you have been a good friend, and we have worked very closely, you are privy to the problems Howard and I have had with the old man."

"Yes, yes, and no."

I went into a detailed explanation of the mounting pressures, the changes of opinion, the overruling of our trades, the renegotiation of our Equatorial deal, and our running the business. I concluded that our health could no longer stand the atmosphere and that we were going to start our own company and needed Multitrade's backing.

Penguin could not believe that Father and son could not work things out; after all, the business would be mine some day. I explained that Howard and I had made a proposal to buy into the company and were flatly turned down. I told him I was thirty-four and had no intention of inheriting the company at fifty years old totally castrated and emasculated. He gave me his total support and suggested he talk to the Hagemeyer board.

I responded, "No, not yet. We're not ready. I only wanted to confide in you as a friend and ask your support—which I greatly appreciate. What do you think about the Reichmeister? Do we tell him?"

"Yes, definitely. He feels the same way about you as I do. He's been in various positions with Hagemeyer for the last thirty years, so the Board will listen to him. It's important to get his support."

He would be on our side of the table: one chalk mark for the good guys.

The plane landed in Jakarta, and the Reichmeister met us. We cleaned up and went to dinner. With little time wasted, Penguin laid out to the Reichmeister Howard's and my plan. At first incredulous, he finally supported us fully. He had never had so much fun in the business as he had since we appeared on the scene. He was prepared to fly to Amsterdam to make a presentation to his board. I calmed him down, thanked him, and told him the time was not yet ripe, but I would take him up on it when we were ready.

The subject then switched to Multicontinental becoming an exporter. He liked the idea, and the next several days set to the task of getting all the information to set up the facilities.

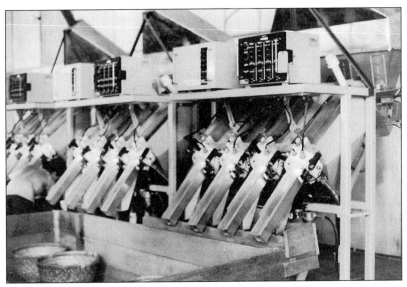

Electronic sorters which replaced women, 1971.

I flew back via Singapore, to touch base with Mighty Mouse and enlist his backing for our future undertaking. It was "no problem."

Back in New York, I gave the good news to Howard, and he told me that he had obtained backing from his roasters. It was time to accelerate our program before the word leaked out.

Christmas and New Year passed uneventfully. Then, in the first week of January, I flew to Kinshasa with Fred. Zaire was in the midst of nationalizing most of the European plantations, as well as all the exporters. Fred and I met at length with the D.G. of the ONC, who was in his glory, revamping all the old machinery, ordering new parts, building a larger organization, and promising to be the largest exporter, leaving only a few political locals. Fred decided to visit the old European exporters, to evaluate how all this would affect his business. I decided to visit Hippo, and then check in on my friend André.

I thought to myself that I had made the right bet on my first visit, not bothering with the old Colonial houses. This would put a crimp in Father's business when the change happened. I could already feel the blood of revenge and competition coursing through my veins. With luck, everything would fall in place when Howard and I set up shop.

My meeting with Hippo was like old home week, and we talked like old friends. He confided in me that he thought that the Zairization of the colonial business system would be in place within six months, and that he was quite confident that he, Hippo, would be made D.G. My intuition was confirmed. I then confided in him my plan to start my own company. He was excited, as much as Hippo could be, and went on at length about how new young blood would carry the day in trading the coffees of Zaire. I concurred and encouraged his plans. Then I asked him if he thought his friend André would survive, or if he would have to go back to Belgium.

"Don't worry about André. He's very clever. You should visit him."

"I plan to."

"Good. By the way, I would appreciate your keeping the information about my becoming D.G. very confidential. In fact, I would prefer you not mention it to Fred."

"That's fine. What about André? Is he up to date?"

"Yes. He is my confidante. We are very close. I hope you can fill the same nook for overseas sales, when you are ready."

"With pleasure. I think we will make a good team."

I bid him farewell. I was ecstatic. All the pieces were falling together. I jumped into the taxi which was waiting outside under the shade of the omnipresent Banyan tree; the temperature was still ninety degrees.

I arrived at André's just in time for lunch, so we went down to the King's Inn, the local hangout in midtown, which still had good food and was known for its preparation of the local shrimp. We each ordered a bowl (about a pound) of shrimp, cold beer, and country bread. I skipped the salad—when in the tropics, I only ate cooked vegetables. The shrimp, slightly smaller than in the States, were boiled in the usual *pilipili* sauce, so they had some real snap. We sat there, elbows on the table, peeling shrimp and drinking beer.

"Tell me, André, how is this Zairization of business affecting you?"

He told me he had anticipated the political change and avoided any losses by selling the company to Hippo's cousin over a ten-year period. He would pay the cousin a minimum salary in local currency and keep all the major profits, in hard currencies, at a brokerage he had set up in Brussels. He and Hippo were happy with the outcome and had met the organization requirements. I congratulated him and told him I thought we'd be able to maximize profits for coffees headed to the States.

I told him about my situation at G.M. and about my plans to start an independent business. I asked for his support. He had met my father only very briefly, so had no hesitation in backing me.

After paying a courtesy visit to the Minister of Agriculture, I met Fred. We had dinner, and he told me all the horror stories about how the old colonial houses were being forced to sell their businesses over a ten-year period at book value—quite a different outcome than André's. I kept quiet about André's arrangements and Hippo's predictions. But I did give him encouragement, since he had a decent relationship with the D.G. Next morning we caught a flight to the Cameroons.

To leave Zaire, I had arranged for an Amiza representative to handle all our passport and currency formalities, and thereby avoided most of the hassle. After takeoff, we had a glass of champagne to celebrate our leaving Kinshasa. Fred relaxed, and in this convivial atmosphere, I calculated that I had over two hours to broach the subject of leaving Father.

"Fred, I would like to talk to you about a delicate matter."

"What's up? You sound so serious."

At this point, I switched to speaking English. Fred's English was very good, and I wanted to be very clear. However, the switch made for a hesitant start; I had become accustomed to speaking French over the past four days. But I forged ahead with a review of the growing difficulties between Father and me.

Fred cut in. "Yes, Claude, but he is your father, and blood is thick. Someday the business will be yours, and in the meantime you are very well compensated."

"Maybe so, but my health and sanity are in jeopardy. Money and stock ownership are not the main issues. I need the freedom to expand trading and build a business without continual conflict and recriminations. And since Howard and I are the main movers, we should also be building stock value for ourselves."

Fred's blue eyes narrowed as he questioned me. "It sounds to me that stock ownership is important to you. Could it be that your father doesn't want to include Howard in the family business?"

"It's not a family business, it's Father's business. And if he wanted only me, then he could have had a conversation with me on a father-son basis, but no such thing has happened. Besides, if we came to an agreement, I would sell 50 percent to Howard. He's earned it."

"What do you mean, earned it? You're the one who's providing all the source connections, who's traveling to the ends of the world and living under continual stress and time changes. You're securing the supplies. Howard is just sitting on his fat rear with an assistant trader to help him, while you are all alone out here. And when major position decisions are made, you are the one who gives the final word, and you're the one who plans all the financing with your father. All he does is make sales, and any decent salesman can do that if he's got the right product at the right price. Don't tell me you plan to go 50-percent partners with him if you start your own business?"

I already felt I was betraying my father, and I needed the loyalty of a friend. I would not abandon Howard. "Yes, I do. Howard and I go back to our fraternity days in school. I trust him implicitly, which is a rare commodity in this world. He has a terrific imagination, which has been very helpful in planning the various approaches and deals at source. And it is not just a matter of selling—it's also a matter of developing customer relationships, so that when the buyers need coffee they will call him and give us the first shot."

"Come on, Claude. Don't give me this stuff. Most of your major customers were initially developed by you. All he's done is follow up and expand."

Fred was making sense, but I did not want to hear the truth, so I defended my position. "Well, he has expanded the relationships tremendously, and got ten new ones that I never was able to develop. Besides, I can't work alone. I need Howard as a sounding board. Howard is the only one who can dissect the market and be a devil's advocate for me. Father just doesn't hack it."

Fred responded incisively, "I think you're similar to your father. You need Howard to hold your hand. You even second guess yourself on position decisions like your father."

This was getting uncomfortable. "Maybe so. Maybe I have some of Father's weaknesses, but I don't have the cash to set up a business alone, and Howard and I work well as a team. One and one is three, not two, in our case. I admit I bring more to the party, but that's life!"

Fred was exasperated. "Okay, your mind sounds made up. All I can do is point out what I think is an unfair split."

I knew I had the courage to travel to the ends of the Earth under difficult circumstances and put large and complicated deals together. But I needed the security of someone at home watching my back door. I could easily handle quick trading and situational changes but had great difficulty with emotional changes. Howard was part of my emotional security. At the time, I felt the cost worth the fifty-fifty split. I got a glimpse of my father's insecurities reflected in my own.

Fred shifted in his seat as he shifted the subject. "Claude, you need to understand: if you go ahead with this, I just can't back you. Your father has meant too much to me. He has introduced me to Africa and to dealing. He has given me the power, vis-à-vis my own father, to be a highly regarded member of my firm."

I nodded. "I understand. All I can ask is that you be a typically neutral Swiss. In Zaire, Indonesia, East Africa, and Europe, I can fend for myself. But I need your support in the Cameroons and the Ivory Coast. This is where I need at least your assurances to them that we would be a viable company and deserve a fair shake."

"I don't know if I can support you *per se*, but I can be neutral, and if asked, I can say that I highly respect you. Furthermore, I would have no problem doing business with you, but you must understand I will continue doing business with your father, as I have a close relationship with him."

He needed to protect his flank, so I said, "I understand your position. And I want to thank you for your understanding, but I need your cooperation to keep it a secret until our plans are definite, so that we can at least get an even start."

"You have my word. Not a word will be said until you tell me to."

"Thanks. By the way, I don't want any leaks in the Cameroons as yet, even though N'Dongo is a good friend. As far as Hayatou is concerned, you have now developed a closer relationship than I have, so when the time is right, I might ask you to put in a good word about your doing business with both of us."

"Hayatou will want to continue to do business with your father," Fred said, "but he is smart enough to know the future may be with you. He will place a limited bet on you to see how it works, and let the better firm win."

I sensed that this statement probably reflected Fred's attitude as well. If he did not have such a large obligation to my father, I felt we would be much closer and do terrific business together. I let the thought pass. Time would tell.

The plane was descending on Douala, and we wrapped up the conversation with some banalities.

Socopao's representative was at the airport to whisk us through customs and luggage pick-up, then check us into the old Cocotier and hence to Jean-Claude's office. We got all the latest information and rumors, including the fact that Hayatou was in town, saving us a trip to Yaounde. Meetings were set up from his office, as well as a dinner with Hayatou and N'Dongo. Fred and I both closed substantial contracts with N'Dongo that afternoon, followed by an elaborate dinner and exotic wines with Hayatou, who had given his blessing to our endeavors. He dropped us off at the Cocotier around 11:00 P.M. Fred and I decided to have a *Poire Willaume*, a white pear liquor, in the hotel's freezing cold disco bar. We began to talk about our fathers and the difficulty in proving ourselves in business. Another *Poire Willaume* and we talked about competition. More *Poire Willaume* and we talked about women. And still more *Poire Willaume* and we were the best friends on Earth. By 2:00 A.M. we had polished off the whole bottle, and decided to go to bed. The bar temperature must have been sixty-five degrees—below zero! We stepped out into the Cocotier's open reception hall where the temperature was still ninety degrees, and the *Poire Willaume* hit us like a hammer. Fred's legs collapsed.

Just then, a call girl standing on the corner decided to solicit some business. I managed to get my mouth to move and told her she could earn 2,000 CFA, about five dollars, if she would help me carry Fred up to his room. She was not having much of a night, so she agreed. All three of us wobbled to the elevator, squeezed in the little box, then wobbled down the hall, fumbled with the key (after five minutes I realized I was trying to open the door with a large coin), and then, with great effort and a real burlesque scene, got Fred laid out on his bed. The woman's mothering instincts took over, and she insisted on taking off his shoes and loose tie and covered him with a blanket. We left. I slurred my thanks and gave her an extra 2,000 CFA, for I never could have done the job alone. I went to my room.

The next thing I knew it was 9:30 A.M. I went for a swim, had two strong French coffees and a croissant, then checked on Fred. He had a very bad head. I prescribed the same formula I had just completed. We finally made our way to Jean-Claude's office after his lunch break. Thankfully, all the important business had been done the previous day. We checked on coffee samples and shipping schedules, and generally did clean-up chores. The next morning Fred flew to Geneva, and I made connections on Pan Am direct to New York.

Fred and I had cemented a close relationship, which would work out well in the turmoil to come. He had forced me to look at my deep self; to understand that I needed to rely on others. And I came to realize that my trust in Howard was well worth the fifty-fifty split. My ego had difficulty accepting vulnerability and this lesson would be forced on me in the future in ways I could not ignore.

10

Delay

... you are killing your father.
This will be on your head forever!

When I returned, I briefed Howard on the success of my trip. I found him in a harrowed state. He had been keeping a lid on the pressure, so the atmosphere in the office was unnatural. Father informed us that he did not want to put up with the charade of the Boca Raton Convention, so Howard and I could handle the convention together. He and Steve would mind the office and the markets. Was he sensing our intentions? He always had an uncanny knack for finding weaknesses in people or situations and pressuring at the point. I dismissed the thought. The convention would give Howard and me the time we needed to consolidate our plans.

This was, at its peak, a convention attended by 500 or 600 people. Representatives from various Central and South American governments were present, as well as U.S. State Department officials, trade people, roasters, brokers, dealers, bankers, packagers, and steamship agents and officers. Everyone vied for the best tables, cabanas, tennis or golf times, with payoffs to those in charge who could obtain the desired results. A continual game of one-upmanship was the standard for the convention. Unpleasant, but a lot of work got done.

We met with Peter Siverson, head of commodity lending for Chemical Bank in New York. The Bank had a relatively small commodity department for their size, and Peter was looking to expand. He had a very quick mind and evaluated people without hesitation.

We explained our predicament in conservative banking terms and reviewed our accomplishments in trading, our volume, clients, sources, and our education. We both had M.B.A.s now—Howard had earned his at night over the past two years. And we indicated how little capital we had.

Peter sat back in his lounge chair in our cabana, the sun beating on the side of his head. "Listen, the deals I finance are always greater than a corporation's capital. I deal in trust, and I don't know why, but I trust you guys." He told us he had the authority to go up to five million without board approval, but that he was thinking in terms of a smaller amount. He asked us for backup paper work, a letter laying out what we had told him.

Howard asked the crucial question: How much money was he talking about?

"Assuming it all checks out," Peter told us, "I would say a one million line of credit with the usual trust receipt, demand loan agreements, and so forth. And, if you have an exceptional situation, we can sit and talk about it."

Howard and I were ecstatic. The rest of the convention went smoothly, and we had time to plan our next move. We needed to draft a shareholders' agreement and find space in downtown Manhattan, not too far from Wall Street.

When we returned to New York, we discovered that Steve had become Father's new protégé. We were informed that we had better toe the line. "You boys are getting too aggressive in the markets for my stomach. Furthermore, you're behaving as if you own and run the company. I'm still the boss, and I make the decisions. I could get an assistant for Steve to do the trading, and work a deal with Fred to help me cover source. That would be a lot cheaper than you boys cost me. So just stop acting like such big shots, or you can do it in another company."

Howard and I were steaming. I gave him the raised eyebrow look to keep calm. I asked Father testily, "Well, does that mean you would like us to quit right now?"

"No, I just want you to understand who is running the show. I want to be consulted more closely on the positions you take, and I want the risk to be minimized."

I matched his bravado and said flatly, "Fine, we'll start lowering the exposure and get the positions neat and orderly."

"Don't be a wise guy. I still want you to take a view of the market but I want to be consulted."

Once again, damned if I did, and damned if I didn't. I stayed calm. "Fine. I still think we should lower our exposure right now."

He agreed and went on to say he was leaving with Mother for the Hotel Beau Rivage on the French Riviera. Following that he would visit Fred in Geneva. So I should run the positions, as he would not be in touch that much. This was a total contradiction to the harangue he had just given.

Father went on. "Howard should plan to take a trip to East Africa, shortly after I get back. It would be good training for him. He might bring back some fresh ideas. Anyway, you have too much of a monopoly on our sources, and being in touch with the roasters would do you good."

I felt him reining me in, to limit my influence at source which he always considered the power base of the company. My intuition was that he was also trying to drive a wedge between Howard and me.

"That's fine. I need to spend some time at home with Bette and the kids."

When Father left for Europe, Howard and I set to work. Through one of Howard's family contacts, we were introduced to an owner of several marginal buildings in lower Manhattan. The real estate market in 1972 was not strong, and so he was happy to talk to two young turks. We located a spacious, well-lit office on the fringe of Chinatown. We shook hands on the rent, and asked him to send us the lease. During this time, we had also consulted with Herb, a lawyer and CPA, who was a cousin of Howard's wife.

Herb was a tall, bespectacled man, with open gestures and a good sense of humor and, most importantly, a clear mind. He asked all the important questions relating to the Shareholders' Agreement: What happened if one of us died? How would the estate be compensated? Did the survivor have enough funds to run the business? What about a lengthy illness? Should we have insurance to cover these unknowns? Did we want to be a sub-S corporation? And many other personal queries. I felt strongly that the company should be named Saks International, Inc., because my name was well known at source and would provide a natural link. The "International" part of the name I felt would depict us as larger than we really were and give us the flavor of a global trading company. Howard acquiesced. Since my name would be on the door, he wanted to be President. I agreed. "Fair enough. I'll be secretary of the company and chairman of the board. That should cover legal matters."

Father was due back the following week, and I felt we should give him one last pitch before we made our final move. He returned on a Thursday and said he was too tired to come to the office. He said he was going out to his beach house for the weekend and would see us on Monday and that we should have a full trading and financial report ready for him.

On Sunday I received a shocking call. "Hello, Claude. This is Dr. Schuyler. I don't want to alarm you, but I just admitted your father to New York Hospital for observation."

"What happened? Is he all right?"

"Well, apparently, as he was driving back from the beach, he started to lose control of his right arm and leg. He barely made it back to the apartment. I admitted him at once, and he asked me to call you."

"My God, do you think he's had a stroke?"

"I don't think so. However, there is a problem in his head, and I would like to run a brain scan. Do you have any idea if he has bumped his head in the past ten days? I've asked both your father and mother, but neither can recall any such incident."

"Well, as you know, my mother is on strong doses of Thorazine and would not remember. He didn't report hitting his head to me. He certainly would remember."

Dr. Schuyler patiently explained. "Not necessarily so. If he hit it hard enough, he could have a loss of memory as well as loss of motor control to some of his limbs." He asked me to come in and sign release papers.

I called my sister and told her I was on my way in and would keep her abreast of the situation. I arrived at the hospital and signed the forms. My father was having a fit about possible surgery and did not want the EEG scan. His speech was slurred. He kept repeating to me that he had not bumped his head, and, except for the semi-paralysis on his right side, he felt fine. He was in real panic and was convinced the neurosurgeons wanted to operate on his brain. He wanted second opinions and refused to budge. I convinced him that the EEG was non-invasive, but the doctors needed a picture before the specialist could give an opinion. Finally, with much objection, he was rolled away to be tested. While the scan was being done, I called Howard and said I doubted that I would be at work the next day. I then tracked down my aunt Denise in London, who had seen my father during his trip to Europe. She told me that he had indeed bumped his head recently.

"He called me and told me that he had slipped in the bathtub and really hit his head hard. He nearly fainted, the bump hurt so badly. He said he called out, that he actually screamed out to your mother, but she was in her usual daze."

I found my way down to the EEG room. Dr. Schuyler said the findings confirmed the knock on the head. A large hematoma had built up inside Father's head. It was putting pressure on his brain, causing the paralysis. He needed to be operated on immediately to remove the pressure.

"What do you mean by operated?" I asked.

"We need to drill a hole, or a couple of holes, in his cranium to drain out the blood."

"What are the risks, and what happens if he's still bleeding? How do you stop it?"

"The risks with drilling are minimal. The probability that he's still bleeding is remote, or he would be in much worse condition. Let's take one step at a time."

"Okay, let me consult with my mother and call my sister, and also call my aunt in London."

Dr. Schuyler was impatient. "Let's do it fast. Every moment is crucial." I felt the burden fall on my shoulders; my emotions raged in all directions.

The orderlies wheeled my father back to his room. I met with Mother and Dr. Schuyler, and the doctor explained the problem and the procedure.

Mother sat quietly and blinked her eyes. "He'll be just fine. Why don't you wait until morning?" Dr. Schuyler was quiet but firm. "Mrs. Saks, unfortunately your husband is at a critical stage, and every moment counts. We need to act now."

At this point, Howard showed up and I bounced the options off him.

"Well, Claude, one of your favorite sayings is 'If there is enough information the decision is made for you—decisions are always made with insufficient information.' It seems to me you don't have much choice."

I turned to Dr. Schuyler. "I agree. I'm just looking for the last out, but there is none. Okay, let's do it. I'll sign the papers and call my sister and aunt. I think my father is still lucid, so you should get his approval as well."

The doctor would not let me off the hook. "I'll try, but you know he does not want to be operated on. In the final analysis, I need to rely on you."

"You've got that. I just was hoping for a smoother decision."

I signed the authorizations and told my sister and aunt, who concurred. My mother sat by smiling, assured that all would be well. I went to Father's room, where the orderlies had already transferred him to a stretcher and strapped him down. Dr. Schuyler had explained the necessity and urgency of the procedure and had informed him of my consent.

My father addressed me in anger. "Claude, you're disobeying the wishes of your father. I do not want to be operated on. You'll kill me! You *are* killing me! You're a murderer! If I live through this, I swear I will disinherit you!"

They started to roll him down the hall toward the operating room. He was screaming from the stretcher as it rolled away. "Claude, you are killing your father. This will be on your head forever!"

The elevator door shut. And all was quiet. What a love-hate relationship! On the one hand, I wanted to save him, and do all I could to please him. On the other hand, I wanted to let someone else make the decision, then quit, and go into a competitive business where I would beat the hell out of him. The clock ticked away.

Mother snoozed in a waiting-room chair in the corner. She was a warm, all-embracing woman, who never had a bad word to say about anybody. I put my hand on hers while she dozed, and Howard kept me company, assuring me I had made the right decision. We talked about our future plans and agreed all had to be put on hold until we knew the outcome of Father's condition.

My thoughts wandered off to my sister Marianne, and how distant we had become. She had recently gone through a difficult divorce, and Father had intervened with lawyers and money. Father had always made comparisons between us, particularly who did best in school or who was most creative. I believe this competition had caused an unhealthy antagonism between us. We were pitted against each other, while Mother had already withdrawn and was unable to provide solace to either of us. Marianne was three years younger than I. I reflected that when we were kids we had fought like cats and dogs. She had scratched and kicked, and I had been known to throw eggs and had even torn her blouse once—she ran to her best friend's house for safety. Somehow, when we got to our late teens, we intuitively understood the acrimony from Father and bonded together for mutual support and became very close, sharing our experiences. Then I was off to college, and Marianne was in boarding school in Switzerland. We drifted apart again after we both got married and Father was back on track, pitting one couple against the other. But at that moment I did not have time to worry about our relationship. I needed to concentrate on my own flight to freedom, then perhaps Marianne and I could be close again.

Dr. Schuyler came into the room and told us that the operation was complete and that the outcome looked good. The surgeon had drained out the blood pool, and no new bleeding was apparent.

"He is back in his room and has already regained a good part of the motion in his arm and leg. And his speech is back to normal. You can go in and see him now. He's much calmed down."

Howard and I had to put our plans on the back burner until Father was well. We let go our option on the office space.

11

Compromise

He knew his bluff had been called.

Father was back in the office within two days, and seemed good as new, except for the bald spot on the back of his head. He showed even greater vigor and a determination that he was in charge and running the show. I kept quiet, and Howard left for East Africa with much relief. I turned my attention to marketing and enjoyed spending time on the phone with old friends to whom I usually spoke only sporadically, due to traveling.

I also got a chance to size up Steve at close quarters and saw that, indeed, he was very bright and a good trader. I could see that if we left, Steve would be able to hold things together, albeit at a reduced volume. Father would not be left in the lurch.

I met with our traffic manager to tell him about our intentions. He took care of all documentation concerning shipments: routing the paperwork to banks, U.S. Customs, docks, shipping lines, or customers. He was from Brooklyn and was street-wise. He knew how to get the weighers and truckers to move cargo off the docks and deliver to customers. Before I had a chance to fully explain, he told me that, if Howard and I left, he would not stay with my father, no matter how much money he was offered. I was jubilant, because we needed a traffic person desperately, and had not yet addressed the issue. I told him we would love to have him join us but would not be able to offer him any raise whatsoever, and the first year might be lean as far as profits were concerned, so I could not assure a bonus.

"I understand," he said, "but I saw what you guys did here, and how you treat people, so I'm willing to take the risk and hook my wagon to yours." Our back office problem was solved.

Father was getting ever more critical and overbearing. My nerves were on edge. I proceeded on the assumption that we would leave. I lined things up with the bank and recontacted Howard's family friend about a potential lease. Ten days later, Howard returned from his trip, jubilant about the experience and now understanding the problems we faced at source. Once back, he quickly became aware of the tone of the office and expressed his desire to quit immediately.

Quoting one of his expressions, I said, "Just gird your loins for another month." That's what we had agreed to. I told Howard things were working in our favor. Father was trying to prove he could handle the business. He was talking to a lot of the customers, not particularly effectively, telling them he was fully recovered. Meantime, we should get our wives to shop for furniture, carpets, and so forth, for the new office so we would know all the locations and prices when the time came. "If things go according to plan, I think we should give notice first thing on Monday."

Thursday afternoon we met with Father, and once again made our presentation and expressed our desire to buy into the company on some sort of formula. This time, Father did not go into his CGS routine. "Claude, I must say that my good fortune has increased tremendously since my partner left and you joined the firm. Furthermore, you saved my life a month ago in the hospital, and I am grateful. As you know, I have always been against selling my stock. However, I want to think about the situation overnight, and I will get back to you boys tomorrow morning at 9:30 A.M. I'm sure that reasonable people can work things out. I want to leave for the beach house by 1:00."

"Fine. We'll see you in the morning."

That evening I got a call from Father. "Claudy, you know we are father and son, and blood is thicker than water." He always called me Claudy when he wanted to be close to me. And I was sure that he had called Margot, his girlfriend, to get emotional support since Mother was not present mentally. Margot must have counseled him to get me to his side against Howard. I could smell a double-cross pitch coming. "Howard is not part of our family. You know I will leave you the company stock when I die, of course, with promises that you take care of your mother, and pay an equal share to your sister. So why make all this fuss? Let Howard remain as an employee. He's not leaving without you. You are the driving force in the business."

"I hear you, Father," I replied, "but I have a commitment to Howard. The situation might never have reached this point if you had expressed this family closeness early on. But you never did. On the contrary, you pit Howard and me against each other. Howard will probably leave, with or without me, and certainly will if he doesn't get any stock."

"You're overestimating Howard. Finding and training a good salesman is not that difficult. Trust me, the business goes to you, and if Howard can't handle that fact, let him leave. We can do wonders together."

I tried to remain calm and said flatly, "Sorry, Father. That certainly has not been the case up to now, so I'm not prepared to go on promises. I want assurances in the form of actual stock up front."

There was a moment of silence, then he went into his CGS routine, blasting my ear on the phone. "Claude, you're being unreasonable. I would sell you some stock, but I know you would sell 50 percent of it to Howard, and I do not want him as a partner. You're my son. That's different."

"Look," I responded, "I don't think this is the way to go. You need to sell at least a small portion to Howard. He might go along with it, as it would show your good faith. It would be a positive starting point."

"What do you mean starting point?"

"Well, that over the years you would continue such a program."

"I'm not prepared to go that far. One thing at a time. Let me think about your proposition, and I will let you know at our meeting tomorrow morning. You know I'm a little superstitious about you bringing me luck. Let's keep the family together. Reasonable men can work things out, especially a father and son."

I hung up and called Howard to report the conversation verbatim. He was not pleased. He expressed his desire to be an equal partner, not a subordinate. He went to say, "There are too many complications. There is the value of the stock, timing, and other problems." He felt I was backing out. He reiterated that the reasons for our leaving was not the stock, but because of the way we had been treated, the way we wanted to live. He said, "You need to make up your mind if you want to live under your father's thumb the rest of your life, an emaciated, controlled empty shell of a man."

I was torn emotionally, although intellectually I knew we had to leave. "You're right. At this point our health and survival is at stake," I said. "Let's see what he has to say. If he really offers a plan worth our while, we can discuss it. Personally, I believe it's likely he won't offer stock, in which case please swallow your gum and stick to our game plan, 'til Monday morning."

At 9:30 sharp, Father showed up, walking very erect; his gray suit jacket was buttoned. This was unusual, as he didn't like tight clothes against his stomach. His face was stern, lips drawn tightly across his teeth. The three of us sat down around the small conference table. Father leaned back, with legs crossed at right angles, lighting a cigarette with his gold Dupont lighter. "Well, boys, I have thought about this carefully overnight. I think you are both extremely well-compensated. In fact, I believe you are probably making more than most others in the industry. As I told Claude last night, I'm leaving all my stock to him at my death. What he does with it at that time will be his business, but for now I will not sell any of my shares, or give any percentage beyond what you are both getting now as a share of the profits. I will not put up with a revolution in the palace by two young whippersnappers, so you can take it or leave it. No more discussion." I guess he must have talked to Margot again and she must have really pumped him up.

Howard was beet red, and I thought he was going to throw the ashtray at Father. Outwardly I was calm, but inwardly I was very cold and very angry.

"Well, Father, this is a very different picture from what you presented last night. For my part, I need to think about it over the weekend and discuss it with Howard."

"Does that mean you accept my decision?"

"Yes in principle. I want to mull it over on the weekend."

And with that he leaned forward, uncrossed his legs, and opened his jacket button—the classic body language of victory.

Howard caught up with me later.

"How could you say `Yes' to him? Aren't we quitting on Monday?"

"I said `Yes' to his *decision*. I accept that it's his decision, but I have no intention of abiding by it. This weekend, we're clearing desks and looking at your friend's lease space. We're going to war."

Father had a sandwich at his desk and left punctually at 1:00. We stayed until 7:00, cleaning up the positions as best we could and eliminating all exposure, so that Father would have a clean slate on Monday morning.

On Saturday morning we were in the office early. We cleared out our desks and made sure we had copies of all pertinent phone numbers and information. We called our traffic man, told him our game plan, and advised him to sit tight.

On Monday morning, Howard and I were in the office early. We started calling all our customers, informing each we were going to be on our own in two weeks' to a month's time. At 9:30 A.M., Father, relaxed and smiling, waltzed into the office. As soon as he saw our desks cleared, he collapsed into his chair and blanched. He knew his bluff had been called.

"Well, as you can see from our desks we are quitting," I said. "We will be happy to stay for two weeks, or up to a month, to help you get organized and provide for a smooth transition."

Father's color went from white to red to purple, and he yelled, "Never! You're no son of mine! I disinherit you! You can both go fuck yourselves! Get the hell out of my office, now! Get out! Get out! I don't want to see you ever again."

We took our briefcases and walked out.

We had not expected to be free so abruptly. However, within forty-eight hours we pinned down our bank line at a million dollars, and gave our lease to Herb for review. Our wives were looking for carpet and sundry office equipment, our business cards were being printed, and we were pressing our AT&T vice-president friend for help with phone and telex lines.

On Tuesday night I got a call from Father, asking to meet me. He said he had a plan that might be acceptable to both of us.

"Look," I answered, "I'm very busy setting up a new office and a new company. I don't have time to go through any charades, so if you have a proposition in mind, say so, and I'll relay it to Howard."

In an unctuous tone he said, "I've heard through the industry that you're setting up your own company. Maybe you could go ahead and set up the company, but operate from my offices. I'm starting to take it easier. I would continue with my European contracts. Steve could handle my end of the business, and you can forge ahead with what you want to do. In the few gray areas we could go joint account, and on any special large business you put together, I could come in and get a percentage by helping finance. Of course, I would charge you a percentage of overhead proportional to your use, which would be a lot cheaper for you than starting from scratch. I would also provide you with professional back office staff."

This was typical of his reversals of mind when events did not go his way. And I further felt Margot's counseling.

"Well, it's an interesting proposition, but fraught with potential complications. I would need to talk to Howard, but, off the top of my head, I don't think the deal is attractive enough for us. At this point, I'd rather go ahead and take the risks. If you'd be willing to put up a half a million bank line against our line of credit, then it might make sense."

"Claudy, I don't want to lose you. You're a strong person, but reasonable men can work things out. I'm bending a lot to stay together. As for the half a million, that's a lot of money. Why don't you talk to Howard, and perhaps I could consider a lower amount guarantee."

"All right, I'll be back to you. But it might be late."

"That's fine. I'll wait for your call."

We hung up, and I called Howard and reviewed the proposal. He had the same reaction I did. He was concerned about Father watching our business, the gray areas, sharing of staff, continued personality conflicts, and our ability to grow without clashes. I agreed that there were certain dangers, but if we could get 200,000 in guarantees, or a standby letter of credit, we could double our line of credit to two million and really continue business as before. Personality clashes should be at a minimum, since we would not be running his positions or vice versa, so no CGS syndrome. I wanted to give it a try, because he was my father. If the situation really did not work after a year, we would have built a base and could move out under better conditions.

Howard agonized but agreed. I called Father back and told him we were in general agreement, subject to the guarantee, but that time was of the essence. We were in the midst of making certain commitments, which would have to be canceled. Furthermore, we were planning to leave this weekend for the London ICO meetings and could not afford to be in limbo. We were going to meet our overseas contacts and tell them our situation and inform our roaster friends of any changes.

"I understand," he said. "I'm glad we can work this out. As far as the guarantee is concerned, the best I can do is 250,000 in a standby letter of credit against actual coffees, no future market positions. If that is agreeable to you, we could meet at Harry's office tomorrow, say 10.00 A.M., and work out an agreement. We have both worked with Harry, and I don't think he favors me any more than he does you. If we both get our own lawyers because of Harry's potential conflict of interest, you know it would take at least a month to hash things out."

Father had known Harry for a long time, and I had worked very closely with him over the past four years on some complicated international deals. He represented companies from Africa and Europe and several important people. He was brilliant and quick, spoke seven languages, and could summarize agreements incisively. We were pressed for time and short of funds, so we agreed. Next morning we met at Harry's office, which was lined with modern paintings by Magrite and Francis Bacon. I figured the value of the paintings at over a million at that time.

Harry quickly summarized the agreement. The only hitch was the 250,000 guarantee, which he thought the banks would not agree to since G.M. had the lines of credit, but not the capital, to give any form of guarantee. We finally settled that G.M. would make available the company's own line of credit for financing of up to 500,000. The negotiations were tense, but not acrimonious. By mid-afternoon, we had a signed five-page document. It was not perfection, and a lot of details were not covered, but Harry assured us it would stand up in court. We could always adjust the document as we went along. I gave Father a hug, hardly the warmest embrace we had ever exchanged. I had the feeling he was not looking at the agreement as the victory of father and son over circumstances, but rather as a personal defeat. If so, this would not bode well for the future. During the next two days, Howard and I called all our friends, told them of the agreement, canceled the telephone line orders, and once again backed out of our unsigned lease, giving full explanations and apologies.

That Saturday, we flew to London for the ICO meetings.

12

Double Cross

La vengeance est un plat qui ce mange froid!

To save a few bucks, Howard and I shared a room at the St. George. It was not the best hotel in London, but respectable and only a four-block walk from Berners Street where the ICO headquarters were located. The ICO meetings would start on Monday. In attendance would be delegates from every coffee producing nation in the world, as well as delegates from all the consumer signatory countries, and a few observers from non-signatory countries. It was a regular mini-United Nations. There were also many advisors from the trade and dealers such as we, who were interested in the outcome of the meetings and the opportunity to meet the important people in the trade.

Sunday was spent resting and phoning, locating who was staying in which hotel, and lining up lunches and dinners for the week.

On Monday morning we were at Berners Street early and mingled with the incoming delegates. We set up further meetings, but could not really talk of our plans because of the crowd milling about in the reception area next to the delegates conference rooms. For the most part, all we could convey was that we were starting our own company and would give details later. The meetings were long, and word got out that the delegation would not break before 4:00 P.M.

We decided to go back to the hotel, call New York, and find out about the market. When we got to the hotel, there was a message for me. It read, "Urgent—call Harry at his office."

This did not augur good news. We went up to the room and I called. Harry was quick and to the point. "Claude, you should come back immediately. There are some major changes we need to discuss."

"Harry, I can't. We are in the midst of very important meetings informing the delegates of our plans. These encounters are crucial. This must be done now, as I don't intend to travel to each country to tell our story. What the hell is going on?"

"Well, perhaps Howard could stay there and you come back. It's crucial that you return immediately."

"Harry, I can't. Let's stop the merry-go-round. It's obvious Father is trying to change the deal. Give it to me plain and simple on the phone. Then I can make some decisions."

"It's worse than that. He doesn't want to go through with it at all. He says he doesn't want any part of you boys. He was red in the face, sputtering and hacking that you pushed him into it, that he's done well without you all these years, and he bloody well can do without you now."

I blew up. "That son of a bitch! Harry, I thought you drafted a fair and straight contract. Why can't we enforce this in court?"

"The contract is enforceable, but will take you two or three years in court. In the meantime, what do you do for a living? Besides, under these circumstances, would you want to work alongside your father?"

"You're absolutely right. Okay, I'll be back in a week when the ICO meeting is over, then we can sign a dissolving agreement. In the meantime, we have a lot of work to do. Harry, you must absolutely guarantee me that he wants out before I reverse gears again."

"Yes—it's over. He swears you can sue him to Kingdom Come. He won't have anything to do with you. And by the way, he says he's disinheriting you."

"So what else is new. Thanks for the call. I think we caught things just in time, before it was a disaster."

Harry sighed relief in the phone. "Well, I'm glad to hear you've calmed down."

"I haven't. I'm just quietly angry, which is much worse. As the French say, '*La vengeance est un plat qui ce mange froid!*' Vengeance is a dish that is best eaten cold."

I hung up. Howard was beside himself as he listened to my side of the conversation. I felt like a tense bowstring, ready to release deadly arrows. I said: "Listen, we don't have time to beat ourselves up because we made the wrong decision. We got doubly fucked. Let's pick up our marbles and move forward. We tried our best. I have a clear conscience, and so I give you my word—our path is clear—we will bury him alive!"

We spent the rest of the afternoon calling home and recommitting to our previous engagements. By evening, we were exhausted and went up to the rooftop bar and restaurant. We each had a double scotch on the rocks. As we were commiserating about our difficulties, in walked Hayatou and the rest of the Cameroon delegation. We immediately invited them for dinner. Over dinner and drinks, speaking a mixture of French and English, we explained our new company and received resounding support and assurances of substantial new business. We were elated. This set the tone for the rest of the week's meetings. We returned to New York in high spirits, signed our lease, and reviewed with our landlord how the office should be laid out and built. Construction started that afternoon.

We went up to Harry's office to meet with Father and sign the disassociation agreement. Father proceeded to tell us how we pressured him into the deal and that he had signed the agreement under duress and consequently would not honor it. He went on: "As far as I'm concerned, you can take the agreement and stick it up your ass. It'll be a cold day in hell before ever you collect on it."

"Look, George," I said, calling my father by his first name for the first time, "I don't intend to waste my energy with your bullshit, so let's get Harry to draft a disassociation addendum. I only want two points in it: a clear statement that you're the one breaking the agreement, and, secondly, that we are willing to accept the break, provided our profit sharing plan and compensation percentage to the day we left be paid in full by good check within ten business days.

Otherwise, while proceeding with my own business, I will sue your ass, and the entire trade will find out. Harry will be our star witness."

Harry was not happy with this confrontation, and took my father aside and into another room. He came back and said, "All right, gentlemen, I will get George to sign the addendum you want and make sure he honors it. I want you in separate rooms until it is typed and ready for signature. Then I want you to sign the understanding without any nasty comments. Do you think you can behave?"

I responded. "Yes, you have a deal. I would like four originals signed, one for you and one for each of us."

He agreed and disappeared to dictate the addendum. A half hour later he came back with the finished two-page product, which we read and agreed to. Father came in. We all signed the cancellation of the agreement in silence, and then the addendum. After thanking Harry, we walked out. Two weeks later, we received his bill for services rendered, the lowest bill I had ever seen. Maybe it was our start-up present.

In three days, Saks International, Inc. was operational, with two phone lines and little else. We had a bridge table, a picnic table, a chair, and an upside-down garbage can as our second seat. We took turns sitting in the real chair. The carpenters were hammering on the framing studs and wallboard all around us. One of our good friends, a small roaster in Chicago, insisted he wanted to give us our first contract, so we closed a deal for twenty-five tons of Indonesians, joint account with Multitrade. We were in business.

By Friday the walls and spackle were complete. The landlord had the place painted over the weekend by his own men. Monday afternoon, the remnant carpet, which our wives had found, was tacked down—just enough to cover the entire office. On Tuesday, our desks, file cabinets, and other equipment were delivered. A telex line and two more phone lines went in the next day, and we were fully operational.

We started to do small contracts, so the paper flow began. We hired a secretary and called the traffic manager at G.M., telling him we would be ready for him in three weeks. He was jubilant and informed us he had been approached by the accountant, a Cuban woman, who also wanted to join us. We welcomed her with open arms. With a full staff, we now proceeded to push for more business.

Between the time a contract is made, the coffee delivered and the funds collected, 90 to 120 days can elapse. We had good profits built into our contracts, so our overhead was covered quickly, but our funds were being drawn down due to the long cycle time.

A month into our venture, Father decided to give us a run for our money. He began to see if he could hit us where his invective would hurt most—in Indonesia. He contacted the Dutch, particularly the mother company, Hagemeyer. He went directly to the Chairman of the Board and told him we were just a bunch of young upstarts. He had the real contacts, and the real thinking in the business was all his. The work I had set up in Indonesia, all my negotiations and deals, were due to his planning and thinking. I was a mere legman, carrying out his orders. The Chairman was not particularly aware of the day-to-day coffee business. One thing Father was marvelous at was making a good presentation. He was suave, worldly, bright, and could put across a concept exceedingly well. The Chairman said he would review the situation and told Father the Board would see whether it wanted to continue with Saks International, Inc., or perhaps support only G.M. Father also went after Walter Matter and Company, as the senior Walter was a good friend of his. I was concerned about the position Fred would take. Father thought he could influence Walter because both were of the same generation. Father tried to convince him that we were just a couple of young guys trying to steal his business and screw him. He was particularly convincing after the traffic man and accountant had joined us; it looked as if we had raided his company for our staff.

We decided the problem was of such importance that we should both go to Europe. We would leave our traffic man in charge of the office for a couple of days. Howard thought that he might not be much help in Switzerland, as he was not close with the people there, but in Holland we should present a united front. We would have to convince these companies that we had operated in an ethical manner, and that George Saks was not at all the person who put the deals together.

We flew to Amsterdam and met with the Chairman of Hagemeyer. Also present at the meeting was Aristocrat, the Director of Commodities and Tropical Products, who oversaw Multitrade. We explained how I had developed all the concepts at the source and Howard had developed the sales programs in the U.S.

The Chairman was very polite. He stated that George had made a very convincing argument, and he therefore felt that a meeting should be set up, to include Penguin, Aristocrat, George, and us. The chairman would then make his decision from the outcome.

A lot would be riding on this meeting. We thanked the Chairman, retired from his office, and went down a couple of floors to Penguin's office. We went through the business detail by detail. Saks International, Inc. was still a start-up business, now in our second month, and we could not show big contracts. But we already had on our books 600 tons of Indonesian coffees, which were very profitable. We were joint account with Multitrade, splitting the profits fifty-fifty; Aristocrat was very impressed. However, he had to follow the Chairman's instructions and try to meet with George Saks. I told Aristocrat that I thought George was in Switzerland, as I had heard he had told the same stories to Walter Matter & Company. He asked me if I would call and confirm.

I reached Fred and found that George was indeed there, having meetings with Walter. Fred said that he was doing all he could to try and keep his company neutral, but I should remember that his father was the boss, and whatever he said would be the way Fred would have to go. At the moment, he seemed to be leaning very heavily toward believing and backing George. I briefly explained to him what had transpired in Holland; that George was taking credit for the business we had developed and was trying to sabotage us.

I asked, "Do you think it would be possible to get George to fly to Holland and speak face-to-face with the Dutch about his claims, and allow us to defend ourselves?"

"That decision is not in my power, but I will speak to George and get back to you."

About fifteen minutes later, George Saks called and asked for Aristocrat. Multitrade's telephone system was different from ours in that each phone had a listening device whereby you could listen but not talk. Aristocrat motioned me to pick up and listen. The device caused no noise, so there was no way George would know I was overhearing their conversation. Father told him in no uncertain terms, "I'm an older gentleman, and not about to be pushed around by two young whippersnappers, or forced to come to Holland to explain my position or my business, which has been in existence for many years. I certainly am not going to defend myself against some young upstarts who have just started a couple of months ago. I have the proven track record. They have little or nothing. I have already replaced one of them and will shortly be hiring another young man. If any meeting is to be held, you can come to Switzerland and meet with me here."

Aristocrat stayed cool about the tone and did not take umbrage. "I will fly to Switzerland, but I feel it important that both Howard and Claude come with me. In fairness to all the parties, I think both should be present to defend their position. We have done a lot of business with G.M. Saks, but Claude is the man who opened the Indonesian business to us, and Howard appears to be the guy who has done most of the marketing. Under these conditions, I would be happy to fly to Geneva."

"Fine, I can receive you in Walter Matter's office but I'm sure it will be unnecessary to have a meeting with all of us together."

Aristocrat insisted that we be present.

The three of us flying to Geneva, instead of Father flying to Amsterdam, was a costly affair, and I recognized that the situation was unpleasant for Aristocrat. But he was the man who was going to make the recommendation to the chairman.

13

Sweet Revenge

Reasonable men can work things out.

We flew to Geneva and were met at Matter and Company by Fred. He informed me that his father and my father were up in the penthouse and would like to meet with me before they met with Aristocrat. This was contrary to what I had expected. I thought George would meet with Aristocrat and not bother with me at all. I went up to the penthouse. Matter Sr. was there with my father, and, as I came in, I was greeted very politely, albeit with heavy tension in the air.

Walter was a tall gentleman in his late sixties. He was imposing, very proper and correct. I could tell George was being aggressive and that he felt he had the situation under control. His jacket was buttoned. He sat very erect, as if to say "I've got you in a corner. Now we shall just see how you handle Walter." Walter started the conversation. "Mr. Saks." (He was from the old Swiss school and still formal.) "Your father and I have been talking about your unfortunate separation. He is very saddened by your leaving him. Families should stick together. A father-son relationship is especially binding and strong."

"Mr. Matter, all you say is true, and you're a fortunate man to have such a wonderful relationship with your own son. But this does not exist between my father and me. How can I—in a few moments—describe to you the mounting tension of the last five years? My father has never had a good word to say about any of my accomplishments.

He has been critical of every decision Howard and I made. When we involve him in the decision process, he agrees to go ahead, but at the same time gives us all the negatives and downsides to a move. It's a no-win situation. If it goes well, he takes the credit for the decision, and if it turns bad, he backtracks by saying I told you so. The tension in the office is unbearable. Howard has come down with a serious case of colitis, and in the past year I have developed elevated blood pressure and recurring asthma, which I have not had since childhood. I'm sorry, but we can't live this way."

My father, in his most unctuous tone, said, "Listen, Claudy. You are my son. We can talk this out. I only do and say things that are for you—for your learning process. You know I have your best interests in my heart. You know I would welcome you back with open arms. Reasonable men can work things out." It was the old refrain. Again I felt Margot's influence. Mr. Matter picked up on the tone.

"Well, you see, Mr. Saks, it seems your father is more than prepared to open a dialogue and really would like you with him in his company. I'm sure the two of you could find a way of working together. Besides, you must think of your difficulties. You deal for the most part in underdeveloped countries, where the father figure is most highly respected as head of family, clan, or tribe. All these people will support your father—not you. Your father told me how well he compensated you. It seems to me that your new venture will cause you to lose a substantial income. Do not cut off your nose to spite your face. It's like the biblical story of the prodigal son. Your father is waiting with open arms to welcome you back into the fold."

"Mr. Matter, this is not the case. I've overlooked most transgressions, and have tried to be part of `the fold,' as you put it. On several occasions, Howard and I have made offers to buy shares in the company. We certainly did not expect shares for free. My father has never indicated any intention of selling or sharing with me."

Mr. Matter raised his eyebrows as he leaned forward in his chair. "I must tell you, Mr. Saks, that it has never entered my mind to sell shares to a stranger, so I can understand your father's reticence about selling to Howard. As for my son, we have a good working arrangement in the company, and when I pass away, he will inherit all my shares. This is what your father has indicated his intentions are for you as well."

Father jumped in and reinforced the concept for ten minutes, stating that Howard had always been the fly in the ointment. He was not part of the family, but otherwise all would come to me. He finished his diatribe with his usual "reasonable men can work things out."

"Father, that is a lot of nonsense. You never indicated any such thing until you were threatened by our leaving. As far as Howard is concerned, he contributes to his end of the business very well. In the early stages, had you been close with me instead of playing Howard off against me, he might have accepted not being a shareholder, or perhaps a minority shareholder. By not treating me as a son, it backfired, and I became closer to Howard. As far as I am concerned, Howard is my partner. Too much water has passed under the bridge. We are fifty-fifty partners. Furthermore, as far as promises go about stock at your death, or any other promises, your promises are full of hot air because you don't hesitate to break them."

Father raised his voice, saying with bravado, "What do you mean? I always keep my promises, as Mr. Matter is my witness. Over the many years we have done business together, I have always kept my word."

"That may be so to an outsider, but certainly not to your family, or your son. I had a signed legal agreement with you which you did not hesitate to break, and told me it would be a `cold day in hell if I ever collected.' You told me to shove it and go to court. Your word in my book is worthless."

He raised his voice higher as if to blanket the situation. "I never broke any agreements. You young turks think you can interpret documents your way. You're the one who backed out. If I had that paper with me I could show Mr. Matter what a dishonorable person you are."

At that point, I reached into my breast pocket and pulled out the canceled agreement with its addendum. He blanched visibly as he recognized the document.

"Mr. Matter, Father has been telling you lies. This is the broken agreement and addendum. It won't take long to read. You will clearly see he is the one who broke the agreement, and, as far as I'm concerned, I can never trust his word again."

I got up and handed the document to Walter. Father, in the meantime, was frantic and started his familiar CGS routine. Mr. Matter began reading the document.

"Claude, you should not have brought that document. You're washing the family's dirty laundry in public. That's not acceptable."

Walter kept reading while the diatribe went on.

"Look, George, as far as I'm concerned you are the one who started washing dirty laundry in public, and concerning family—I do not consider you part of mine anymore. For me, you're dead. And as far as business is concerned, I will bury you alive."

Mr. Matter had finished reading and handed the document back to me.

"Mr. Saks, I now understand your motives in going on your own. Still, I think it would be nice if you and your father could part as friends."

"I'm sorry, but that is not possible at this time. I would like to thank you for your patience and understanding in the midst of this squabble. We've been talking here for two hours and I have no further words to add. The Hagemeyer director has been waiting to talk to Father. Shall I send him up when I go to the conference room?"

Mr. Matter looked at my father for guidance. Father said, "You tell him [Aristocrat] that I have no interest in seeing him, or any of his associates from Holland. Hagemeyer supports the two of you, and I'll be damned if I'll do business with those Dutchmen."

"Okay, fine with me. Mr. Matter, again thank you."

I shook his hand, turned my back to my father, and took the elevator down. I stopped in Fred's office for five minutes, thanked him, then went to the conference room where Howard and Aristocrat were waiting. I could immediately tell that the tension had reached a particular high. Howard was looking at me with raised eyebrows; Aristocrat was absolutely fuming and said, "What do you mean keeping me here for two hours?"

"I certainly didn't keep you here for two hours," I replied calmly. "My father tied me up with Matter. I indicated to them, several times, that you were waiting here, and that he had requested your presence so that he could present his side of the story. I'm sorry to inform you that we just had a rather nasty meeting, which, unfortunately, is typical. I've tried to explain to you that my father is unreliable, and, in fact, he just informed me he does not see any reason to meet with you. He said he stated his case to the chairman on the telephone. I'm unable to apologize for my father, since this is why we're breaking up. You could try to reach him and confront him."

Aristocrat stood up, very erect. "I have no intention of doing any such thing. If that is his attitude, I don't want to meet your father or do business with him. You therefore have Hagemeyer's and Multitrade's 100-percent backing, and we'll never do any business with him. Should he ever find himself in Indonesia, we will go out of our way to sabotage his endeavors." Aristocrat raged in his best Dutch accent, with a few Dutch profanities thrown in.

Howard was looking at me. I could tell he was jubilant, and so was I. Aristocrat calmed down, and as he relaxed, we relaxed. It was an absolute victory for us. This fiasco sealed our relationship with Hagemeyer, and with Multitrade, and proved to be our most important calling card as we started our business.

I already knew the rules by which my father would play—subterfuge, underhandedness and criticism about us to our customers and sources. I knew he did not have the balls to take me on one-on-one at source or the market. I decided I would not play on his turf; I would beat him by being quicker and smarter and by offering better deals at source and to the end user.

The die was cast—I was at war with my own father.

14

Opportunities

All I had seen were Europeans in positions of authority.
That would change.

Back in New York, we set to the task of expanding our business based on a quick turnover, as we could not afford to finance slow moving, big positions. Thank God for Multitrade's financing of the bulk of our joint Indonesian business. The Cameroons were true to their word and supplied us on a regular basis.

During our first six months, we kept expenses to a minimum, and I did no traveling. I made up for the lack of movement by putting in sixteen-hour days. I rose at four in the morning to telephone Africa before their lunch hour and worked until seven at night, reviewing contracts, positions, and financing. Bette and the kids suffered the consequences and did not see much of me. Even when I was with them, I was consumed with restlessness, as if I needed to be in the office constantly doing deals for the business. Because of my ambition to conquer the world and secure a financial future for my family, my children were growing through their wonder years without my joyful involvement. Most times I was lucky to give them a hug goodnight. I shuddered at the idea of traveling again, but I had to renew my close relationships with our sources.

I called André to get updates, and he told me that the ONC had completed its transformation and that the French D.G. was on his way to Paris the following week. A trip to Paris was cheaper than going to Kinshasa, so I made arrangements to meet him. He was staying at the Bellemont, a small older hotel, but clean and reasonable, situated on the Avenue George V. He brought with him his attractive young Zairian mistress. The three of us went out to dinner at a quaint bistro, and I pressured him to obtain contracts. The D.G. was evasive and noncommittal, all the while assuring me he would give us full support. He kept telling me he wanted to develop a European market outside of the Belgian and Italian users. His intention was to increase France's share in particular, and he felt the U.S. would never be a big market for Zaire. He did say he would consider giving me some trial contracts. I got the message: he had a "special relationship" in France, and would give us some crumbs both to satisfy us and the political record. I was frustrated and understood how my competition felt when I would negotiate large contracts and lock them out. I was polite, however, and accepted the outcome. I believed the status quo never remains the same in Africa. I would get another shot down the road.

We returned to the hotel, and my other shot came sooner than expected. There was a message that Howard had called. When I called him back, Howard told me, "André called. He says there is a strong rumor going around Kinshasa that the D.G. is being replaced by his assistant, Hippo."

"That's great. I'm sorry about the wasted funds for this trip. If the change is confirmed, I need to go to Kinshasa immediately."

Howard concurred. I would still need to make a sales pitch to get Hippo to open up quantities for the U.S. market. I caught the first flight back to New York. A week later, an official announcement was made deposing the French D.G. and appointing Hippo, *Directeur Generale*. What a joy. The wheel turned. I reached Hippo by phone, at three in the morning New York time, avoiding the usual phone traffic. I congratulated him and set up an appointment for the following week.

Landing in Kinshasa was not my favorite experience, but at least I had an Amiza rep to take me through passport and currency control. By 1973, the Intercontinental Hotel was finished, and, compared with previous accommodations, was a delight.

I was on pins and needles because I had to succeed in beating Father and proving my worth in source supplies for Howard's marketing. I took a taxi to the ONC and met with Hippo. I congratulated him again on his promotion and expressed my concern about obtaining large quantities of coffee for the U.S.

Hippo sat relaxed behind the enormous desk. He assured me he had the blessing of the ministry to do large contracts with us.

I was astonished by Hippo's quick acceptance when I asked for a contract of 700 tons a month of the better coffees. "You have a deal, starting with the shipments for September, October, and November."

"That will be fine," and mentally I said, "Up your ass, George."

The next morning I flew to Bujumbura, Burundi. You can't appreciate the vastness of Zaire until you fly for three hours across dense jungle to reach Bujumbura. The town was still a sleepy, backwater corner of Africa, where old, low colonial buildings lined the four paved roads that made up the "downtown."

Although Bujumbura sits in a valley at 5,000 feet, the town does not have the coolness of Nairobi. Bujumbura is enclosed by the Kivu mountains of Zaire to the west and Rwanda's and Burundi's mountains to the north. To the east are the Ugandan mountains, and to the south lies Lake Tanganyika, stretching 600 miles down the backbone of Africa. It was hot and humid, but with a spectacular view: blue water with blue skies on top.

With the exception of its natural beauty, the area's only attraction is a little monument, located a few miles out of town, marking the location where Stanley met Livingstone. The main excitement available was fishing on the lake, which yielded an incredible number of species. Swimming was not recommended. The small rivers feeding the lake had microscopic parasites, which would enter your anus and eventually eat your intestines away. Of course, if you were a real nature buff, you could go to the Burundi/Rwanda mountains and observe the gorillas. The power of nature here made me aware of my insignificance.

As this was my first trip to Burundi, I planned to lay seeds for future developments and get the lay of the land. When I was with Father's company, we had done business with two firms, one Belgian and the other Greek. The Belgian firm tried to preserve its former glory—the director still drove about in a large Mercedes—but the business was now nearly nonexistent. The Greek firm was wealthy but small, and operated in a conservative and unimaginative way. I paid them both a visit. I knew that Father had not done business with them since we broke up. The owners were supportive, but I knew that business would be limited. I discovered that both were unhappy with the Burundi authorities, who were beginning to control coffee sales.

Burundi wanted to control more of its own production and diversify its sales and was offering coffee through a local European broker. Golf, the code name we gave him (the reason will become apparent later), was a self-important Belgian. As well as claiming to know all the technicalities of the standard coffee contract, he was convinced he was the ultimate authority on Burundi coffees. Golf was about 5' 8", with thinning brown hair, a bulbous nose, and small mousy brown eyes. He considered me a young upstart, but was most expansive in dispensing his wisdom. He told me that the government was planning to nationalize all the exporters. The Government would set up a parastatal organization headed by Golf as part owner. He went to great lengths to tell me he would stop payoffs at all levels. A line from Shakespeare went through my mind: "Methinks the lady doth protest too much." I filed the thought away for future reference.

I went to visit the Ministry of Agriculture. Up to that time, all I had seen were Europeans in positions of control or authority. That would change. The native Burundians would take their destiny into their own hands. I obtained an audience with the Minister quickly. He was a tall, handsome, very dark man. I could see his Watusi heritage.

The division between Burundi and Rwanda occurred along tribal, rather than purely geographic, lines. The tall people of the Watusi tribe (up to seven feet), more generally called Tutsi, were in control of Burundi, and the much shorter Hutu, who averaged about five foot five, were in control of Rwanda. Tribal antagonisms had broken out a few months prior to my arrival. Rumors circulated that 10,000 Hutu had disappeared—possibly massacred. While I was there, everything seemed orderly and quiet—maybe too quiet. There was still a very large population of Hutus in Burundi, but mainly in menial or clerical jobs.

The minister had been educated by the Jesuits in Burundi and then had gone to the University of Uganda in Kampala, when it was still considered a very fine school in Africa. It became apparent from our conversation that the main concern of the ministry of agriculture was the growing of crops, purchase of fertilizers, the health of farm animals—particularly African cows—and the general welfare of Burundi's native farm production.

"The government is going to take a firm hand in the marketing of coffee," he told me. "One of my up-and-coming young assistants is going to be in sales under the D.G., at the new parastatal coffee organization. Would you like to meet him? Perhaps he could show you around the facilities to be used once the transition is in place."

I was introduced to Kabwa and knew right away we would get along and do well together. He was a soft-spoken man of about twenty-six, with a broad, smiling face. He was a graduate of Brussels University. We toured the facilities, which the government had purchased from a defunct shipping company. Kabwa knew the coffee business well, and I was convinced he was being groomed to eventually take over the parastatal organization, much as Hippo did in Zaire. I had hit the jackpot! Now it was up to me to nurture the seed.

At the end of our tour I excused myself, and went to the men's room, where I took an envelope from my briefcase and stuffed it with local currency. Kabwa drove me back to my hotel in the ministry car. I thanked him for the tour, and handed him the envelope as a token of my appreciation.

It is interesting, in retrospect, to look at my total lack of moral or ethical attachment or judgment about paying someone off to obtain a preferential position. I considered this practice no different than giving a tip to a maître d' to obtain a good table. Yet if I discovered within my own organization anyone who was on the take, that person would immediately be dismissed. As my future path of spirituality unfolded I would find this double standard inconsistent and unacceptable.

15

Miracles out of Crisis

She must have dialed the wrong company.

Howard and I were concerned that we would not be able to finance the Zaire quantities. We had developed a close relationship with Abba, who was now working for a medium-sized dealer. We quickly sold to him, at a small profit, 200 tons out of our first 700-ton September commitment, and also 200 tons out of the October portion on a cash-against-documents deal, so no financing.

Over a pleasant dinner meeting with Peter Castelano, head of coffee purchasing, and John Buckley, V.P. of overall Purchasing, of the Nestle company, we sold 500 tons.

The next few months saw me traveling extensively. September came and went with no Zaire shipment. I was in touch with Hippo, and he assured me the coffees were on their way from Kinshasa to Matadi, the shipping port. I spoke to John Buckley, and explained the situation. He said he could accept an October shipment because Nestle had more than enough supplies for the time being.

October rolled around, and we knew we were going to have a problem. Again I called John Buckley and again he extended the contract one month, but this time he was adamant that Nestle needed the coffee shipped in November. We got an Advice of Shipment for 100 tons in October and, since Abba was screaming, we applied the coffees to his contract to soothe his nerves.

I got no satisfaction from Hippo and was getting frantic. I knew I could not threaten him with late shipment penalties and price revisions due to the falling market, because that would have meant the end of our relationship in Zaire. I did say to him that I was being threatened by my customers of such an eventuality. He responded: "I realize the ONC is very late, and appreciated your not claiming, especially considering that we also owe you 700 tons each for October and November and these shipments will also be late. I suggest that as soon as the contracts are complete you fly down to Kinshasa. The ONC will make good on any problems."

Knowing Africa, this meant our losses would be covered but he could not say more on the phones; the lines were always tapped. Meantime, it was most important for us to come up with a coffee equal to or better than the Zaires we owed to our major customer. I called my friend at Amiza in Kinshasa to see if transport delays might be occurring. He explained that Matadi was a bottleneck between incoming and outgoing cargo. Despite good intentions on the part of the ONC, once on a train the shipments were always late. I was extremely anxious as this was my first big deal since Howard and I were on our own and my self-worth, reputation, and money were on the line. Was I going to fail right from the start?

In the midst of our first major shipping and market problem, I got a call from Paris. I did not have any ties there so the call was unexpected, and the caller unknown. He introduced himself in French as Bernard Veysseyre and said we had met at the gala opening of the Paris Cocoa exchange. He was calling to get some market information.

"I'm sorry Mr. Veysseyre. I wasn't at the opening of the Cocoa Exchange. I suspect you met my father. We're no longer together, so you've reached the wrong number. But we did meet briefly about a year ago when your boss took me out to lunch. Anyway, let me give you my father's number."

"No, no. That's quite all right. I have it. I told my secretary to call `la maison Saks.' She must have dialed the wrong company. I do remember meeting you when you were visiting my boss."

"Please give him my regards—"

Bernard cut in. "Oh, I'm sorry, you mustn't have heard the news, but he died in a car accident two months ago."

Bernard told me the suddenness of his death had left company affairs in a mess. "I'm trying to sort out all the various positions, some of which don't make much sense to me. And that's the reason for my call. I would like your market opinion."

I decided, okay. I would give him a market run down. It was his nickel on the international lines. I proceeded to give him a forty-five minute analysis and dissertation on the market, which had been dropping steadily.

"Mr. Saks, that is the most comprehensive market analysis I've ever heard. If I may, I would like to call on you from time to time to compare notes."

"My pleasure, and, by the way, my name is Claude. Can I be of any help in unraveling your positions?"

"Well, Claude, actually you might. We own 750 tons of Angolan 2 BB, spot in warehouse, New York. I don't know what to do with them! Maybe you could find a buyer?"

I could not believe my ears. "Yes," I said quickly. "The quantity is no problem. Robustas are our main business, so if you could make us a firm offer, I'm sure we could market them and give you a reply by telex for your morning opening."

Evidently delighted, Bernard made me a good offer at a price cheaper than the delayed Zaire coffee.

I accepted and bid him goodnight. When Bernard's confirming telex arrived, I picked up the phone: "Peter, Claude here. I have some good news. I think we've come up with a terrific solution to our Zaire problem. We can offer Nestle the full 500-ton replacement with Angolan Two BB's which, as you know, is better coffee, at the same price. The coffees are in storage, with thirty days privilege, which means you can draw the bags out as you need them. No shipping schedule headache."

Peter was pleased and readily accepted. "I have great faith in you two guys," he told me.

He said they would still be interested in Zaire coffee provided we could straighten out the shipments.

Howard was concerned about the large quantities of coffees we still had coming from Zaire at full prices and questioned our entire relationship in that crazy country. I calmed his anxieties, assuring him that a deal would be worked out with Hippo. I would go to Zaire to work on the problem directly, flying via Paris to meet first with Bernard.

Bernard's company was located a few blocks behind the Madeleine in a typical, older, Parisian walk-up building. His office, on the third floor, was reached by a staircase that was exceptionally steep due to the twelve-foot ceilings in the rooms. By the time I climbed the three flights, I was exhausted. I was overweight by thirty pounds. My custom Hong Kong shirt and Hermes silk tie were sticky with sweat. I took off my jacket, wiped my brow and rested on the landing to cool down before entering the office.

Once I met Bernard, I knew we would get along like a house on fire. He was a thin, wiry Frenchman with dark thinning hair and dark flashing eyes. He smoked Dutch cigarillos while continually on the move and talking. I was very impressed by his detailed knowledge of the French African robusta business, including its related geography, shipping lines and routes, and existing anomalies.

It was on one of these anomalies that the conversation settled: Ivory Coast grade threes, and how they were sold to Morocco.

Bernard proceeded to tell me that, for political reasons, the Ivory Coast always did deals for the lower grade threes, at a much greater discount, with Morocco. Though it was an Arab country, Morocco was also a full ICO member, which none of the others were. Morocco would negotiate a deal on a government-to-government level, for Ivory Coast threes based on their importers' estimates. Each importer, in his zeal, would overestimate the quantity needed and end up with huge stockpiles of threes in Morocco and no buyers.

Bernard's Moroccan importer, Habib, was anxious to unload his overbought quantities. We called him and set up an initial deal: Habib bought overage from the other Moroccan dealers, added it to his overage, and sold it to Bernard for reshipment to the United States.

Over the next two years, the three of us developed a very profitable business, which was split three ways, and our status as major robusta dealers was consequently reinforced.

The incredible solution to our problem and greatly increased business through a chance phone call from Bernard was later explained to me by an astrologer. I had my sun in the twelfth house, which is the house of surprises both good and bad.

I went to the ONC soon after arriving in Kinshasa and was immediately ushered in to see Hippo. Sitting behind the big D.G.'s desk, he seemed well pleased with himself. "Hello Claude, I hope you had a pleasant journey. I'm glad you've come down so we can resolve our late shipments."

No preliminaries—right to the problem.

I told him we needed an allowance of four and a half cents a pound to come out whole. I appeared relaxed, so he knew I was exaggerating the situation. The market had fallen just under two cents a pound and a good part of the rest of the claim was for Saks International's profit. We had made a big profit covering the Zaire coffee with Bernard's Angolans.

"You are claiming this on how much of the quantity?"

"On the September and October shipments. November is still open, so a total of 1,400 tons."

"That's a lot of money."

He punched up the figures with his pudgy round fingers on a small calculator.

"That's over $123,000. The minister will never accept it. I don't know how we will resolve this. If it were ten to twenty thousand, I think it could be managed politically, but $123,000, no, my friend. It can't be done."

"The other alternative," I said, "is that we sign an additional contract at a reduced price, reflecting the allowance. That way you don't have to ask for an official hard currency check. It will just come out on our end when we sell the coffee."

"That's a possibility. I would still have to present it to the Minister, so that on the official records it would not appear that I'm selling you coffee below the market."

We were back on track. And adding the allowance to new contracts assured us of a flow of supply and a serious presence in the market.

Hippo suggested we get together for lunch after he met with the Minister.

I met Hippo at the outdoor Zoo restaurant. The tables were far apart, so we could talk easily. Hippo's meeting had gone well. The Minister agreed to additional contracts at a reduced price to make up the allowance.

"How do you propose spreading the $123,000 cost?" I asked him.

Hippo responded with his mouth half full of food: "Come on, Claude. We are friends. You know that's too high an allowance. I'm prepared to let you make additional profit because of the difficulties the ONC caused, but it must be within reason. Further, I need to talk to you on a personal basis as one of my confidantes."

I saw the scenario coming. If he wanted me as a confidante, there would be money involved. I had better show all my cards.

I told him we were out of pocket two cents a pound because of market movement. "We were able to move other coffees to cover our customer, but I assure you it would have cost another two cents had we not been able to cover. The situation was saved by our being a large dealer and having other coffees available. What is that worth? That's the whole story. I leave it to you. Now what can I do as your confidante and friend?"

Hippo began by reminding me that in the industrialized world, we had insurance—insurance in case of death, insurance in case of injury, insurance on your cars. He explained that in Africa, insurance was expensive, when it was available at all, and payment of claims was not always assured. "Our real insurance is our family, our tribe," he told me. "Whoever is in power or has wealth must look after his family and help his tribe. If something happens to me, my wife and children will be taken care of by my brother, cousins, or others. Now that I have a position of wealth and power it is my responsibility to be the insurance for my extended family. This job will be rotated politically every two years, so my time is short." He then asked that a 10-percent commission be paid on the allowance through Andre's company which would provide a coffee quality inspection service for Saks International.

I calculated mentally that after paying the commission we would still be ahead $60,000, above costs and market risks, due to the larger quantity involved.

We shook hands on the deal.

When I called Howard to bring him up to date, he told me about the situation in Burundi—reported hostilities between the Tutsis and the Hutus, in which as many as 100,000 Hutus may have been massacred. Another 100,000 had fled the country.

I called Bette that night. "I just wanted to let you know I'm still alive and kicking. Thank God I didn't go to Burundi. How are the kids?"

"They're fine. They're all here and want to say hello to their Dad. Here's Claire."

"Hi, Claire. How's my little girl? I miss you terribly. What have you been doing?"

Claire was now six years old, and she proceeded to tell me all the things she had done in first grade and how she had played with her friends. Eric and Marc got their turns and described the events of a sixth and third grader respectively. After sending then all hugs and kisses I promised I would call at length from Amsterdam and be home in less than a week. With all my traveling I felt I was missing my kids growing up.

I called Howard again from Amsterdam—and we spent the next hour updating each other on the markets. Our main concern was that our lines of credit were too small for our volume. Peter, at Chemical Bank, had already increased our line by half a million, but could go no further until our year-end financial statements were available, even though we were doing well. I said I would see what I could do with Multitrade.

By 8:30 A.M. next morning I was in Multitrade's office. Things were quiet, and Penguin had not yet arrived. London trading did not open for another hour, and New York was sleeping. I was astonished that the traders were not taking this time to review, analyze, and in general develop their plan of attack for the day. With the reverse time sequence, Howard and I always used the quiet time after four P.M. to develop our game plan for the next day.

The office had expanded and, including their small spice division, had thirty-seven people. We had only six, but I was prepared to match profits any day. I took the opportunity, with Penguin out, to snoop around the back office. All documentation was done by hand, and the staff seemed to be phobic to the point of making duplicates of all systems. The traders never traveled to source and from the business I saw, I concluded that we provided the bulk of their profits through the Indonesian contracts.

Penguin finally arrived in a flurry of activity. "Hi, Claude! Good to see you. I've been working so late that I slept right through the alarm. Forgive me, but I need to see what's happening with the market. Then we can spend some time together. Please feel free to use our office as your own."

He continued bustling, picking up phones, giving instructions to the back office, speaking to the traders, but I was not convinced that much real business was being conducted. I called Fred and Bernard and got up to date on the market.

Penguin and I lunched at the Oyster Bar in a windowed alcove overlooking Rembrandt Square, where an old, bundled-up woman was feeding the pigeons and the trolleys clanged their bells rounding the corner. Penguin was full of himself, telling me that he now had a small office in Trieste, and that Multitrade was doing good-sized contracts out of the Brazilian coffee depots located there. I was astonished that he was involved, as he had never been to Brazil and the firm was not known for that business. He explained that he relied on people in his Trieste office who knew the Italian market well and had brokered Brazils in the port. I congratulated him, not having any further interest and feeling it was not my business to question him in depth.

He told me he was doing increased business in the spice division, selling pepper, cardamom, cloves, rattan, cow hides, rice wine, and other things. Again I wondered about his expertise.

I talked about our need for more financing for our increased business in Africa and Indonesia and asked him if Multitrade would consider helping.

"I don't see any problem, but I will have to check with Mama Hagemeyer. She may want to charge larger interest costs," he explained jovially.

"If she has to, so be it," I said. "But I think that between our paying one quarter of a cent per pound for inspection in Indonesia, and my coming up with the ideas that have allowed you to become a shipper over there, and the fact that the office is now a profit center, I would think you should do the financing at cost. I need it for four months until I can meet with Chemical Bank."

"I agree with you and I will present your case to Hagemeyer."

For the rest of the afternoon I continued to observe Multitrade's operation. That evening I had dinner with Penguin and the traders, where my view of their lack of professionalism was reinforced. I filed my impressions in the back of my mind.

A week later, Hagemeyer's Treasurer Yella, a great supporter of our endeavors over the past year, telephoned and agreed to the financing at a very slight premium to cost.

Back in New York, our business was growing swiftly. It pleased me to know that George was no competition for us either at source or in the United States. I settled in to clean up paper work, review operations and financing, and generally keep in touch with suppliers by phone. I was grateful that I could spend time at home, enjoying the family and catching up with my children, yet somehow I felt distant and noncommittal. My mind was on the coffee world; I was unable to be interested in the details of my family's daily life.

Two days before Thanksgiving, I got a call from the Secretary General at the Burundi Embassy telling me that the Chairman and the vice Chairman of the Burundi National Bank would be in New York on Monday and would like to make an appointment to visit us.

"It would be with great pleasure that we would see the Chairman and the Vice Chairman. Shall we say 11:00 A.M.? And could you give me the reason for their desire to see us?"

"Yes, certainly. As you know, there have been certain disturbances in our country."

Christ, I'm thinking, 100,000 dead and 100,000 fled and he calls it disturbances. "The flow of coffee has been halted," he continued.

"The National Bank has been given the directive to sell the stocks on hand. As far as the time is concerned, could you make the appointment a little earlier, as the gentlemen are visiting other importers?"

"I see. I was hoping we could take the Chairman and his colleague to lunch after our meeting."

"I'm sorry but both are already booked."

Howard, who was listening to the conversation, whispered, "How about over the weekend? If they're going to be here, let's tie them up."

"How soon are they planning to come to New York?"

They were arriving Saturday. They accepted our offer of a Sunday morning tour followed by lunch.

We would have them to ourselves for Sunday before the rest of the trade got their hands on them. I smelled a deal, and Sunday was the day. Thanksgiving rolled around and Sunday morning was upon us.

Howard and I picked up the Chairman and his associate at the Biltmore at ten sharp. Both men wore typical bankers' suits, dark, pin-striped, with conservative ties, white shirts and black shoes. The Chairman was a soft-spoken, erudite African, who had been educated at the University of Louvain. The Vice Chairman seemed to be along for the ride, agreeing with all of the Chairman's thinking. The Chairman's English was fairly good, which was helpful for Howard. However, he occasionally struggled with words, so I would switch to French and get into lengthy discussions, reinforcing the fact we had similar backgrounds and common areas of interest— which I knew they would not find the following day when visiting the competition. Howard was fully cognizant of the strategy and understood the gist of the conversations when we digressed into French.

After touring New York, we went to the King Cole bar at the St. Regis for lunch. Before it was remodeled, the King Cole dining area had deep leather banquettes in a U-shape. The Old King Cole bar had tables far apart for easy conversation, impeccable service, and great food.

The Chairman explained Burundi's predicament: they had not sold any of their new crop, which had been completely picked and processed. They did not have the warehouse space or the financing to ship and store such large quantities. In Washington, they had met with the World Bank and U.S. financial advisors to request help during this difficult period. Provided they could demonstrate sales contracts for their coffee to World Bank representatives, they had been assured of the necessary financing. "Your name was given to us from our Agriculture Department," he said. "We also obtained other names from your Green Coffee Association here in the U.S."

The Chairman told me that, as most of the European exporters had fled, the government had created a sales committee, which would eventually constitute a new parastatal organization.

Burundi had lost a lot of production because laborers had fled before all the coffees were picked. His best estimate of available coffees was 160,000 bags of all grades, not including the amount in the hands of the few European shippers who had stayed. I asked for the breakdown. The conversation was fully in French and accelerated.

I could tell that Howard, who understood pieces of the conversation, was getting concerned that I was trying to negotiate the whole crop. He was not far from the mark. The assistant remained quiet, nodding his head from time to time.

I said, "We are entering the latter stages of the shipping period for the crop, so the coffees could lose some of their acidity and color. This could be a problem because the new Central American crop starts shipping in January, and these coffees take only a week to ten days to get here."

He told me that only the sales committee could answer my questions.

He was a member of the committee. The others were the Minister of Agriculture; Golf, whom I had met and who would head up the new Burundi Parastatal Organization (BPO); Kabwa, from the Ministry of Agriculture, and the present director of quality control.

The committee was made up of people who knew me and would probably vote for us if we presented a reasonable deal. The position of Golf, the main man, was an unknown, however. He had been a small broker all his life, and he had to know that this problem could not be resolved by making small contracts. I came out of my reverie in the middle of the Chairman's sentence. ". . . a commitment on your part for 50,000 or so bags would resolve part of our financial problem and give us the respect needed to market the remainder."

"Mr. Chairman, if we were to make a commitment to Burundi for a large quantity, we would need assurances we would not be undercut by our competitors, who would buy smaller quantities and ruin the entire market. What I propose is that we buy 100,000 bags, 75 percent higher grade and the 25 percent remainder of lower grades."

Howard, hearing "*cent mille,*" 100,000, gave me his raised-brow, wide-eyed look, meaning, "Where the hell do we get the financing?"

I winked back at him, so he knew I had worked an edge. This deal would put us on the map as arabica dealers and garner us a substantial position in Burundi. I could tell by the Chairman's countenance that he was warming to the idea that he could resolve the bulk of his problem in one fell swoop.

After two hours of talks I summarized the deal with all the price differentials and shipping positions. The chairman expressed his confidence that we would be able to conclude an arrangement.

It was 3:30 in the afternoon, and our coffee cups were long cold. The waiters were anxious to clear us out. In 1973, late brunches were not the fashion. We took the two bankers back to their hotel.

As we drove home, Howard turned to me, "What the hell are you doing? How are we going to finance such large quantities?" I always felt free to let my imagination and creativity go wild, because I knew I could rely on Howard to find the negatives and rein in my expansive side. I always felt comfortable pushing the edge of the envelope with Howard as my partner.

I told Howard I had set up a lot of loopholes and that shipment did not start until January so we had time to maneuver on both counts. I went on, "I'm worried about Golf, who will probably head the B.P.O. The committee will listen to him. I get a niggling feeling he plans to make personal money through his own brokerage house in Brussels, which this deal obviously short-circuits. I think he will dot every 'i' and cross every 't' to pin us in a corner, either forcing us out of the deal or, if it goes through, showing the great job he's doing for Burundi, securing his future position."

We had come to a red light at Forty-Third Street and Eleventh Avenue, just before the Lincoln Tunnel, and we were engrossed in our conversation. It was a bright, cold and blustery day. There was a tap on my window. I looked over and saw a mini-skirted hooker with garter belt showing, leaning over and smiling at me, her full breasts three-quarters exposed. I whooshed down the window. "Yes?"

"Gentlemen, last blow job before the tunnel?"

"Thanks anyway, but we're in a rush."

And I whooshed the window back up and drove off as the light changed. We broke into hysterical laughter at the absurdity of New York. When we finally regained our composure, I said to Howard, "I think it's imperative to add arabicas to our marketing, and Burundi is a good way of doing this without having to lock horns with the big boys in Central America."

We concluded that we wanted to do the deal.

The next morning, as we walked into the office, we were handed a telex from Burundi, signed by Golf, who had tightened my loopholes and made us a firm offer that was tough in price but workable. He asked for our reply in time for Burundi's next day's opening. It was a neat, tight package. We immediately set to work to see what demand might exist. Howard sold all the lower grades but was unable to find any interest for the better qualities.

The Burundi bankers came in, and we showed them the telex and told them we felt the asking price was quite high, considering the very large quantity we were prepared to take to solve their problem. Golf probably was thinking that if the bankers were unsuccessful, he could sell quite a few lots, piecemeal, through his Brussels brokerage.

I pointed out that Burundi had missed its main marketing months so to try to market small quantities would be disastrous. They didn't have the luxury of time. The coffees would begin to fade, and the new Central American crop would start shipping in about thirty to sixty days. Golf needed to understand that, without a price concession, there was absolutely no attraction for us to take the risk on such a large quantity. I said, "We are negotiating 100,000 bags—that's 6,000 tons of coffee, worth over $6.6 million."

The message sank in. I told them we would be telexing a counteroffer that afternoon. Meanwhile, we went back to the task of trying to drum up interest for the better grades without alarming the market with our quantity. In desperation, I called my old Lebanese mentor, Camelari, and made him an offer for 10,000 bags a month, January through March. After some bantering, he came out with his famous line: "Don't geeve me dis djazz, geeve me di cohfee. How much total quantity you have? I don't want to compete against you in the market—I want it all or none."

I knew this was a tight offer, but our main desire was not to make a big profit, but to get a solid footing in Burundi.

I told him I had the better qualities tied up, with a guarantee that the remainder would be offered only outside the U.S.A. "I can offer you 25,000 bags a month, a total of 75,000 bags, for January, February, and March."

"All right, let's stop di ball, I geeve you a bid for the entire quantity."

His bid was below our costs so we bid down and telexed Burundi that evening, knowing that the bankers would have reached Golf by phone and softened him up. Since the bankers, the minister, and Kabwa were probably voting for the deal, Golf would be alone. Nevertheless, he was the marketing expert. We bid fifty-one for the better coffees, with substantial discounts for the remainder. The next morning, we had a telex countering at fifty-one and a half and accepting the other differentials. Hooray!!

We had a nice profit built in for the lower grades, but what to do about the higher grades? I went back to Camelari. The best he would do allowed for an extremely small profit of one-quarter cent per pound. I closed the deal.

I accomplished all I wanted in Burundi. When the country was totally calm, I would visit and be in position as a regular large buyer, particularly now that I had the National Bank of Burundi as a backer. Golf was isolated, and I would deal with his little fiefdom when I met him on his own turf.

Many years would pass before I understood my relationship with Howard during these crucial times. We were partners in business and as in a good marriage each partner accepts the other's strengths and faults, mirroring each other, and forming a successful combined whole. In hindsight Howard's greatest contribution to me at this time was his giving me full permission to be who I was. He gave me the confidence to create and engage all the energies around me with my never having to look over my shoulder. Something I never had with my father and certainly a new perspective in my life in relation to other men.

16

The Chairman's Surprise

What I have to say is not for phone conversation.

The next eight months, from December 1973 through July 1974, were wildly hectic. By February, Herb had completed our audit, which showed that we had covered our overhead, which now included six staff members and us; we had paid ourselves a decent salary, and we had quadrupled our capital and had left our loans to the company intact. The official statistics published at the end of 1973 by the New York Green Coffee Association showed us as twenty-third out of the top fifty importers, and not far behind George, who was seventeenth. Many of his larger imports were at the beginning of the year, reflecting our old contracts. We were proud of our accomplishments. And I was determined to bury G.M. in the dust of our success.

In retrospect I believe my success was due to my "engaging the energy," as one of my spiritual teachers would say. My teacher taught that the life force always flowed to the most dynamic and present consciousness.

When I started on a spiritual path, I began to see the process as important as the goal. At the time, although I played a tough game and felt some remorse, I knew I was helping underdeveloped countries market their coffee, I was building security for my family, and, most importantly, I was determining my self-worth.

Based on our financials, our reputation in the market, and our import statistics, Peter agreed to increase our line of credit to three million. This relieved some of the pressure, although we would soon be probing the edges of our new limit at the pace we were growing. Apart from being involved with the financing and back office organization, I traveled over 50 percent of the time to visit our sources. My energy level was high, and so was the tension. Time flew by. The political situation in Burundi had stabilized; they had honored our coffee shipments without a single problem, and we had made a decent profit.

In the first week of August, the phone rang. Another call out of the blue! "Good Morning, Mr. Saks, one moment please. I have the Chairman of Hagemeyer on the phone for you."

"Good morning, Claude. I hope I'm not catching you at an inopportune time in the midst of a busy trading day."

"No, not at all. It's always a pleasure to talk with you. What can we do for you?"

"Well, I'm planning a visit to our operations in the U.S., Canada, and the Far East, and since I have never visited your offices I would like to come by and say hello. I plan to be in New York next Monday, and, if 2:00 P.M. is convenient, I will see you then."

Always a man to go right to the point and have his own way. I knew the Chairman never paid casual visits.

"Two P.M. will be fine. May I ask why you honor us with your presence?"

"I will discuss it with you in person. What I have to say is not for phone conversation. See you Monday." And he hung up.

The Chairman arrived punctually at 2:00 P.M. He was in his early sixties, with thinning blond hair and clear blue eyes. After some preliminary niceties, he got right to the subject.

"I would like to buy your company. What can we work out?"

Howard and I were stunned.

I recovered first. "This is the last thing we expected. I would need to consult with Howard, but for my part, I would not have any interest in selling."

Howard concurred and continued, "We are just starting, and doing extremely well. We haven't hit our stride yet. What would you be buying except cash, a position and nothing else? What makes the company work is Claude and me. Why do you want to buy?"

"I will get right to the point." As if he had not before.

"Multitrade has run into some difficulties. By buying your company, I could have the two of you in charge of the entire commodity group, and I'm confident it would do very well."

I had just got out from under George's thumb. There was no way I was going to get into bed with a powerful overseas company, even though our relationship had always been very correct and amiable.

I replied: "We are flattered by your confidence in us, but as Howard pointed out, we are just starting, and even if we considered selling, our capital is not large, nor have we been in the business long enough to obtain a high enough price, equal to multiples of a proven record." Multiples in the recession of 1974 were low.

"Forget your multiples. Let me put it simply. Hagemeyer wants to buy you at an attractive price to you. If we can't, I will close Multitrade down. I have sent our treasurer, Yella, with his team of accountants to analyze Multitrade's situation. All their contracts on a joint account with the two of you are very profitable. The other businesses into which they expanded have been a disaster. Since we receive consolidated statements, we were not aware of the extent of the losses, as your profits were covering up their other mistakes. As of this meeting, Multitrade has lost one million dollars." He went on to say that he realized that the joint account Indonesian business with Multitrade probably represented close to 50 percent of our business, and without their financing we would be strapped and unable to continue on our own. He continued, "I say this not to threaten you, but to explain that we are in a predicament, but so are you. Because, without us, your business will look quite different. By the way, the million loss is over and above the profits you have generated. They could hide it no longer. I need to make decisions and move quickly." He said the bleeding had to stop and he had instructed Penguin to make no new contracts, except jointly with us. He asked that our talks be kept confidential. He then said, "I have ordered the Reichmeister to travel from Jakarta to Amsterdam to oversee the changes and install some semblance of order so that I can understand fully the existing situation. I have the highest confidence in both of you. So, Gentlemen, you need to come up with a solution for me and for yourselves. I leave for Toronto in the morning. I will be there for two days, and then I am off for Singapore. Think about what I have said, and call me in Toronto."

With that, he closed up his briefcase, indicating that the meeting was over—which was just as well, as I had no ready answer. My temples were pounding at the idea of no Indonesian supplies or financing from the Dutch. I was appreciative of how candid he was, and we parted, not as negotiators on opposite sides of the table, but rather as partners looking for a common solution.

Howard and I stared at each other in disbelief.

"What do we do now?" I asked.

"Claude, as far as I'm concerned, there is no way I'm going to work for Hagemeyer. I've worked too hard to get to this position, and the Dutch can't come up with enough money, based on our present net worth, to make selling attractive to me."

"I agree. But I'm not prepared to go back to square one. I broke my balls in the armpits of the world, and if they close Multitrade down, we don't have the financing to pick up the lost volume. We would be half our size in one fell swoop. I can't go back to Fred, because we have done very little with him, and his terms are much costlier. It makes you appreciate how fairly Hagemeyer has treated us." I was not going back to the bush for new sources.

Howard sensed my rigidity. "Okay, I agree with you on that one. Have any brilliant ideas?"

We talked for hours without much progress except that we needed to retain Indonesian coffees and Hagemeyer's help.

Finally, I exposed my inner desire: "My dream has always been to build an international organization." As I said it, I thought how I wanted to prove to my father beyond a shadow of a doubt that I was the better man in business. "This might be our chance to give some further meaning to 'Saks International,'" I said. "Let's think big—really big. We both know that our capital is too small to get any really large cash out of Hagemeyer by selling to them. Our limitation is financing. What if we got daring and made the following proposition to the Chairman: we sell Hagemeyer 50 percent of our company, at book value, in exchange for 50 percent of Multitrade's stock. They recapitalize it at one million dollars net, and take all outstanding losses for their account. On top of that, Hagemeyer guarantees that they will make any and all necessary financing available to Multitrade and Saks International, including an unsecured cash line of credit, large enough to meet any margin calls we might have for the futures markets."

Howard ran his fingers through his thick hair and responded, "You do have balls. But he will never go for it. Half of a recapitalized Multitrade is half a million dollars, which he is giving us for selling half our company at book. Hell, that's more than twice our entire capital, plus we get half our capital back. That's too high a price, on top of which Hagemeyer provides all necessary financing. It would be great, but you're dreaming. Besides, we don't know the first thing about the intricacies of the European market. This would be plunging in with both feet without even testing the water."

He had a point, but the concept felt right in my gut. And when my intuition felt right I usually plunged. Besides, I wanted to go international and beat George.

I told Howard that Multitrade had some good people. They only needed guidance from a really solid trader or deal-maker. They could be found once Penguin was fired. I said, "As far as the money goes, put yourself into the mind-set of a big corporation. Half of Multitrade is only paper for Hagemeyer until we get paid out down the road. They are not out any hard cash. As far as financing is concerned, the Chairman considers our needs to be peanuts. Even if we doubled our volume again in the next twelve months, it's still no big deal! In fact, Hagemeyer may just put up a guarantee against any excess we need. I'm sure Chemical would agree. You know damn well with all that financing, we could substantially increase volume and profits, and would make a lot more money, even if we only owned 50 percent. And, in the final analysis, we may not have a choice. If we are to compete with the big boys, we need the big financing that Hagemeyer can provide. We have nothing to lose, so let's make the pitch and let him turn the deal down, or make a counter proposal, because right now I don't see the alternatives as very attractive."

Howard put his hands up in surrender. "Okay, you call him tomorrow. In the meantime, let me bounce this off Herb, and see if he has any objections."

Howard called Herb and explained our predicament and my far-fetched proposal. Herb, only three blocks away, said he would be right over. This was too important for a phone conversation. Herb listened patiently to the pros and cons.

"I think you guys are making a mistake by giving up your freedom. Hagemeyer is a very large company, and by the mere fact of their size, they will control you. You will be submitting corporate financial reports, budgets, projections, and every other kind of report, which will take you away from your trading, and from your liberty of movement and ideas. I have looked over your financials. You have doubled your capital again since your last balance sheet. Maybe you lose some size, but you keep it all for yourselves. You will arrive where you want to be a little later, but it will be on your own terms. Jumping into Europe may prove to be your undoing. What do you know of the market, except for some peripheral deals? I think you're taking too big a risk with too little information."

I responded: "Herb, that's what life and decisions are all about, moving forward with incomplete information. I understand where you're coming from: being a CPA, all numbers need to fit neatly in a predetermined box. But my gut tells me to go for it, if the Chairman accepts a concept somewhere near my proposal." I explained that as far as Europe was concerned, I had watched their traders and systems carefully each time I went through Amsterdam. My opinion was that they had the capability and a fair knowledge of the markets. What they needed desperately was training, a rigorous *modus operandi* in their market analysis, and simplified back office procedures which dovetailed into their trading systems. I thought we could do that, and in one fell swoop become international dealers and be in the major leagues in the U.S. I could taste this deal. My energy was electric.

Howard cut in, "Herb, it's not any different than coffee. It's just that we are dealing directly with the ultimate product--money and power. It is power because it will give us incredible clout at source, to be able to purchase coffee for open world destinations and then send it to the place which commands the best price."

Howard was getting on the bandwagon; this would work.

Herb continued to be the devil's advocate. "You guys certainly paint an optimistic picture, but where are you going to find the time? You are both working twelve-to-sixteen-hour days to make the company grow. Add to that worldwide traveling on a nonstop basis. Who is going to teach the traders and revamp their systems?"

I told him I could cut back on my traveling, as most sources were now established. I would have more time, which would free either Howard or me to spend an intensive period in Amsterdam, putting them on track. "I think it can work," I said. "Change hats, Herb, and put on your lawyer's *chapeau*. Do you see any legal problems?"

"I would have to research it, but off the cuff, if you are a 50-percent owner or less, I don't see a problem, as long as you do not have control of overall decisions."

Early the next morning, I telephoned the chairman in his Toronto hotel, and in great detail laid out our proposal, listing all the advantages for Hagemeyer. He listened without interruption until I had completed my presentation.

"I knew you boys would come up with an ingenious solution. That's why I want to be in business with you. There is one major technical difficulty which I cannot change. Because of Dutch laws regarding corporate integrity, Hagemeyer needs to retain 100 percent of Multitrade's stock, offsetting losses and consolidating the financial statements. However, I think that we could work around that by simply paying you 50 percent of the profits every year. We would also pay half a million dollars at the termination of our relationship, representing half of Multitrade's restated capital. I realize this will raise other questions, so you will need to think it over. I must tell you I am in agreement and back your proposal totally, except for that one hitch. As you know, I'm on my way to the Far East, so I will report our conversation back to the board in Amsterdam."

"Sounds as if you are confident the board will go along with it."

"Yes, there is no doubt of that in my mind. Prior to my trip, I sounded them out. So if this is my recommendation, which it will be, they will approve it. Do you think you will be ready to discuss details in a fortnight's time? If so, we can have our treasurer, Yella, in New York for the length of time it takes to work out an agreement."

My head was spinning. I told him Howard and I would discuss it and I had to go to Burundi. We would be ready to talk during the second half of September.

"All right, that sounds feasible to me," the chairman said. "I would like to have all this concluded by the end of the year and start together as partners January 1, 1975." It looked like we had a deal.

Howard was wide-eyed. "Wow! Now my concern is that if Hagemeyer controls all the stock, all we are to them are glorified consultants. As soon as we have straightened out the mess and built up the company, they could say `Thank you' and bid us `Goodbye'!"

"That crossed my mind, but it can be solved by building in some onerous penalties if such a trick were pulled. All the deals I have set up around the world have always been on just a handshake. As J. Pierpont Morgan once said, `I wouldn't lend a penny on all the bonds of Christendom to a man I didn't trust.' Either we trust the chairman, and Hagemeyer as an organization, or we should not get into bed with them."

The next day we met in Herb's office, and, as usual, he brought to the fore the issues that had only vaguely touched our minds. What rights would Hagemeyer have to get out or get rid of us? What should their cost be for that right? The list went on for three pages.

I decided that we should structure the best of all worlds for ourselves, without being overly greedy. My feeling was that they would go along with most propositions as long as no cash came out of their pockets except for payment to buy our stock.

We were convinced that we would conquer the world of coffee, and were prepared to be compensated down the road. Restructuring Multitrade at one million dollars, with Hagemeyer owning all the stock, was only a book entry, not an actual cash layout; then half a million at the end of our relationship, if successful, would be cheap.

The only catch was that Hagemeyer would have to cover all outstanding losses. But in any event, whether we were involved or not, they would still have to pick up that bill. I left for Burundi with plenty to think about during the long flight.

17

Arrangement on the Fairway

This little piggy was buttering both sides of his bread.

I was met at the Bujumbura airport by Kabwa. He was now Head of Sales at the BPO under the watchful eye of Golf, the D.G. He brought me up to date as he drove from the airport along the dry open plain to the new four-story hotel built by an Italian concern and completed barely one month prior. Everything seemed sleepy and quiet, and I could not imagine that recently this backwater of the world had experienced a genocidal confrontation which resulted in 100,000 deaths.

Kabwa told me that Golf had assigned him to help me in any way he could: I had become a well-known personage from having helped the country out of its financial dilemma. When I checked into the Italian hotel, Kabwa quietly told me to make sure my room was not above the second floor. There was no assurance of water pressure for either showers or toilets on the third and fourth floors. Welcome back to Africa.

At my request, Kabwa drove me to the National Bank where I paid my respects to the Chairman. The Chairman told me he had organized a dinner in my honor that evening, which would include the original members of the coffee committee who had approved our deal. The Belgian Common Market Economic Advisor would be joining us as well.

Kabwa and I had a pleasant lunch, and I got further confirmation of my support. It became apparent that Golf's idea was to market, piecemeal, 500 to 1,000 bags at a time, but his efforts had not gotten very far. Golf still had a broker's mentality, and it appeared he was trying to make money on the side by doing many of the contracts through his own small brokerage firm in Brussels.

Kabwa and I went to the office after visiting the Ministry of Agriculture, and Golf greeted me, all smiles, and began to show me the office. Explaining the communication difficulties—even on telex—particularly to the U.S., he suggested it might be easier to have all communications go through Brussels. His office there could relay any information necessary. My suspicions were confirmed. He was trying to set me up to use his brokerage. If he wanted to make money, that was okay with me, but it would have to be on my terms. I did not answer him or comment, but let the conversation move to quantity movements, which is what we needed for the U.S.—a minimum of 1,000 bags at a time, but preferably 5,000 bags—especially now that Burundi's main market was North America. He in turn did not comment—a tough poker player!

It was 5:00 in the afternoon and all the employees including Kabwa had left. He turned to me. "I guess it's time to close up shop. I'm going to go for a round of exercise, then I'll pick you up at your hotel at 7:45 for dinner."

"That will be fine. What do you do for exercise here? I need some myself, and I don't trust the hotel pool. I once came down with a skin fungus in Zaire."

"I go down to the golf course. It's only nine holes," he told me. "I walk around it a couple of times."

"Mind if I join you?"

His countenance softened. "Not at all. It will be a pleasure to walk and talk."

As we walked around the golf course under the deep blue African sky, he seemed to relax.

I congratulated him on the excellent performance for our large contract.

"Thank you. Yes, that was some job to get it all out on time. I wasn't concerned on the Burundi end, because we are well organized, but once the coffees cross Lake Tanganyika by barge to the Tanzanian side, we are at the mercy of their train schedules down to Dar Es Salaam. Their railroad is narrow gauge, and their trains are in very poor condition, with virtually no supplies left in the world for replacement parts. I went personally down to Dar to visit Belbase and make sure they could handle it. I enlisted their support to convince the rail authorities to put all available railroad cars at our disposal."

He was loosening up and talking freely. I sensed that he resented all the old European shippers who had made a lot of money in Burundi, and that he—a European—had not participated. It was now his turn, and he was going to show them through his control of the BPO.

I began to state our position on shipments. Offers of 250 or 500 bags were too cumbersome for us to market. Since most of Burundi's coffees were being handled by the BPO, we wanted to see offers of between 2,000 and 5,000 bags at a minimum.

"I think we could do that from time to time, but not a regular basis," he told me. He was concerned, he said, about the potential interruption of overnight telexes or cables relating to negotiations in progress. Again he suggested that we transmit all our bids through his office in Brussels. "With the time difference, it will dovetail perfectly. They can always reach me by telex and most times even by phone. I think this would solve all our problems, and I think a small brokerage fee would not be inappropriate for the work they perform."

I felt like saying "Cut the shit. How much do you want? A small brokerage is not going to make you rich." Instead, I replied, "That may be a possibility. How much would they want to perform the service?"

"Normal brokerage is one-quarter cent a pound, so say half of that."

"May I suggest a better setup for all of us? We would be willing to pay the brokerage to your office in return for a more personalized and in-depth service." I could tell he was warming to the way this conversation was going.

"What do you have in mind?"

"As I said before, we would like to see offers of 2,000 and 5,000 bags. We would telex the BPO directly with our bid, and you would reply directly to us. However, during the New York morning trading, which is our most active time, Brussels would still be open. We could call your Brussels office by phone and explain our need for an adjustment, either greater quantity or a lower price, depending on the market. We would not want to lose the business by taking the time to make a counteroffer. Your office could then indicate to us at what levels we could safely counter and know we would be accepted. So whenever we bid, we would word the telex 'we bid for prompt reply.' The 'prompt' would tell you that the bid included a quarter-cent brokerage for your office in Brussels." We quickly worked out a code for various situations, with a brokerage fee in certain instances as high as one cent.

This little piggy was buttering both sides of his bread. We had gone three times around the golf course, and the sun had dropped behind the Zaire mountains, leaving a chill in the air. We had reached, by perambulated and convoluted conversation, a complete understanding. And so it was that the D.G. of the BPO became known as Golf.

Before returning to the hotel to shower and change, we dropped by the office and I typed, in my slow hunt-and-peck way, a telex offer of 5,000 bags of the better grades, which Golf had just made, and told Howard that everything was under control.

The dinner that night was a complete success, and with the encouragement given me by members of the sales committee, I had no fears that Golf would perform up to expectations. The next morning I went to the BPO and saw that Howard had accepted the offer. I took Kabwa aside, thanked him for all his help, and gave him a token gift, which, in the local currency, filled the envelope. I wanted to make sure he would root for us.

The need to make these payments left an unclean feeling in my spirit. But disparities of personal income between the buyers and the government employees was too great and too apparent. I knew that this was the only successful way to do business in Africa.

I flew out on Sabena and decided, since I had a one-day layover in Brussels, to check out Golf's brokerage operation. The office turned out to be a one-room cubical in the back streets with a secretary—the entire staff. By the way she referred to Golf, using his first name and other very personal references, I was convinced she was his mistress. She was already up to date and privy to the conversations I had with Golf and explained she would always be available to facilitate any transaction. She gave me her home number, should there be a need for a late-night communication. I thanked her for being so helpful and assured her we would be in close communication as business developed.

Over the next couple of years, Burundi became a key supplier to our ever-growing presence in the market.

18

International Cleanup

How dare you sell our own company back to us!

Two days after my return, we got a call from Hagemeyer's Treasurer informing us that he would arrive Friday for negotiations. Howard asked a question. "One point we would like to clarify in advance: to whom would we be reporting, assuming we can get together on this proposition?"

"Technically and organizationally, you would report to Aristocrat. However, as you will be representing a high portion of our volume and be a very different undertaking from most of our other businesses, I will be an overseer of your progress. In simple terms, Aristocrat for the monthly reportings and me or the Chairman for any special or major developments. Whomever you recommend hiring to run Multitrade we will accept, and he will report to Aristocrat."

Howard and I both felt confident. At 8:30 on Friday morning Yella arrived, ready to sit down to serious work. He was a study in monochrome—gray hair, gray pin-striped suit, dark striped tie, and steel-rimmed glasses, with intelligent, small gray eyes.

The commodity business is a complicated, unpredictable affair; it is very difficult anticipating all the possibilities. However, if we could skew our negotiations in such a way that the financial data appeared to fit in neat cubbyholes, then Yella would eventually come around to our viewpoint. We started on Friday at 9:00 A.M. and worked through Sunday evening, at which time we had a rough outline for Herb and the Dutch lawyers to review.

After the lawyers became involved, it took nearly another month to hash out the details. Finally, on January 1, 1975, the deal was signed by all the parties concerned. In one fell swoop we were, *de facto*, an international organization, with representation in Amsterdam, Jakarta, and Trieste.

The question now was how to straighten out Multitrade's mess. Initially, the job would have to be done hands-on, until we could find the right people to run the company. We would each spend three months in Amsterdam. During this time, I would greatly curtail my traveling. Since Howard's children were preschoolers, we decided he would be in Amsterdam March through May, and I would take June through August. My family would join me as soon as school was over.

The Reichmeister had been moved to Amsterdam, and was our only reliable person in Multitrade. Penguin had been fired. Howard left for Amsterdam and settled into the Marriott Hotel.

Beyond saying hello, we did not know the traders and back office staff. This was to be one of Howard's shining moments. He dug into every nook and cranny, like a terrier on a hot scent. The surprises that popped out of the various holes were amazing. Positions in Russian pigskins, sausage casings, and "warehouse" coffees: all unsold. Howard had them all liquidated one at a time, with substantial losses to Hagemeyer. He and I were in continual daily contact, spending a minimum of an hour a day on the phone. Howard had Multitrade place ads in the *London Financial Times*, the *International Herald Tribune* and *The Figaro*, for a Senior Manager of Operations in a commodity firm and, separately, for a Head Coffee Trader. He located a Dutchman who had spent more than fifteen years in East Africa with a competing Dutch coffee company. He knew the business, and all we had to do was indoctrinate him into trading procedures. By the end of April, he was in place and quickly got down to the nitty-gritty. He turned out to be a great Operations Manager and eventually became General Manager. Our main concern was to find a head trader who would be responsive to our advice and whom we could trust. The problem was left open for me to deal with, as our newspaper advertising for the position came to naught.

The last problem left was staffing. Multitrade, with its in-house spice subsidiary, Apparak, had forty-three people—way too many. The organization's volume was about half of SINT's and we had only eight employees. (I admit that with eight we were strained, however, a situation we corrected shortly after Howard's return.) We had lengthy discussions as to how to reduce the Dutch staff. In Holland you could not fire an employee without just cause, and at great expense—one month's severance pay for each year worked. After further consideration, we decided one way to lower staff was by selling off the subsidiary Apparak, even though the Company was marginally profitable on its own. Apparak dealt in spices, rice wine, and rattan. The business was made up of many small contracts, one to five tons, which had high margin but created reams of paper work and back office follow-up. We decided this was not our business, and Apparak had to go.

Howard and the Reichmeister started to put out feelers, through financial brokers, to sell the company. They were about to place ads in major papers. Word got around Hagemeyer and particularly to Aristocrat, who called Howard. "Look here, Howard, I don't agree to Multitrade's selling of Apparak. Even though it's a small company, it is quite profitable in its own way. It's a decent little profit center."

"I quite agree with you but it's just not our line of business. We want to concentrate and expand the profitability of coffee. Claude and I have discussed Apparak and have decided to spin the Company off."

"Howard, I am group director of Hagemeyer and Multitrade falls within my purview. I do not wish you to sell Apparak. If you do not want it in Multitrade you can transfer it over to one of my other group companies."

Howard set the parameters. "Our deal with Hagemeyer was that they would take loss positions for their account, and reconstitute Multitrade at a million dollars, which included Apparak. So if I transfer it to one of your other companies, I'm losing capital. If you won't let me sell to outsiders, I'm more than happy to sell it to one of your group's companies. Besides, the chairman has given us full authorization to do what is necessary until this mess is cleaned up."

The Chairman, Vice Chairman, and Yella were all out of the country on a major negotiation, so Aristocrat had no way of corroborating Howard's position, nor did he deem it necessary to trace them down for authorization of his actions.

He said to Howard, "Let me think about it overnight. In the meantime, why don't you put a presentation together so I can review it in the morning."

In the most glowing terms, Howard and the Reichmeister made a presentation on Apparak to Aristocrat the following morning. The presentation included seventeen employees, some of whom had been moved over from the coffee back office to reduce staff. Before he had a chance to cool down, Howard had the in-house lawyer draft up a sale agreement between Multitrade and one of the group companies.

A week later, the higher brass returned to the office, and that weekend Howard was invited to the Vice-Chairman's house for dinner. It was a large stone house with various collections of artifacts from around the world. Delightful smells emanated from the kitchen, and the atmosphere was cordial, warmed by several rounds of scotch. The Chairman and Yella were there with their wives. The group proceeded to dinner, a magnificent *risstafel*, a Dutch and Indonesia rice dish, with many bottles of white wine, then many bottles of red wine, all consumed over stories of the good old days in Indonesia. After dinner, the party moved to the parlor for coffee. A few moments elapsed, and the Vice Chairman suggested the gentlemen move to the library for cigars and brandy.

Between the food, all the drinks and now the second round of cognac, Howard was feeling quite warm and content, the cigar smoke swirling around his head. The Chairman, suddenly purple in the face, turned to Howard screaming: "You fucked me! You fucked me! How dare you sell our own company back to us! You are a fucking outrage."

Howard was stunned but recovered quickly. "Mr. Chairman, you cut a deal with us because you believed we were the best deal makers you had seen in a long time. Well, I cut the best deal possible for Multitrade, and I can't help it if it's one of your group directors who bought it."

The Vice Chairman, a large burly dark-haired man, was sipping his cognac with one hand, while in the other, he held a large lit Davidoff cigar. Suddenly, he exploded the cognac out of his mouth in a roar of laughter. "Howard, you are absolutely right, and if our directors are not smart enough to negotiate with you, we should change directors."

The Chairman, feeling no pain from all the booze, saw the humor in the whole affair and also broke out laughing. Yella too joined the fracas. The ladies, curious, came into the library, and so the whole story was recounted with much ribaldry. Two months later, Aristocrat was no longer with Hagemeyer.

The last problem Howard dealt with was the tea department. Multitrade's Tea Department, although relatively small on a global scale, was quite profitable. The department specialized in Indonesians, low-grade Turkish, low-grade Russians, and some Ceylon teas. Multitrade had their own blending warehouse and were masters at lowering the cost of blends by adding the Turkish and Russian teas. The old man running the department quit after seeing the brash young American who was calling the shots. His leaving was a godsend, because his young assistant was more capable and did not keep old speciality teas forever in the warehouse. Teas had no futures market, and trading was conducted as if it were 1870. Howard had him clean out the old positions and taught him coffee trading techniques. Multitrade's tea business flourished. Howard had done an incredible job; we had a clean-running international organization.

A week later, Howard packed his bags and came home. When he returned, we spent three days together, briefing each other on the latest developments, and then I was off, stopping in Paris to talk to Bernard.

Arriving at Amsterdam, I checked into the Marriott and walked to the office. What a change! The staff was reduced, and they were happy and eager to move forward with our guidance.

I got a call from Bernard, who said he had been thinking about our conversation and my plans with Howard. "Your projects sound exciting and very promising. You expressed the need to find a Head

Trader for your European operations, and depending on your requirements, I might be interested in the job."

Bernard's joining us had never entered my mind. He seemed happy running his own show in Paris. I expressed great interest in his joining us as head European trader. Two days later, he flew to Amsterdam and we negotiated an agreement. The only hitch was that he was not willing to move to Amsterdam full time. He would commute the first six months, and then we agreed to open a representative office in Paris, from which he could run Europe.

I reported all the details to Howard. We were both pleased with the outcome.

"Listen, Claude," Howard said. "I think we should hire a trader here in New York. There is just too much work. I'm here until 8:30 every night." After much discussion, we agreed on my old cupping mentor Abba, who was currently working for a competitor. Ten days later Abba joined SINT.

Meanwhile, Bernard found an office on a back street in Paris, which had a connecting courtyard to the *Champs Elysees*, so Multitrade would have an address of 32A *Champs Elysees*, Paris—very swanky.

While all this was going on, I had the Reichmeister summon Peacock, the head of Multitrade in Trieste, for a showdown in Amsterdam. Peacock showed up dressed in his best Italian attire and immediately told me the great job he was doing. He had just sold another 1,000 bags of Brazils out of our position, bringing it down to 16,000 bags. I informed him that the amount was totally inadequate, and I wanted the full 16,000 bags sold in the next two weeks. Also, I was going to shut down the Trieste office. He was stunned, and replied that we could not shut the office down because that would be equivalent to firing him, which, under Italian law, would force us to pay penalties and to give him a year's compensation. Besides, there was no market for the Brazils, and he was doing a great job moving them out.

I told him to cut the crap. "You've been living off Multitrade long enough. I've checked your record. In the two years Multitrade has been associated with you, there is not a single month with a profit.

The funds have flowed only one way—in your direction. As far as closing the office, if you don't cooperate with me, I will simply let Multitrade in Trieste go bankrupt, as the organization is an independent company. I'm sure bankruptcy does not provide for your year's salary and other penalties. Furthermore, since you are a 15-percent owner of the stock, you will lose that money as well. I suggest we come to an understanding."

He was not aware that I was only a consultant and would have to get Hagemeyer's approval.

"Mr. Saks, I consider you a very uncouth and ungentlemanly person. This is not over. You will have to deal with me and the Italian authorities."

"I'll show you 'couth.' Get the fuck out of my office."

The Reichmeister, who was silently following all this, blanched, took Peacock by the elbow, and led him out. A few moments later, the Reichmeister, having put Peacock in a taxi, reappeared. "You can't let Trieste go bankrupt. Hagemeyer will never go along with it."

"Relax. I apologize for the scene, but besides being a peacock, he's a leech. He keeps lining his pockets. Multitrade pays him a salary and replenishes the capital monthly, so his 15 percent is never exposed. I intend to talk to Yella and get him to go along with my bluff. Peacock will be back, and we'll come to an agreement once he is convinced my scheme will cost him his own money."

"Are you calm now?" the Reichmeister asked. "I want to talk to you on another subject."

"Yes, I'm calm. That was just playacting. What's on your mind?"

"Well, it seems to me that you and Howard have cleaned up the company, so I don't see any necessity for me to stay here. I would like to go back to Jakarta. That's where I operate best and am most happy in business."

I agreed, telling him I would miss his support and counsel.

"Well, if everything is cleared up, I'd like to go next week."

The Reichmeister was elated to be returning to his beloved Indonesia. In the meantime, I spoke to Yella, asked for his support, and explained to him my dilemma with Peacock. Later that afternoon, Peacock called Yella, crying about the terrible person I was, but got no satisfaction when Yella told him he would go along with my suggestion to let the Trieste operation go bankrupt. When Peacock walked into my office the next morning, the whole scenario had changed.

After some discussion, I offered full reimbursement of his 15 percent, plus two months' salary. This meant no personal loss to him which I felt was more than fair.

"You are a difficult man. I have worked so hard for—"

"Peacock, stop the melodrama. Do we have a deal or not?"

"Yes. We have a deal."

"Fine. I will have Hagemeyer's house lawyer draft up a letter of understanding, which then can be formalized with your attorneys."

And that was the end of Multitrade's Trieste office. Within two months, everything was cleaned up, and we made a nice profit on the Brazils, the reason for which will shortly become apparent.

That morning, immediately after Peacock left, Fred, with whom I had kept in close touch while in Europe, called me. He said that Hippo had just been deposed, and replaced by N'Daka, chief of Zaire's Secret Police and a close associate of President Mobutu. That was definitely a major change. Fred was tied up with Central American problems. Nicaragua was heating up, and he was concerned about his office there. He could not travel to Zaire. If I was going, could I give him a report of the situation? I explained I was just at the end of cleaning up, and could break away in a week's time. I would keep him posted. I had not traveled to Africa in a while, and since all the pieces of Multitrade were in place, it was high time I went again into the dark continent.

I was under tremendous stress and working insane hours, as was Howard, continually making fast and dramatic decisions on markets, people, and organizations. But I was having a ball—I was like an addict who needed continual and greater fixes, deals, to keep the adrenaline flowing at a high pitch. I always liked pushing the envelope, placing myself on the forefront of new ideas and concepts in business.

During this period of my life I did not know or accept failure— that was about to change.

19

Black Frost and Black Fear

For the moment, Americans are personae non grata.

I landed in Kinshasa and cleared the usual airport mess. Shortly after checking into the Intercontinental, I dropped in on André to get the latest input. He gave me the grim news that the new man, N'Daka, who was connected at the highest levels, favored either Zaire firms or very large European firms. He was taking full control of all coffee production and exports through the ONC. All the plantations were nationalized, André concluded: "The good old days of lucrative contracts with Hippo are over. I can't help you with this one. I have no entrées."

"I get the picture, old friend. Sorry you're going through rough times. I haven't been able to get an appointment with the D.G., but his secretary set me up with his assistant. Looks like he's going through a serious screening process."

"He is. But I don't think he trusts his assistant, who is a political appointee from another tribe, definitely not his confidante. Don't forget, he was head of the secret police, so he has files on everybody. The staff is frightened of him."

I immediately got an audience with the new assistant D.G. Mawabe was extremely tall and thin, with long arms and legs which hung about at odd angles when he sat down.

We had a pleasant conversation for an hour and finally started talks on a new, larger contract. We quickly got down to terms for

1,500 tons a month for six months—the largest contract Zaire would ever have done with the U.S.A. The Italians and Belgians were able to do such quantities, but no one else. But it was coming too easily. If the real decision rested with the D.G., a whole new negotiation would have to start. Mawabe said he would take the contract to the D.G. in the morning and have an answer for me in the afternoon. I pushed for an appointment with the D.G., but to no avail. Five days later, I still had no reply on the contract and no appointment with the D.G.

I was going crazy. There was nothing to do in Kinshasa except check up on old contracts, quality, samples, Amiza interior news, and all the small peripheral details. Finally, after I convinced Mawabe that I had a flight out on Monday, he set up a meeting with the D.G. at his home on Sunday afternoon. The Sunday paper headlines read "Coup attempted but failed by the Americans on our President Mobutu Seseko"; the meeting did not look promising. The government had ousted the American Ambassador, who they claimed had been in Chile when a coup there had installed General Pinochet. Americans were not wanted, and I wanted out. Picking me up at the hotel, Mawabe was extremely casual. He told me to relax—everything was just fine. This was not the sense I was getting in my gut.

The D.G.'s house was very large, completely walled in, and had spikes on the top of the entrance gate and broken glass imbedded on top of the surrounding walls. Marble tiled floors, heavy modern Chinese carpets, and an oversized yellow-gold velour sofa with matching armchairs on either side greeted me. High ceilings with slow-moving fans and slotted paneled windows allowed adjustment for the airflow. I sank down in one of the armchairs. The servant who had brought us to the living room retired to get his master. Mawabe was draped over the other armchair with both legs straight out, head resting on the back and arms dangling over the side.

N'Daka, the D.G., walked into the room—his presence felt throughout. A large, bulky, solidly built man, in his mid-forties, with very dark skin and brown watery eyes with yellow background rather than white. I struggled to get out of the low oversized armchair to greet him. He was a master. He had me on his turf, had made me wait five days, and was about to demonstrate that no decisions were made without him. After a few preliminary introductory sentences, he proceeded to ask me why he should give me such a large contract. Mawabe did not get up to greet him, remained quiet as a clam, drooped in his chair with a beatific smile on his face. I found it quite disconcerting. He seemed like a child and gave me no support.

I described to N'Daka the history of SINT and its growth, our major involvement in helping to market Zairian coffees, bypassing the old colonial system, and now our association with Multitrade through the ownership of Hagemeyer. In the strangely quiet and somber atmosphere, I tried to give as enthusiastic a pitch about our abilities and advantages as I could. I finished twenty minutes later. N'Daka never reacted throughout my discourse. He just sat on a hard chair, both feet on the ground, leaning forward, one elbow on his knee, with a white handkerchief in his hand slowly wiping his nose. Silence prevailed. These were the days before I had become involved with Eastern tantric practices and meditation, so I was quite disconcerted by the silence and his dark presence. I did not have the confidence to sit quietly and accept the outcome. I felt like a total amateur in front of this imposing African.

After a few more of my babbles, he finally cut in. "Mr. Saks, I see you have done quite some business with Zaire through my predecessor, which I'm sure was very lucrative. However, it is my intent to support the countries and large companies who have been associated with Zaire for several decades through our ups and downs. Belgium and Italy have been our largest customers and have consistently paid the best prices, and I therefore must favor them. The United States is a secondary market for us. I will review your contract and lower the quantity to an appropriate amount. There is no purpose for you to stay here. I will have Mawabe contact you when we have concluded all our commitments. You must excuse me now but I have some family matters to attend to." And with that, he got up and left. I felt totally intimidated and insecure; my sense of self-worth was smashed. I was responsible for reliable and lucrative supplies for the business and I had failed.

N'Daka clearly had a "special arrangement" that benefited him personally, and I would have to live with it. I could not handle failure and took this one very personally. I tried to reach Howard with no success.

The next morning I boarded Lufthansa. What a relief to be out of Zaire. In Frankfurt I had a two-and-a-half hour layover on my way to Amsterdam, so I called Howard and brought him up to date.

He listened patiently to my report but had another matter on his mind. "They've had a frost in Brazil, looks like a black frost—potentially a killer black frost—perhaps the worst frost in the history of the coffee business."

A black frost occurs when a large, freezing air mass travels over the Andes and descends into Brazil's coffee-growing areas. What makes a black frost special is that it usually occurs during a full moon, and the following day there is no cloud cover. The leaves and trunks which have been frozen overnight are then suddenly baked in the full sun. The leaves turn black within a few days and the branches and trunks wither within a couple of weeks. A black frost is always damaging, but the major question is whether the trunk and roots survive.

"Jesus, when did it happen? Why didn't you call or telex?"

"Impossible to get through to the hotel, so I telexed Socopao. I didn't want to alert André or the competition, so you could get a leg up purchasing if possible. It happened Friday night, so we could not act, and the situation really was not scary until Sunday morning, when the leaves started turning black." Howard's telex had never reached me.

Howard explained that Abba had a plantation owner friend who had chartered a Piper Cub to fly over a wide area of the region. He reported that all the leaves were turning black. "It will take a few weeks to see if the trees are lost," Howard said. "It's an absolute disaster for the farmers and the economy."

"What are we doing? Have you covered all our shorts and are we now long?"

"I've covered up the position and started to go slightly long."

"What do you mean? Let's buy the shit out of the market."

"Claude, slow down. I got my hands full. I called Multitrade and instructed them to do the same. Bernard is in total agreement. You have to understand we will not know for a couple of weeks if production is totally destroyed, which would mean five to seven years to get back up to speed. On the other hand, if just next year's crop is wiped out, there may not be much of an upswing. Remember, the official count shows Brazil with over sixty million bags stockpiled, enough to supply the entire world's consumption for a year, and that's without counting the huge stocks in Columbia, as well as stocks in all the other producing nations." The ICO agreement restricted shipment, but not production, so all the producing countries were apparently bulging with stocks.

Howard told me the market had moved up so far only five to eight percent.

I was certain the market was going to take off. "Everyone is short supplies from the importers to the supermarket and even the consumer," I told Howard. "I don't believe all the stock statistics. All these countries are lying, trying to get an extra quota from the ICO. I don't think half the quantities exist. If we really have a black frost, this market is going up. I also think you have to figure that we're going to have some defaults elsewhere, particularly in Indonesia. Tell the Reichmeister to buy with both hands."

Howard replied, "You are not going to believe this, but the Reichmeister went riding, and his horse had not been exercised while he was away, so it was skittish and threw him. He cracked his skull and is in the hospital making no sense. The doctors think he will come out of it and be all right. But Anette, his wife, is in the office and has issued orders like a storm trooper to buy all coffees in sight. I've been up all night on the phone with Jakarta."

"Christ, I can't believe this. Everything is turning against us at the same time."

"Relax. We're in great shape. We have a great team. Bernard in Europe will take hold of things, and Abba here will be a great backup. On top of that, we have a contract with Hagemeyer guaranteeing us all the financing we need. What more would you want in a bull market?"

He was right. What was really upsetting me was the Zaire fiasco and losing our premier position there at a crucial time. I calmed down and told him, "As soon as I check on Multitrade, I'll turn around and go back to Zaire. I'll sit on top of N'Daka until he signs a contract."

"That's up to you, if you think it's worth it. Just don't waste time on a lost cause. We have other fish to fry. Abba is fairly friendly with the Uganda coffee board here in New York. Uganda's coffees are much better than Zaire's."

The hour's flight to Amsterdam felt like an eternity. I was making notes and lists like crazy, and I wanted to talk to all my connections in the world. In that two-hour conversation with Howard, I had swiftly turned from a bear to a raging bull. I checked into the Marriott at 9:00 P.M., got Howard on the phone. We talked intermittently until 1:00 A.M. We planned strategy. He bought coffee. Abba bought coffee. We talked. Abba was getting reports from Brazil and on and on. . . . By the time I had finished on Tuesday afternoon at Multitrade, we were in pretty good shape. I had apprised Hagemeyer of developments, and the Chairman assured me of financing availability for any quantity.

"We" included all of Hagemeyer's coffee companies, Saks International in New York, Multitrade in Amsterdam, Multitrade in Paris, and Multicontinental in Jakarta. All our positions were covered, and we were comfortably long, with a doubling up of longs in coffees where we thought there might be a default. By Wednesday, we were ready to make offers to roasters again. I called my sources and obtained large quantities of Cameroons as well as Tanzanians. We were ready to do battle. The market kept moving up slowly but steadily.

The week before, my family had arrived in Amsterdam. On the weekend, I took off with them to a Dutch beach on the North Sea. Although it was early August and the days were partially sunny, the sea was gray and cold, which did not seem to inhibit the children in the least. For Bette and me, after having spent summers on Long

Island and in Maine, the North Sea was a big letdown. The sand was grayish with a very long tide. We bought the children the usual pails and shovels, and they proceeded to build a huge fort against the tide. They wanted to show the Dutch kids that they could build a bigger fort that would last longer in the rising sea. But the Dutch kids had more experience, and their forts lasted twice as long. While our children were playing in the sand, Bette and I, hand in hand, went for long walks. I explained my trips, the adventures, the excitement of a major bull market, and our luck at being properly positioned; business, business, business. She told me about touring Holland with the children while I was away: canal trips, visits to the Anne Frank house, the Van Gogh Museum, and the Rijksmuseum; of Gouda, flower markets, dikes and windmills. She told me of the kids' curiosity and wonder. I was envious and sad that I had not been there to share in their joys.

The only thorn left was Zaire. I had no leverage to pressure N'Daka, but I was stubborn and could not accept defeat. I was about to learn my lesson the hard way. I booked flights and landed in Kinshasa ten days after leaving. The plane was the last flight in—10:00 P.M.

I had not been able to contact Amiza to assure a representative would be there to facilitate passport and currency control. The airport was empty except for our flight. The lines were long and slow as usual, but they kept moving, which indicated the officials were tired and not hassling people too much. I went through currency control without a problem, but ran into a blockbuster at Passport control.

"Mr. Saks, I'm sorry, but I can't let you in the country. Your visa is not in order."

"What do you mean, *Citoyen*? Check the stamp. It was issued by your Embassy in Washington for multiple entries and is valid for three months."

"I regret to inform you it is no longer valid. There are people behind you, so step aside and I will deal with you later in my office."

What was the problem? I was sure I had a multiple entry visa. I watched as the big hall cleared of all the other passengers, and the currency officials closed their stations one by one. One by one the customs people closed their stations. The lights in the main waiting hall were shut off. Two soldiers, submachine guns dangling from their shoulders, lazily patrolled the building. The facilities were being shut down. The official I was waiting for closed his station and told me to follow him. As I followed him down the dimly lit corridor, I saw, from behind, a figure in dark blue pants and shirt. Could it be an Amiza rep? I called out and sure enough, as he turned around, I saw the red Amiza emblem on his shirt pocket. As I got closer, I recognized him. What a relief; at least someone would know I was in the country, in case I got thrown in jail. "Am I glad to see you!" I said, uneasily but smiling. "Were you sent to pick me up at the plane?"

"No, we never got a message about your arrival. I'm only here to drop off a package for a flight out tomorrow."

"Well, in any event, please stay with me, as I may have some difficulty and need a ride into town. I'm sure all the taxis have left."

"Yes, they have. I'll bring you in with pleasure."

At that point, the customs official motioned me to move along and join him in his office. The building was pitch black outside, and the soldiers' boots echoed off the concrete floors in the hollow building. I stood in front of the official's desk as he examined my passport and visa. He repeated himself. "Your visa is not in order, and I can't let you into the country."

"*Citoyen*, I specifically requested a multiple entry visa because I do a lot of business here. There [I pointed with my finger] it states right in the embassy mark, 'multiple entry, good for three months.' I was here only a week ago, and that was the first time this visa was issued."

"I see all that; I can read as well as you can. However, the entry stamp from your last visit is stamped 'Final Entry,' which means no more entries after that."

"I never heard of such a thing. How can it be final if it's my first entry?"

"As you probably know, the American ambassador has been asked to leave Zaire. For the moment, Americans are *personae non grata*.

All Americans have had their visas canceled on exit from Zaire. When you left your visa was canceled and stamped 'final visit.'"

It was time to get help. I excused myself and stepped out of his office to explain the situation to the Amiza rep.

"Why don't you go in there and review the situation with him in his local dialect and see if he'll take twenty zaires and simply stamp my passport. No one will ever know the difference on the way out."

"I will try, but you need to understand that our dialect is different. We are from different tribes. I can't promise you a result."

He stepped into the office. A dialogue began, then a banter ensued, lasting about twenty minutes, during which I paced the floor, incredulous. Did I do the wrong thing, and was I going to end up as the scapegoat in some tribal game of one-upmanship? The Amiza rep stepped back out.

"He says there is no way he can stamp your passport because he has to put his initials on the stamp and could get into trouble. He would be prepared to take forty zaires, and let you in the country by keeping your passport, provided you come back within forty-eight hours with a letter from a minister and a proper pass. Otherwise, he would have to issue an alert to look for you."

This was a mess, and this customs official was starting to push his weight around. Time for me to bluff.

"You tell him that I'm good friends with N'Daka, the previous head of the Secret Police. I'm here specifically to do business with him. I'm not going to put up with this nonsense. I will not leave my passport with him. I never leave my passport. Tell him I will pay the forty zaires, but he has to give me my passport and let me into the country. That way, there is no stamp, and no one can trace it to him. Therefore, there is no need for him to issue an alert, because as far as he is concerned, I don't exist. He has no passport that needs papers or stamps. That's the deal. Tell him I'll work the situation out with N'Daka."

I was half scared to death to flaunt N'Daka's name, because I knew he would not even give me the time of day, let alone help me out with a customs problem. I would just have to come up with a solution once I was in the country. I was not going to stay in the airport or a jail overnight. I was determined, although scared, to get in with my passport and get on with business.

The Amiza rep went back into the office and another twenty-minute discussion ensued.

He came back out. "You've got a deal. He wants to be paid in zaires."

"Are you kidding? The regulations say no one can come in or out of the country with zaires. I don't have a thing. Can I borrow it from you, since all the exchange offices are closed? It's past midnight. I assure you I will take good care of you."

"Thank you, but that is not necessary. I'm afraid I don't have forty zaires. All I can scrape up is twenty zaires."

"Well, will he take dollars? I'll even give them to him at better than the official rate. I'll give him twenty dollars, which he can change on the black market to his advantage."

"They're not used to dealing in dollars, but let me get his reaction."

I gave him the twenty dollars and he disappeared once again.

Five minutes later, he reappeared with my passport, and we hightailed it out of the airport. The beat-up red and blue Amiza van looked like an angel's chariot in that desolate airport.

"When we get to the Intercontinental, wait a few moments so I can change some dollars. I want to give you a present. You've been terrific."

"Well, thank you. But that's not necessary. It's part of my job to help incoming Europeans."

"Maybe so, but I would have had to pay a taxi, and besides, I want to. Would you rather have dollars?"

"Yes, that would be nice. Thank you."

"By the way, are there any checkpoints or patrols out in the city now? I'm concerned about the state of my passport."

"I haven't seen any checkpoints in a few weeks, but I'm usually not out this late."

I took a deep breath, and we rode in silence until we reached the Intercontinental. I handed him a fifty dollar bill. His eyeballs almost fell out. I gave him a double handshake of thanks and retired for the night.

The next morning I was up early, and I decided that for the first time in my life I would check in with the U.S. Embassy. I never had much faith in our embassy officials' ability to resolve problems, but, technically, I was in the country illegally, and did not care to spend time in a Zaire jail. When I arrived at the embassy there were a lot of people milling about in the entrance hall. Some time elapsed before I found the Sergeant at Arms. I told him I had a passport problem and needed to talk to the person in charge. After a few minutes, a young attaché came to the door and ushered me into his office. I explained my predicament, and asked whether he could help.

"Well, sir, at this point in time we are without an Ambassador. I'm afraid there's not much we can do vis-à-vis the Zairian administration."

"Look, I don't want to make a big deal out of it. I just thought you might have an entry stamp in a drawer somewhere that you could put on my visa."

"Sir, that would be illegal. This is not a practice that the U.S. Government undertakes. I'm afraid we can't be of help."

I felt like saying, "Give me a break. Nothing would ever get done in these countries if you didn't circumvent the rules," but I kept my mouth shut.

"I'm a U.S. citizen. There must be some way to resolve this."

"There is an ex-embassy employee who has just started a business facilitating business people with paper work. I hear he is also handling cases like yours. Hold on, I'll look up his number."

He pulled out a piece of paper and wrote down the man's name and number. He then escorted me to the door, wishing me best of luck with my problem.

Suddenly, as he was about to close the door behind me, he exclaimed, "Hold on! There's the man I was talking to you about."

He was in the corner of the hall talking to a woman. I went over to the corner and waited a few feet away until the two were finished with their conversation. When they parted, the man looked up at me expectantly. I introduced myself and explained how I had gotten his name. I detailed for him my predicament.

"I would say you have a bit of a mess. The lower echelons here can be quite difficult, and should the officials find out they could throw you in jail. A few days might elapse before a friend found you. However, I am handling a few similar cases so I could try to help."

"What do you mean, 'similar cases'?"

"I have two other people who are here with passports without entry visas or entry cancellation stamps. I am handling their cases."

"You mean they are still in progress?"

"Yes."

"What would be the cost, and how long have their cases 'been in progress'? When do you expect the situation to be resolved?"

"The handling will cost you 300 dollars. I turned over their passports to my Zairian contact three weeks ago, and I'm not sure when I'll get them back, nor for that matter, can I guarantee to resolve the problem."

I thanked him and told him I needed to try some other avenues.

I walked out of the Embassy. I definitely had a problem. I decided to delay seeing André until later and try another route.

Socopao had set up a materials handling and warehousing operation in Zaire in competition with Amiza. Jean-Claude, who was head of their Cameroon operations, typified the high quality management that Socopao had in each country. I had made a point to meet their manager, Pierre, when Socopao had first established their office in Kinshasa. I had been very impressed with Pierre's ability to circumvent red tape and get operations moving—always a miracle in Zaire.

Pierre was a big, round, joyful Frenchman, with dark hair and sparkling eyes.

I was explaining the situation, and at about the midpoint he interrupted. "Hold on. Let me call in my young Zairian assistant. He is well versed on how to solve problems in this country."

"Whoa! Can he be trusted with this situation?"

"Be assured that he has handled much trickier matters for us. I trust him implicitly. He is very efficient and will take over my job in about two years' time. Be confident. I put you in good hands."

He called in his assistant. My immediate impression was of sharply pressed khaki trousers and white shirt topped by a smiling, intelligent face.

Pierre laid out the problem and I filled in the details.

The assistant manager said, "I have a friend in the Ministry of the Interior, which controls Customs, who I think will be able to work it out. Why don't you leave me your passport so I can get working on the situation this afternoon?"

"I'm very reluctant to leave my passport. It's liable to get lost in the shuffle. How long before I get it back?"

He turned to Pierre, "Is this important and urgent?"

"Yes. Number one priority. You can drop other matters. I will handle them."

"In that case, I will set up lunch with my friend, and if he can resolve the problem quickly I will give him your passport. Otherwise, I will hold on to it and then we can discuss the options."

I agreed to leave my passport.

I went to see André for the latest update on coffee developments. I was in the middle of telling André about my difficulties with customs when he suddenly interrupted. "If you want to see N'Daka, you'd better get down to the ONC right now, because my informants tell me he is flying out for Europe this afternoon."

"Thanks. I'll see you later."

I dashed out the door, got into my waiting taxi, and recrossed the city to the ONC. I got in immediately to see Mawabe, who confirmed N'Daka's travel plans. In fact, he had already left for the airport, as it was after 1:00 P.M., and his flight left at 3:00. I asked the status of my contract. He said, "No change. He has not reduced it, and he has not signed it." I decided I would try to intercept N'Daka in the airport. I got back into the taxi and sped toward the airport. After some enquiries, I found N'Daka in the V.I.P. lounge, and noted that the couches were the same as in his house, yellow and gold velour. I apologized for disturbing him, but explained I flew back to Kinshasa especially to meet with him. In light of the frost occurrence in Brazil, I needed to know our quantity commitment from Zaire. He did not bother to get up to shake hands and barely acknowledged my presence. He sat hulked over, continually wiping his nose with his handkerchief. Finally, he blurted through the handkerchief that he would probably sign a contract at 200 tons a month to keep a presence in the U.S.A.

"Thanks, I'll be in touch from New York." I was pissed, but knew there was nothing to be done.

First thing the next day, I went to see Pierre and get a progress report on my passport. He was his usual joyful self. "Well, Claude, tell me how much you are willing to pay to get your passport in order?"

"Listen, this is no joking matter. This whole trip has been a bloody mess. I can't wait to get out of here. We have a major bull market on our hands and I need to be in touch with people who can supply coffee. Where do we stand with my passport?"

He smiled and handed it to me. I picked up my passport and flipped the pages. There was the visa in the middle—a full page stamp with the leopard head and a statement that I was an important and privileged guest of the Zairian state, who should be accorded all the courtesies of a dignitary. The visa also had scrolls of green ink along its side with tax stamps included—quite a production. To my eyes it was a miracle.

"That beautiful work will cost you twenty zaires and a bag of rice."

"Pierre, I owe you one. This is the most gorgeous piece of scrolling I've ever seen. I presume the visa is genuine? By the way, where am I going to find a bag of rice?"

"Yes, it is genuine, countersigned by the Ministry of Interior. As for the bag of rice, I will take it out of our warehouse and add it to your bill."

We shook hands, and for the first time on this trip my step was light. I stopped at the hotel bar for a drink. The Brussels director of one of the Belgian colonial houses hailed me to join him. He proceeded to tell me about the large contracts that he signed with N'Daka for Europe and said the excess would go to my father's firm. He rubbed my nose in my failure. Many years would elapse before I would be able to accept vulnerability and yield to failure.

The next morning, with my Amiza rep handling the formalities, my beautiful visa and I flew through customs and boarded Air France for Douala, Cameroons. The doors closed, I ordered champagne, the plane taxied and lifted off the runway. Unbeknownst to me, that was my last trip to Zaire.

In Douala, everything was familiar, and after visiting with Jean-Claude, I flew to Youande and cut a deal with Hayatou for 1,000 tons a month. I felt like a whole person again.

20

Problems and Resolutions

What's going on? Amin is crazy!

The next day I flew to Amsterdam. I got in late Friday afternoon, which afforded me the weekend with Bette and the kids.

We had planned, long ago, to take two weeks vacation in mid-August, ten days away, and I vowed not to put the trip off because of business. I wanted time with my family. I wanted to make up for the absence of a father on a daily basis. Yet I knew I had to watch myself, because if my expectations for that vacation were too high, tensions would accelerate and catastrophe would ensue. I had made reservations at La Belle Etoile in Concarneau, on the Brittany coast of France. The plan was to spend one week there and one week driving and visiting the Normandy Coast and Belgium.

After a hectic work week, my family and I finally drove off, shedding our cares and concerns. In Brussels, we stopped to visit my aunt, my mother's younger sister, an attractive, vivacious woman only fifteen years older than I. She took us touring around Belgium for three days.

Our time in Belgium was full of fun and wonderful sights: museums, cathedrals, and the picturesque countryside. From there, we visited Normandy, including Mont St. Michel. The kids loved clambering on the old fort's walls and running through the cobbled streets. We finally arrived in Concarneau, half exhausted and pleased to stay put on the beach for a week. We explored the rocky coast of Brittany, sailed in small boats, played tennis, and ate fine French cuisine, which did not help my weight problem. Most importantly, we felt like a family again, exploring and sharing experiences together. We "introduced" the frisbee to the French beaches, and the children made sign language friends, as all children do when on the loose and on vacation. A week later we were on a plane back to New York; the children headed for school and I to the gladiator pit of the coffee market. Bette, in the midst of all this, juggled all our needs to keep the family in balance.

The office in New York had grown in my absence. Brazil was estimated to have lost up to 40 percent of its trees. We had a good long position, and only 600 tons of Indonesians from a small shipper were in danger of default. The futures market was getting quite active due to dealers, roasters, brokers, and speculators jumping in for the game. This activity was good for the business because all the players gave liquidity to the markets.

In the midst of the hustle and bustle, I found out that my father had given up his pretense as a dealer and had sold his company to a competing dealer. He had stayed on, collecting a percentage on all the contracts he was negotiating in Africa and Europe. I was still at war with him mentally and emotionally, but I had agreed under pressure from Bette and my sister to attend family holidays for the sake of the children and Mother. My relationship with my father did not change. We were competing businessmen, two peacocks showing off their feathers.

On the business front I was becoming overwhelmed. My responsibilities covered all our sources plus our relationships with our banks. I was the one who had set up the back office procedures and, as our growth catapulted forward, was often called upon to update them. For the first time in my life, I realized I could not do it all. My brain and body were being short-circuited. I began to listen to an inner voice.

We held a meeting and I transferred the responsibility for East Africa to Abba. We also agreed that I would turn over most of my responsibilities in Indonesia to Howard, since in both cases they were English-speaking areas. Howard and I would continue to overlap in Indonesia, depending on who was most needed in the office. West Africa and all the French speaking areas would continue to be my hunting ground.

Business continued to prosper and I asked Abba to introduce me to Sam, head of the Uganda Marketing Board in New York. We went to lunch at a small pub on Fulton Street, around the corner from the office. Sam was slightly on the portly side, with large flaring nostrils and black pupils. His blue irises were very unusual for an African. He was quiet and observant. Abba, as was his habit, was a chatterbox and Sam interjected only a few words to keep the conversation going. I was also slow to talk, as I tried to dissect this stolid yet bright African. I could tell he was following the action and body language, interpreting all the nuances at the table. I decided to pull an old trick which had often worked in Africa. I smoked a pack a day then, and had recently switched from Lucky Strikes to Gitane's. I had a gold Dupont lighter, decorated with maroon Chinese lacquer. The lighter was small but heavy and elegant. I tapped a cigarette out of the pack, lit up and put the pack down on the table with the lighter on top of the cigarettes.

"Mr. Saks, would you mind if I tried one of your cigarettes?"

"No, not at all. And by the way, the name is Claude. Mr. Saks is for when I get to be eighty." And with that I extended the pack in his direction with one cigarette sticking out. He took it and I lit it for him.

"Thank you, that's a beautiful lighter."

"It's a Dupont, the French equivalent of Dunhill, but I think it better made, more reliable and more attractive. Do you like it?"

"Yes, it's quite attractive."

"Well then it's yours! My gift to you as a new friend."

Abba was awestruck by the action. The conversation moved on to coffee technicalities, the market, crops, and so on. The next morning, instead of Abba calling Sam, I did and tied up 600 tons.

We became regular large buyers of Ugandas, and we developed a market for their lower grades, which were called B B Bits, meaning Broken Brown Bits. These coffees were extremely discounted, as most people did not know what to do with them. Howard had found a roaster who had a closed cylinder, so there was little loss in weight.

My father and mother, 1976.

We made a fortune. By the end of the year, we had done over 5,000 tons of Ugandans. Overall, we were rated the fifteenth largest importer of coffees, and we had not yet shifted out of third gear.

The year 1976 started with a bang. Prices continued upward and we sold ever-increasing quantities. The ICO quota system had disintegrated, and the trade was finally enjoying a free market. Bernard had done well guiding Multitrade, which was fully operational and in the black. Communication between Multitrade and Saks International was excellent, and with the Indonesian operations' time difference, we always had a trader watching the markets. We negotiated an increased line of credit to seven million, plus an additional unsecured million, for margin calls on the futures markets. We were trading heavily both on the New York and London futures markets.

Howard and I took turns getting up at 5:00 in the morning to cover the London opening. With prices moving up, our financing needs kept increasing, and we were calling on Hagemeyer for additional lines of credit. Having promised to supply all the necessary financing, the Dutch started to take our contracts very seriously. Overall, Hagemeyer was not complaining. Their financials showed sales increasing by 20 percent and profits by 30. They had a good deal.

We were up early and worked late, taking frantic calls from all parts of the globe. Our nerves were on edge. But we were in our glory—growing, profitable, and having fun.

There was a setback. The Indonesian shipper we were concerned about defaulted on the 600-ton contract. Howard went to Jakarta in the hope of collecting some lost profit and came back reporting a tremendous increase in modernization, both in communications systems and in the upgrading of coffee production. As far as the defaulted shipper was concerned, we got a lot of promises and local lawyers' bills, but no coffee.

I left on vacation three days after Howard returned, and had a wonderful time up in Maine with the whole family. Three couples had rented two houses, and between us there were nine kids. It was raucous, but great fun. On the fogged-in days all the children were in one house playing Monopoly or some other game. The other house, with its big open fire, was reserved for the quiet readers. Two weeks flew by, and I returned to the office.

The day after I got back, an Air France jet from Israel was hijacked by a faction of the PLO and flown to Entebbe, Uganda. In disbelief, the world watched the predicament of the hostages. I called Sam. "What's going on? Amin is crazy!"

"Yes, I know. I can't reach Uganda. They're cut off. I have no news."

"Jesus Christ, we've got over 3,000 tons due us! The contract was supposed to have been shipped out last month. We're already late to our customers. Can you find out at least if they're in your Mombasa warehouse? If so, set up a ship and get them out."

"I can reach our Mombasa warehouse and inquire, but even if the coffees are there, they won't ship out without instructions from Kampala."

"Yes, but at least I will know that the coffees are ready to go as soon as things clear up. I can then report to my customers and obtain some delay."

I hung up and consulted with Howard and Abba. We agreed to review the problem with our customers before covering the position and creating a loss.

The bulk of the position was sold to two customers: Nestle and one of the top three importers, a good friend of ours. The remainder was sold among various smaller roasters. I called John Burkley at Nestle's since supply problems were always my bailiwick.

"John, I presume you heard the news coming out of Uganda?"

"Yes. How do you think it affects our coffee? Any luck in getting it loaded onto a ship?"

"No, it's definitely not on a ship, but we're checking to see if it's in their Mombasa warehouse, which, personally, I think is unlikely. Let's assume the worst, that the coffee is still sitting in Kampala. What would you like us to do—sit tight for a couple of weeks, or cover in the market for you?"

"I would sit tight another week. We're in pretty good shape with coffee, but with the five-week shipping time we'll need to know definitely where we stand. If, in one week, you can't confirm that the coffees are in Mombasa and a steamer is lined up for loading, then we'll have to ask you to cover, either on the spot or the afloat market."

This conversation was reminiscent of our Zaire problems with Nestle, early in SINT's career. In the meantime, Howard had contacted our dealer friend, who agreed to hold for another two weeks.

The most difficult problems were with the small roasters whom Abba telephoned. They were operating on tight supplies in this volatile and increasingly costly market. We had to cover and supply the roasters with other coffees immediately. The losses were manageable. The big question was going to be the outcome with our two large customers.

In the midst of all this, we were renovating the offices; we had outgrown our space. We had rented the empty floor above us, broken through the ceiling, and were building a connecting staircase. Dust and noise pervaded, adding to the mounting tension.

Howard was bouncing from one leg to the other, trying to decide what to do. He was due to leave on vacation for Cape Cod.

"Howard," I finally said, "just leave. There's nothing you can do here. It's a waiting game. At some point I'll make a decision with Nestle as to whether to cover."

"You're right. I'll leave first thing in the morning."

I called the Chairman of Hagemeyer and explained the situation. I emphasized the potential of the robusta market accelerating upward because of the lack of coffee. The longer we waited, the more expensive it would be to cover. He listened quietly.

"I have full trust in you boys. Whatever you decide is acceptable to me. I will inform my colleagues. Thank you for the call."

The next day the Chairman called. "I'm planning a trip to our various offices in Canada, so I thought I would drop by New York and we can chat a bit. I'm taking this evening's flight."

I got hold of Howard in Cape Cod and told him, "Hagemeyer is taking this very seriously. The Chairman will be here tomorrow A.M."

"Oh relax! I think he was planning that trip. I don't see the market running away just because of a lack of Ugandans. There's plenty of Ivory Coast, Cameroons, and even Zaire's, and also some Angolan robustas around."

"Maybe so, but they're either spoken for or in strong hands. This situation could turn very nasty. I intend to give him the worst-case scenario."

"Well, don't scare him to death. Do you want me to fly back? I can catch a small commuter or a plane out of Boston."

Howard seemed relaxed and in his beach mode so I said, "I can handle the situation by myself. I'll be fine. Got to run. Try and put this out of your mind." I had decided I wanted to handle the crisis by myself.

The next morning, bright and early, the Chairman arrived in the office. Our second floor with the new, expanded trading room, a large, private office for Howard and me, as well as a conference room, was now complete. We met in my new office. We sat down face to face, and as usual he jumped right into it.

"If you covered all your contracts right now, what would it cost?"

"I estimate in round figures, in a worst-case scenario, that the loss would be about two million dollars."

"That's a lot of money. What would that do to your financials?"

"Well, if we closed the books right now, we would have a loss for the year. We would be giving back all our hard-won profit, and wiping out part of our capital."

"I see. Assuming you did this, what happens then to the Uganda coffees?"

"Uganda has always honored their commitments, albeit late at times. So, assuming they shipped within the next thirty days and the market did not drop, we would recover our profit and capital."

"Could you not hedge the shipment on the futures market to lock in the profit?"

"No, because, in the final analysis, if they don't ship because of a war or some other unforeseen activity, then we lose on our short positions on the futures market. We're damned if we do and damned if we don't. So, in the end, I would rather take my chances on the market staying steady or moving higher, without complicating our problem further."

"That's your judgment call? What if they ship and the market has moved down?"

"In that case, I think the worst scenario would be that we are flat, meaning we lost our profit. I'm sure I could renegotiate the contract lower, due to their failure to ship on time. So I think the downside is that we would be out our profits."

The Chairman continued the full court press. "Are you prepared to take such a big loss now? Do you want to wait longer to see how the situation breaks?"

I took a deep breath and said, "The old dictum is that 'the first loss is the best loss.' If we wait longer, the market could move even higher, and the loss would be greater."

"Okay, I agree."

"One last thing. We are not going to be able to finance with the bank, since this is not a documentary transaction. We'll need a cash infusion."

"How much?" His voice was flat.

"To be on the safe side, two and a half million dollars."

"I'll have Yella make a transfer to your account tomorrow."

"Great. I really appreciate your support, and Hagemeyer's conduct in our partnership."

"That's the story of being partners. In the same soup together, for better or worse."

"Hopefully, for better, when this works itself out."

"It will. Give my regards to Howard. I'm going to try and catch the KLM flight back to Amsterdam tonight"

"I thought you were going on to Canada?"

"No, I did not want to alarm you by saying the big boss was coming personally to look into the situation. I am pleased with your report. Let me know how it works out."

The Chairman left, and I went to work looking for cover, informing John and the importer of our actions. In two days we covered all the contracts.

When it was over, I called the Chairman to give him the damage report, and again I thanked him for the transfer and support. Two days later Israel attacked Entebbe Airport and freed the hostages. That crisis was over, but would Uganda ship?

Ten days passed. Howard returned from vacation, and several events happened at once. The market had continued upward. Uganda sent us advice of loading a ship in Mombasa, and Sam was transferred to London with a reorganization of the sales board in Uganda. The new head of sales, Musoke, was a friend of Abba's. Interest in robustas had increased, as the coffees were substantially discounted under arabicas. We easily sold the 3,000 tons and ended up not only recouping our loss, but making an additional profit. Hagemeyer was jubilant, and our financing was straightened out.

Our position as Ugandan buyers had taken another turn for the better.

A week later, I got a call from Golf informing me that the Burundi government had kicked out all Europeans who were in a position of authority in the coffee business. Golf was out of a job and was retiring with his nest egg in Belgium.

Kabwa was to be the new D.G. As the Brits say, "The King is dead, long live the King."

When the statistics were published in early 1977, we were rated among the top ten importers, by far outstripping George's best accomplishments. Since we did virtually no Central or South American coffees, our growth was amazing. But we didn't intend to stop there.

Central America had become part of Howard's and my Sunday strategy sessions. Every Sunday, when I was in the country, we would get together at one of our homes. The host would provide the red wine, and the guest the french bread and cheeses. One of the cheeses usually was an *explorateur*, a double creme. It was like pumping globules of fat into our cardiovascular systems.

Work was my entire life. My passion to succeed was in full force—nothing else mattered. The more I worked, the bigger the deals, the more adrenaline produced, the more I craved for still bigger deals, the more I ate, the more I smoked, the more I partied, the faster I went. It got to the point that Bette was embarrassed to accept invitations to friends' homes, because I would have a couple of martinis, tell dirty jokes, get boisterous, and be full of myself. I was big time, I was an "International Trader."

We kept growing. I was cutting larger and larger deals with Sam in London, always obtaining the offer before the New York opening. This gave us the advantage of looking the market over for a few hours before making up our minds. When the market was really hot, not only would we accept the tonnage in hand from Sam, but we would clean up the remaining scraps from the New York office and Abba would buy from Musoke in Kampala. Our import statistics from Uganda were enormous, and this fact was picked up by a columnist at *The Washington Post*. We were lambasted for supporting Idi Amin's fascist and inhumane regime. Other newspapers picked this up. We received letters from the New York Archdiocese, Protestant churches, humanity groups, and concerned citizens.

Howard and I had a lengthy discussion and decided to temper our purchases from Uganda and in the meantime get some legal advice. I had developed a friendship with Rod Dayan of Cadwalder, Wickersham, and Taft, and called him about our publicity problem. He advised us not to respond to the letters and newspaper articles as we were within our legal rights, and see if the storm would pass. Indeed it did. My friendship with Rod grew further as our wives became friends. My relationship with him, unbeknownst to me at the time, would prove to be crucial toward the end of my career in the coffee business.

21

Awakening

Where had I been all those years?

On Saturday of the Labor Day weekend, 1977, I was warming up with Bette for a mixed doubles tennis match.

Suddenly, I was unable to move my racquet. Pain shot up under my armpits and up into my throat. I wanted to rest and then resume the game, but Bette would have no part of it and drove me to the emergency room of Mountainside Hospital in Montclair, New Jersey. At the time, I owned an Austin Healey MK-3000 and was more concerned about Bette stripping the gears than my pain and muggy condition.

Once I was in the hospital, events moved swiftly with little input from me—totally out of my control. I was hooked up to an intravenous solution and Dr. Horowitz, the cardiologist in charge, gave me some nitroglycerine under my tongue. He informed me I was going through an infarction, a heart attack. I was in total disbelief. How could a young, vibrant man of thirty-nine be undergoing a heart problem? Blood was taken, and I was wheeled up to the cardiac care unit, the CCU, and hooked up to every imaginable monitoring device.

I asked Bette to call Howard, who was vacationing in Cape Cod, and tell him I did not think I would be at work after the weekend. The next day Howard was in the hospital by Bette's side. I was reluctantly relinquishing control. My body had been speaking to me; I just had not heard. The Most High had kicked me in the chest, in my heart center, to shift my consciousness away from business. At that time I did not understand I was being called, asked to switch from being a material warrior to a spiritual warrior. My first lesson in yielding was starting. I did not yet understand that yielding was not to the hospital or its staff, but to my higher self, to the Most High. There were other agendas at work of which, at that time, I had no comprehension.

The blood test came back and the enzymes indeed indicated I had had an infarction. Dr. Horowitz did not believe that serious damage occurred; however, he wanted to keep me in the CCU for a few more days. By midweek I was moved to a private room and began to receive visitors. I was to be kept under observation for another couple of days and, once I was stabilized, Dr. Horowitz wanted to perform an angiogram.

At this point I had Transderm patches taped to my body to keep my blood vessels dilated. Otherwise, I felt chipper and happy. I was not even trying to follow the coffee market. I had much time for reflection, and much of what was happening to me made no sense. It would be years later, through a spiritual teacher, that I would come to understand that a heart attack was the stoppage of the flow of the life force due to hatred—in my case, self-hatred. I had finally reached a point of success where I had surpassed my father; but by doing so, I had become like him. I lived for money, power, control, total hedonism, and the satisfaction of my ego. In winning the confrontation, the competition, against Father, I had lost myself. I had lost my dream quality, the painter, the artist of my youth whom Father had so effectively suppressed during my confrontation with him at college, when I had vowed to beat him at his own game. My dream quality and imagination had been redirected into the narrow channel of competition, into the concrete world of money and power. Without understanding the *why* at the time of my heart attack, I knew I had to redirect my life.

On the eighth day in the hospital, Bette and Dr. Horowitz walked into my room. They looked rather somber. Bette sat on the side of the bed and held my hand. She informed me that our oldest son, Eric, had been hit by a car while riding his bicycle but that he was all right. I pressed for details. He was in the same hospital, two floors down.

I was wheeled down and stood up next to Eric's right side. He had a black-and-blue eye. His left leg was three feet up in the air in traction, and his left wrist was in a cast with his friends' signatures on it. He had a few scratches here and there, but otherwise he was smiling. I just stood there holding Eric's hand, fighting back the tears. I leaned over and hugged him, my eyes watering, the tears sliding down my cheeks. Bette joined the embrace and we all cried.

Where had I been all these years? Eric was a fine young man of sixteen, and where had I been? I sat on the edge of his bed and we just talked. He did not want to talk about the accident. He was having nightmares. We talked about his interest in art, and in particular his desire to be a filmmaker. I listened. For once I really listened. After a while Dr. Horowitz came back and insisted I go back to my room. Eric and I both needed rest.

A few days later I was back home, still on Transderm. Two weeks passed and Eric came home in a hip-high cast. Bette set him up on the ground floor of our house, in the family room, where he could wheel about. I spent more time with Eric, Marc, and Claire, but there was a distance between us. I could not express my deep love for them. I needed time. I was starting to move around a bit, but still under strict orders not to do any business. I would call the office, but Howard would not tell me anything. In any event, the company seemed distant and unimportant.

Each time I went up stairs I would have chest pains. At Dr. Horowitz's insistence I underwent an angiogram at Columbia Presbyterian. The Columbia cardiologist spoke my language—he was quick and to the point.

"Mr. Saks, your angiogram shows that your left descending anterior artery is 90 percent blocked, so I consider you in a very critical condition. I recommend that we do bypass surgery immediately. I mean now, as soon as we have an operating theater free. One of our best surgeons is standing by. He will come and visit you shortly."

"What about a second opinion or alternative method?"

"In your case, there is no time for a second opinion. You are a walking time bomb. There is no alternative solution for your blockage."

"Okay, I hear you. Let's do it."

"Fine. I'm going to have the nurse give you a shot to keep you calm. It might be several hours before we can do the operation. In the meantime, we'll have you prepped and ready to go."

"Assuming I get through this, can you suggest a method to lower my blood pressure and calm down?"

"I read your background. You're a trader, a Type A personality, like me. I suggest you read two books, if you can get them before the bookstore closes; one is *Type A Personality and Your Heart*, and the other is *The Relaxation Response*."

"I'm a slow reader. I'll never finish two books in a couple of hours."

"It may be more than a couple of hours. Besides, you might be astonished how fast you read under these conditions."

Howard had come in for the angiogram and was giving tremendous support to Bette during these trying times. In fact, he was with her to give advice when the local police had called about Eric's accident. He was a godsend in helping her get all the top doctors for Eric. Here he was again in my hour of need. My feeling of having my family and business protected when I was traveling to the ends of the world was further strengthened. He volunteered to try to find the two books while Bette kept me company.

After covering half the Bronx, Howard returned with the two books. It was now 6:00 P.M., and no operating theater was going to be available for a while. The surgeon checked in with me, reviewed the risks, and assured me the best team was standing by. I rifled through the books. It was obvious that my life had to change. My personality had to change. I had to change.

The orderly finally rolled me out at 10:30 P.M. I was put on the operating table and was told to breathe deeply, as a mask was lowered onto my face.

I do not have recollections of meeting the Most High when I was under anesthesia, but I knew instinctively, or intuitively, that I had received a message or information that would change or reorient my life to its real purpose.

Within three days, I was walking feebly around the hospital. My parents came to see me. My father was walking with a cane. These days, I saw Father only at official family gatherings, such as Christmas and Thanksgiving, and had not realized how his health had deteriorated. His kidneys were failing, and he was in dialysis twice a month. He had made a great effort to come and see me, but the words we exchanged were inconsequential. Our feelings stayed unspoken, nor would I have tried to express, or he understand, my perceptions. My sister also came to see me, but I have no recollection of anything said. What had happened to the days in our youth when we could talk about our feelings? Indeed, many years would pass, and many walks on Long Island beaches, before we could reconnect as brother and sister and share our experiences once again.

Within a week, I was discharged and wheeled to a waiting car. Once at home, fear set in. I became conscious of every little pain or abnormality. Now that I had life, I was concerned with death, or being crippled. I was not yet equipped physically, mentally, emotionally, or spiritually, for the reality of being in a weakened condition.

I spent a lot of time with the children—trying to make up for the years when I was not around. A dramatic change had happened to me, but I still lacked the means to really be in touch with my children beyond a superficial level. I loved them so deeply, yet my external self could not translate my inner emotions.

A few weeks passed, and I started to go to the office for half days. I was once again seeing the problems, and the adrenaline flowed. But I was not comfortable being at the office.

A month and a day after my operation, November 18, 1977, Bette held a surprise fortieth birthday party for me. My friends brought a lot of silly gifts, and I laughed a lot, did not get drunk, did not overeat, and thoroughly enjoyed myself without the intensity of past occasions. Howard made a toast to Bette, thanking her for her strength throughout Eric's and my crises, and congratulating her in keeping the whole family calm and together. I listened, realizing that I should have been the one making the toast. Why was it so easy for me to give, and to control, but be unable to receive, or simply to acknowledge Bette's help, her abilities and strength?

I decided to address the problems of my body and my mind. My spirit was to follow, initially without my conscious decision. My resolve was soon tested. Our operations manager was in a serious car accident the week after my birthday. Howard became very involved in helping her find the right doctors and avoid having her leg amputated. She was being treated in a rundown hospital in Queens, just off the highway where she had been injured, and her leg was not improving. I was propelled back into the business full time. I had to get involved with operations and back up the assistant. Our manager would be out for a long time. Since Howard was out of the office visiting her at the hospital, I moved back up to speed on trading and positions. In order not to revert to old patterns, I realized I needed to find extra time for myself. I signed up for a monitored cardiovascular exercise program three times a week and joined a transcendental meditation group. I had stopped smoking and got my weight down to 185 pounds. Earnestly, I began to get in condition. The seeds of change had started to germinate.

I visited our office manager several times, and each time I entered the hospital, I had pangs throughout my body. Howard finally arranged to have her transferred to Mountainside Hospital so that the same orthopedic surgeon who had attended Eric could help her. From that point on she improved dramatically, and was able to return home the week before Christmas.

My sister called me in early December to say my father was deteriorating rapidly, and that he was in dialysis twice a week. I agreed to join the entire family at my parents' house for Christmas, as this might be the last holiday I would spend with him.

Father was immaculately dressed, and Mother, with all her fine jewelry on, smiled at having the family together for Christmas. Father was emaciated. He had lost more than forty pounds and was very weak, yet he tried to carry on normally. He was still in control. I felt sorry for him, not understanding compassion yet, but I still could not connect on a human level beyond the bravado of business talk. My children, happy to spend time with their two cousins, were lavished with gifts from my parents.

Two weeks passed and the demands of business exerted ever-increasing pressure on me. My heart attack had started my inward look trying to discover who I was. I had always been inclined artistically yet I was now embroiled in big business beyond my original youthful dreams. I wanted to reconnect to my family and I felt financially secure; these feelings slowly made me question my need to continue in business. I felt a tremendous dichotomy of wanting to keep building a corporate empire and wanting to find a solitude within myself where I could be at peace without proving anything to the outside world, my father, or my own ego. The New Year rolled around, and I resolved to get out of the business. Exactly how to get out and how long the procedure would take depended on Howard and Hagemeyer. My brain was set in motion.

Father worsened, and dialysis was increased to three times a week. Two weeks later, Doctor Schuyler admitted him to New York Hospital. My sister had taken the responsibility of being close to him and coordinating with the doctors. My mother, in her usual sedated state, kept insisting he would recover. After a week, my sister called and said I had better come to the hospital. I told her he could burn in hell, but she insisted I come, as the prognosis did not look good.

I entered New York Hospital with trepidation. His private room was full of flowers, and death was in the air. My mother and sister were by one side of his bed. I approached the other. He was in pain. He was a frightened man. He kept calling for his mother. "Maman, oh Maman."

Father turned his head slowly and looked at me. "Claudy, I'm glad to see you here. I don't think I'm going to leave this hospital?" He had said it like a question.

His eyes were moist and pleading. I held his hand. The only thing going though my head was the scene of my grandfather's funeral, years before, in the summer of 1971. My grandfather was laid out on his bed in his best double-breasted pin-striped suit. His face and hands were colorless and the texture of wax. The energy of this grand European gentleman was gone, except in my mind. Father and I had stood silently at the foot of his bed. The window was open and the curtains fluttered ever so slightly. Lake Geneva lay below Grandfather's window, blue, still, quiet. Father had turned to me. "He never did anything for me except put me down," he said. "I shall not miss him nor shall I shed a tear for him."

Were my feelings now so different? I questioned how it was that I could never give Father joy at being his son. I was unable to talk to him about death, nor was I open enough for him to feel my love and compassion. So I leaned over and kissed him on the forehead, squeezed his hand, and walked away. That was the last time I was to see him alive.

I had been too bombarded with hospitals, operations, accidents, and death, to deal with my emotions. My anger and frustration with our relationship did not die with him. Many years went by before I could speak of my father with compassion, understanding, and appreciation for the many things I had learned from him.

A week after my father's funeral, I went to see Vincent, a psychic friend of mine. He had wavy black hair, always well groomed, and deep dark eyes which had a soft, penetrating quality about them. We had met a few years before and become friends. Although of Italian descent, he was a Francophile, and spoke French quite fluently. Many times we would spend an entire dinner conversing in French. I met him at his apartment in New Rochelle, a modest building, the interior spotless. We sat in his consulting room.

"Well, my friend, you've had quite a dramatic six months."

"Yes. I've had enough. Tell me things are going to get better."

"Do you really want to know? I would think you would want to live and work through your own karma."

"Yes, but Vincent, I could use a little guidance."

"I'm always happy to counsel you when you want," he said. "You know we all choose our own rebirth on earth with issues we have come to work on."

"Vincent, you're getting ahead of me."

"Well, I think your time has come to start on your spiritual path."

"What do you mean? I'm not very religious. My father was a Jew, my mother a Catholic. I'm married to a Protestant, but I was brought up Catholic."

"We'll see about that. May I suggest a book for you to read?"

"Sure."

He got up and walked to his bookcase, searching without success.

"Well, let's try another way."

He put his hand out and scoured the bookcase. Vincent's hand came to an abrupt stop about midway through the third row down. He pulled out a book and handed it to me.

The Mysticism of Tibetan Buddhism by Lama Govinda.

"Vincent, what is this? I don't know a thing about Eastern religions."

"I know, but you've started transcendental meditation, which is the first little step in that direction. Besides, I know you don't have an interest in religion, but my sense is that spirituality will become important to you."

"I don't know where my energies are going to take me," I said,

My father reading speech to his father on his
80th birthday.

"but I do know deep inside that it will be in new directions. I've decided to get out of the business. Does that make sense to you?"

"Yes, but getting out will take a lot longer than you think, and there will be many surprises along the way."

"How long, and what surprises?"

"You know that I always have difficulty with precise dates. I just see time passing by. As far as the surprises, let's leave them as surprises. You will have your work cut out for you, and I can assure you that you will be tested. But if you really are going to take a new path, and you want to become a more open human being, then you need to arm yourself." He leaned back in his arm chair smiling.

He convinced me that, besides my physical exercises and meditation, I should also avail myself of psychotherapy. He recommended a Dr. Morano, a friend of his who had an office in New York as well as his home in New Jersey, not far from Montclair.

I decided to meet Dr. Morano at his home office. He was also of Italian descent, with thinning hair, a tightly cropped beard, glasses, and generally a rounded, soft appearance to his body. Not soft in the sense of flab, but rather soft in the sense of not being an outwardly muscular, aggressive type. He was a panda bear; underneath the panda's soft exterior was a tough animal.

I explained that I wanted to shed my Type A personality and become more involved with my family and surroundings.

And so started my seven-year process with Dr. Morano.

While I was undergoing psychotherapy, I read numerous books about mystical teachings and became intrigued by all their ramifications. I did not understand everything I read, but my interest was awakened. I wanted to know more. I kept up my TM (transcendental meditation) practice faithfully, five times a week. I found my mind more alert and conscious of what was around me. Slowly, I started to understand my family. I became more responsive. While beginning this spiritual path, my business continued rolling along. I verbalized my feelings of love to my children, which in turn helped them to express their feelings. Bette and I talked of my need to get more deeply in touch with myself, both through psychotherapy and the spiritual path. I could not explain to her what happened to me in meditation except that a deeper knowing seemed to be present. My urge was to pursue the way of spirit. She responded, "Honey, don't bring your rage to succeed to your desire to be spiritual. My feeling is that you need to follow your intuition and not your head."

I did not appreciate her comment until years later, after I had read book after book and my rational intellect had brought me no closer to what I sensed existed in the ephemeral. My gnosis would eventually manifest, but only after years of inner work.

22

On the Road Out

We would need to build a top management team.

Soon after my father's death in 1978, I brought up to Howard my resolve to get out of the business. I said, "My head is just not 100 percent in the business anymore."

"What do you mean?"

"I find I've missed out on too much of my everyday living, my involvement with my family, participating in my children's growth. I think I want to get out."

"You can't have it all. In a few years' time, we've grown beyond most peoples' dreams. If you're really serious about getting out, okay, I'm tired as well. These have been excruciating times. I'm prepared to get out with you. We'll take our money and reinvest in a slower, more conventional, business."

I was astonished that he agreed so readily. Perhaps I had misjudged him and he did not have the fortitude to run the business alone. My long-ago conversation with Fred came back to mind. Had I overvalued Howard's strengths? My old attitude of strength versus weakness and control that I had learned with my father came back. Could I really relax and assume Howard would not take advantage to gain the upper hand? We had worked together as a powerful team against the outside world; could we continue to do so on amiable terms in getting out of the business? I was relieved that he was willing to consider the possibility, as I felt too weak to work my way out of the business alone. "That's great. But I'm not sure about reinvesting immediately in a new business. I need time to see where I am, and anyway, if you agree and we go ahead, it's going to take some doing to negotiate with Hagemeyer."

Howard looked at me, puzzled. "What's to negotiate? Our contract is clear. We have the right to sell to them our 50-percent share in Saks International, Inc. for its book value. Whatever we're due in consulting fees for Multitrade, plus the half equity, they pay in cash, and that's it."

"Well, not so quickly. I would not be prepared to simply sell to them our 50-percent share. I think it's worth a premium."

Howard raised his eyebrows. "How are you going to accomplish that?"

Although I was physically weak, my mind had been working on the possible scenarios. I gave an example to Howard whereby we could buy back our 50 percent from Hagemeyer and then flip the whole company for a premium. In any event we would need to develop full management for Hagemeyer to buy our 50-percent; otherwise, they would fight us legally if we tried to leave with no one to take over, so we could sell to a third party.

Howard shook his head as he leaned back in his chair. "Sounds like you've been thinking about this, but this is a hell of a way of getting out. Your method is going to cause us to get bigger, and do more work to accomplish it. Why ask the Dutch for a premium on 50 percent?"

Perhaps I was still fighting my father's ghost and was out to build the largest U.S.A. coffee importing firm. I just didn't think we had a choice; we had to build management in any case. The other option was to die at our desks of old age, or shut the company down, which certainly would not be financially rewarding.

"Okay. You make the call. You have always played the black hat role and dealt with the chairman. I'll play the nice guy going along with you."

I called the Chairman and went through the same sequence with him as I did with Howard, putting all my cards on the table, including our possibly selling to third parties. I intimated we wanted a premium for our shares without actually naming the price. He was quite taken aback, as he had not expected such an occurrence. He needed a few days to think and talk to his colleagues. He called back right on schedule and suggested we fly over the following week for in-depth talks. He made one condition clear as a prerequisite: we would need to build a top management team operating under us for at least five years. If we could accept these conditions, Hagemeyer would then pay a premium for our shares, the price of which would be negotiated. Howard could not believe that the idea had been accepted so quickly. He felt that in light of the positive response we should touch base with the young traders we had in mind for management.

Later that afternoon, we called each trader and set up individual lunches over three days. Each was in his mid-thirties. Vic had worked for a broker and knew the entire trade. Mike had worked in East Africa for Nestle, as well as in their New York office, then had moved over to one of our competitors. Last was Benjamin, a free-lance maverick from Israel whom I had met on a Columbian deal. He spoke French, Spanish, Hebrew, and Arabic. I felt he could be a good replacement for me with our sources.

We explained to each one of them our intentions of expanding in Central America, building a larger company, and eventually turning the company over to the three of them, as we intended to bow out.

They responded very favorably, but the whole idea was conditional on our meetings with Hagemeyer. We flew to Amsterdam the following week, and immediately we were sequestered with the Chairman, the treasurer, and Hagemeyer's in-house lawyer. After forty-eight hours of intense talks, we came out with a broad meeting of the minds. The details of the actual sale were to be negotiated by our lawyer, Rod, and Hagemeyer's New York lawyers, to minimize any tax consequences.

We met with our young traders. We explained that we had cut a deal with the Dutch and were ready to welcome them aboard. Our young traders gave notice to their respective employers and, as is usual, were asked to leave immediately. We had a fully staffed pro-fessional team.

We discussed with Rod our new direction with Hagemeyer. Rod and his top tax attorney came up with a concept to accomplish our goals through a complicated tax-free reorganization. Now it was up to the Dutch attorneys to review the proposal.

I took this opportunity to take Vic to Indonesia, so that he could take over my responsibilities there. After that trip I went to the ICO meetings in London with Benjamin to introduce him to all the African delegates.

While in London, I met with Kabwa. The United States laws had changed concerning overseas payment to government officials. Although we were paying through a brokerage for our ongoing Burundi business, I wanted to be extremely conservative. I told Kabwa we would stop payments above any normal brokerage. He told me if this was the U.S. attitude that all business would end up going to Europe. "So be it," I said. This was my last formal meeting with Kabwa, and I never did return to Burundi. My personal with-drawal from the business was beginning.

In the meantime, we had the problem of being without guaranteed large supplies of arabicas. Even though our intention was to get into Central America, we were still at the bottom of the learning curve. However, as often happens in my life, an opening would occur. Although we had recovered our market losses from the market downturn, the end of 1978 and early '79 looked grim. Hagemeyer's lawyers had advised us that Rod's tax-free proposal was unworkable and would cause massive problems with the Internal Revenue Service. Rod's team disagreed violently, as good lawyers can violently disagree, and the impasse was finally resolved by deciding to go to the IRS for a ruling. We were advised that if we were lucky the ruling would take three months, but that we should be prepared for a year. I wanted to get out of the business, but the sums were too large to take shortcuts. We and the Dutch agreed to wait for an IRS ruling.

During this time, we hired Richard, a red-headed Puerto-Rican, to do our Central American trading. By mid-March, we began trading Central American arabicas from shippers in Guatemala, El Salvador, and Mexico. We were not getting large quantities, but enough to say we were in the business and competitive. We were now a full-service importer, although not a major factor in Brazil and Columbia, the two largest producers. Although I was, by far, the least experienced in centrals, as Central American coffees were called, I had a definite feeling we could be a more important factor. The break came when Mike asked me to join him for lunch.

"What's up?"

"A friend of mine, a junior member of the Mexican Coffee Institute in Mexico, has just been made head of the new Institute's New York office. I think it would be good for you to meet him because you know how to deal with government officials."

Mike and I met Javier at the old Dutch Tavern on John Street. The minute I shook hands and looked into Javier's eyes, I knew we would get along well. Introductions were made, and I slowly probed his background. He was a lawyer by training and came from a well-to-do family in Mexico City. He was about thirty-five, and I could not determine whether he had political ambitions or was in the *Instituto* as a stepping stone into the commercial world.

"Tell me," I asked, "I'm rather a novice in Central America, but are not most coffees out of Mexico handled by private shippers? The question is, what is the *Instituto's* role in the coffee business?"

He smiled an easy smile, his dark eyes sparkling. He explained that the Institute was set up to support the small Indian coffee grower, bulking their coffees and selling them to the world market. He confided that eventually the Institute had ambitions to market the larger private plantations. The conversation was sounding to me like a variation on the theme put forth when Zaire took over the marketing of their coffees. Mike and I proceeded to convince Javier to use and rely on us to market the lower grade Indian coffees.

We had a strategy meeting with all our traders, deciding to support Mexico even at a loss sometimes to get a major foothold. We were taking all of Javier's offers, and he looked good vis-à-vis his boss. Once again, I was developing a new country, in addition to coordinating our young traders as they slowly took over source operations. Within two years, we were to become the largest buyers of

Mexican coffees. They more than replaced the Burundis, as their crop was ten times larger.

I was impatient for an answer from the IRS. I wanted to build a solid foundation to hand over to the Dutch. And I still wanted to prove to myself that I could build an organization beyond my father's wildest dreams.

In the midst of all this, my spiritual search expanded in new directions. I joined a zendo in lower Manhattan and learned how to sit Zen. I started to understand that meditating was not to relax, but rather to develop a heightened internal awareness.

Once a week, after work, I would go to the zendo and sit. Twenty minutes of sitting, ten minutes of silent walking, and then another twenty minutes of sitting. I also continued my T.M. I slowly found myself more centered. Issues floated up in my head while I sat. I then would discuss these issues during my sessions with Dr. Morano. I marveled how my deep love for my children was finally being expressed. We were communicating on a deeper level.

I am a slow learner. But with the help of Dr. Morano and my spiritual investigations, I began to understand that God had kicked me in the chest to get my attention. I became more accepting of my surroundings, and with this acceptance my urge to get out of the business increased.

We finally got an answer from the IRS giving us final approval. Hagemeyer's lawyers were in shock. We plunged into the details of closing the deal and ironing out open contingencies. Hagemeyer sent over a battery of accountants to look at our books. Events were moving fast, and I was joyous.

By 1980, we were one of the top three importers in the U.S. By April 30, Howard and I closed all accounting with Hagemeyer, and collected all our monies due both from SINT and Multitrade. We were now simply employees, compensated with a large percentage of the profits. We remained consultants to Multitrade, but at a much lower percentage.

Both the financial dealings and contracts were completed with Hagemeyer. I woke up one day with my goal accomplished—the road out of the business was clear and open.

In retrospect, I realize that the entire negotiation had come out of my automatic business brain—much as someone driving down the road reacts automatically to the changing patterns of traffic. What I had not dealt with were the emotional consequences. Suddenly I found myself in an employee-employer relationship with Hagemeyer. Although the language of communication and relationships stayed the same, I felt disempowered at not being a partner anymore. I felt like a man split in half, with my old knee-jerk reflex of rage to succeed, conquer the world, and wield my power on the one hand, and my desire and deep-seated call to find a new way of life on the other. With great difficulty I decided that the only way to walk my talk of a new life was to remove my decorations of authority. I resigned all my titles at Saks International, including chairman of the board and director of the company.

Howard remained as president and seemed to take my resignation as a signal that the company was his personal fiefdom, although Hagemeyer still wanted my full input. I had let go the outward appearance of authority but was not yet ready to let someone else take the full reins of decision making. Howard had just started a difficult divorce which further seemed to exacerbate the situation.

At this point, I increased my sitting time at the downtown zendo to three times a week and started spending more time with my family. As I was slowly trying to reduce my responsibilities, Howard started directing the trading room like an orchestra leader. Every afternoon at 4:30, when the market slowed down, we reviewed the day and planned strategy for the next day. We would work out the pros and cons of the market until we had a clear consensus of our direction. It appeared to me that this process became his personal forum, with much bravado exhibited in the trading room; he no longer looked for consensus but imposed his will. As he increased his bid for power, I watched with a mixture of annoyance and bemusement.

Benjamin, who was similar in temperament to me, participated less and less in the market deliberations. I felt Howard could not stand Benjamin's lack of response to his orchestration. Benjamin left to join a large London trading house. His leaving was a tremendous blow to my West African purchasing plans, as he spoke all the languages and had relieved me of my continual traveling.

Then Abba decided to leave the company because he no longer felt at home with the competition from the young traders. Our position in Africa suffered and we lost ground, due in large part to my refusal to return to my pre-heart attack schedule. Bernard covered Cameroon for us, and we increased the quantities of Ivory Coast from a Parisian shipper with whom I was friendly. All in all, we retained our position as the largest African importer, albeit with smaller quantities.

My view of Howard's need for competition and supremacy within the company came to a head one evening when he dropped me off at home.

I expressed to him my understanding and feeling about his difficulty with his divorce and his need to establish his sense of control, which I felt was spilling over into the company. Intuitively I also believed there might be, at a subconscious level, a need to exaggerate his strength because of my seeming weakness. He knew I was no longer willing to engage the full energy of our fast-paced world and he was compensating for my lack of commitment. I said that in taking his macho tack we were losing our direct source connections. I reviewed with him our friendship of twenty-five years and the incredible success in our partnership and accomplishments, and I told him I now felt pressured by his macho and superior attitude in the trading room. He expressed to me that indeed he had increased his participation because he felt he had to balance my withdrawal; and he was sorry about Benjamin leaving but that from his perspective he was not contributing fully to the trading room discussion or, for that matter, bringing as much source supplies as when I was in charge of source. He was sorry that I felt pushed but he assured me our friendship was the most important element in our relationship and working together.

We shook hands, but I had no conviction about his sincerity. His tone had been conciliatory. I decided I needed to get away from Howard and the trading room—our paths were radically diverging.

I took each of my three children separately on trips to Third World countries so that they could experience how most of the rest of the world lived. I took them along on business meetings as well so that they understood the flavor of my life. I was overjoyed to be away from the intensity of the office and in the old haunts of Indonesia and Africa that I knew so well. I knew that these trips were my swan song to the source operations.

23

Changes

I almost became an energy freak.

By the fall of 1981, Saks International, Inc. was the largest coffee importer in the United States, a distinction that, when it finally came, I found I did not particularly care for. I wanted to be out of the business, yet I had become more involved than prior to my heart attack. My contract had three more years to go. I was still sitting Zen, but I wanted to expand my spiritual endeavors beyond sitting and waiting for something to happen. I still had a deal-maker's mentality; I needed more energy in my spiritual practices.

That fall Marc went to the University of Colorado at Boulder. Two months later I got a call from him telling me he had joined an ashram which practiced a form of kundalini yoga. I went out to Colorado to ascertain for myself what Marc was doing. I was pleased to discover that he had found a fine spiritual teacher in Swami Sambavananda. I meditated with the ashram and felt Swami's love energy all about me.

When I returned to New Jersey, I initiated a plan to find out more about Swami Nityananda, the lineage holder of Marc's practices, and read more books. I felt a conflict developing between my Zen, which required sitting totally quietly, and kundalini, which seemed to work on moving energy through the body. Some days I would sit Zen style and others I would try and visualize the movement of energy through my body. I began to get tingling sensations at the base of my spine and in my sex organs. I could not tell if the sensation was a figment of my imagination or an actual opening. It seemed I was leaning away from Zen and trying kundalini yoga, but I had no teacher. I needed to resolve my dilemma.

The break came when I decided to get more information on the second chakra, the sex chakra, the Chakra of Creativity, the Chakra of the Human Life Force. A bookstore attendant suggested that I read some books by Master Mantak Chia. I rummaged around the Eastern religions and philosophy sections and picked up *Awaken Healing Energy Through the Tao* by Master Mantak Chia.

That evening I began to read the book and could not put it down. This was it! He had the answer and laid the process out in clear and simple terms. Master Chia's teaching of the Tao used the grounding concepts of Zen, but worked toward attaining the higher energy planes of kundalini. After a few calls I located Master Chia in Chinatown in New York and said I wanted to learn. He told me that a couple of weekends later he would be teaching the basic formulas of the energy principles.

The first practice I was to learn was called the "smile down," which I now recommend to all beginners on a spiritual quest or to the busy person who simply needs to calm his mind before an active day. My interpretation of Chia's teaching is as follows:

Sit in a comfortable chair with legs perpendicular to thighs. That is, thighs parallel to floor—for a tall person a cushion is recommended to raise the level of the seat and avoid lower back pain. Both feet should be on the ground and the back, the vertebrae, should be straight as a string of pearls hanging by an invisible thread through the crown. Sitting away from the back in the chair usually helps keep a better posture. Keep the shoulders relaxed, with the chin slightly tucked in. The tongue should be placed at the roof of the mouth anywhere it feels comfortable for the practitioner. The tongue acts as a switch between the back and front energy channels which are used in further meditations. Place your left hand, palm up, in your lap and clasp your right hand over it, palm down. This closes the loop of energy; just keep your hands relaxed in this position in your lap. This basic posture is the basis for all Taoist meditations.

The actual "smile down" meditation consists of smiling to your-self, particularly in the eyes because they affect the parasympathetic nervous system. Picture in front of your eyes a light golden mist which is gentle, warm, and full of unconditional love just for you. Close your eyes and smile inwardly as you breathe this golden mist of unconditional love up into your cranium and say thank you to your brain for all its work as you feel the gentle energy spread. Breathe in and smile more energy down into your cheeks and jaw and feel your muscles relax. Continue and smile down into your neck and shoulders, feeling them relax and giving thanks as the golden energy moves down. Breathe deep into your lungs and give thanks for converting air into body energy. Do the same for your heart and all the other organs, giving thanks for their work. Keep smiling down and feeling unconditional love spread all the way down to your feet. This meditation can be as short as three minutes or as long as half an hour, depending on your schedule. This practice will get you centered. Then, most importantly, when the smile down is complete, let your mind go blank and enter the void. From this very quiet internal space you may develop a great inner gnosis or a new business idea or revelation for a creative project. Whatever the case, the practice will bring you revelations or issues that need to be looked at. At times you may feel heat develop in your body, partic-ularly your hands—this is quite normal and just indicates energy movement. During a busy day you can always close your eyes for three seconds and reconnect to this quiet centered space. From the smile down practice, Master Chia went on to teach me the micro-cosmic orbit to open the outer energy channels of the body.

During the next couple of years, I almost became an energy freak, continually refining and moving into higher energy planes through the teachings of the Tao. When I could not get the knowledge directly from Master Chia, I would work with his top certified teach-ers, one of whom lived near me. As my growth process continued, I would visit Marc in Boulder and meet with Swami to compare notes. It became apparent that kundalini work and the Tao followed par-allel paths as related to energy work. I would sit and meditate with Swami and I felt ever-increasing clarity. I began to understand the

Tibetan books I had read. Years later I took refuge in the Dharma, and did some empowerment teachings with His Holiness Drikung Kyagbon Chatsong during his two-month visit to the ashram. Each little piece from different paths added to the puzzle, with the Tao providing the overall foundation.

Along with the meditative work, I started to incorporate physical energy work into my learning. Under Master Chia's guidance, I practiced Iron Shirt Chi Kung, which is a form of martial art. It is used to learn how to absorb hits by building energy, chi, in the organs, lower abdomen, and generally the entire body as well as by strengthening the tendons. The practice helped open my psychic channels further and strengthened me. With Master Chia, I also took up Tai Chi, a part of the same martial art. Where Iron Shirt is static with internal energy movement, Tai Chi is physical movement with the build up, direction, and discharge of energy. I concentrated on the short form only to work on my chi, because the martial arts were not my primary interest.

While my spiritual growth was continuing, I received a call from my aunt Denise who introduced me to Pierre, a young Frenchman, as a potential candidate for source operations. Pierre spoke fluent English and Spanish, and had a good knowledge of Italian, Portuguese, German, and some Russian. He was used to negotiating all over the world for a large French military contractor and wanted to change jobs while moving to the United States. After several interviews with everyone on our staff, we decided to give him a try as my replacement for Africa.

Pierre joined us, and we went through all the legal requirements to get him a green immigration card. He got up to speed very quickly, and so I decided to take him, along with Mike, to the ICO meetings in London. While Mike was making his rounds, I introduced Pierre to those African ministers whom I knew. The Africans seemed to take a liking to him. In fact, Hayatou invited Pierre to join him at the Cameroon delegation in their closed-door meetings. And so, with Pierre inside, we could get all the up-to-date information as to discussions on quotas, prices, and other details of the new International Coffee Agreement. Pierre became so proficient that he was invited by other delegations, including the Italians on the consumer side. He had the incredible ability to ingratiate himself with the delegates. I relate here a typical Pierre anecdote:

A year later, during the ICO meetings, when he was well-entrenched in the West African circuit, he asked the Head of Coffee Sales (HCS) for the Ghana delegation to lunch. HCS accepted with pleasure, but requested that his boss, the Chairman, be allowed to join. HCS explained to Pierre that his boss did not know coffee, and was an ex-sergeant who had received a political appointment. Not being a civil servant, he had less than perfect manners. Pierre, with his typical *savoire faire*, invited both officers for lunch at the Savoy Hotel's very prim and proper dining room that was frequented by the British gentry.

The Savoy dining room is decorated in light beige tones, with pale yellow table cloths and beautiful bouquets of flowers in the middle of each table. The armchairs at the tables are very comfortable and are covered with flowered fabrics. Pierre, HCS, and the Chairman sat down, the attentive waiter unfolding their napkins for them. The waiter took drink orders and left the diners to chat. Pierre and HCS were involved in heavy coffee conversations, when suddenly the Chairman reached into the floral bouquet, pulled out a flower, and ate it. Pierre took the situation in without breaking the flow of conversation. A few Brits at the next table caught the action, which prompted some lively talk. The waiter came back with drinks and was taking the lunch orders, when the Chairman once again reached for a flower and ate it. The waiter could barely contain himself, but with proper Savoy manners finished taking the order and left. A few snickers could be heard at the nearby tables. At this point, HCS felt he could not let his boss down, so he too ate a flower. The snickers at the other tables became louder. Pierre, with his French aplomb, wanted to support his guests, so he too reached into the bouquet and ate a flower. The three of them happily polished off the bouquet before the appetizers arrived.

This was Pierre's forte—never to lose his cool and to handle all situations with diplomacy and tact. I knew I no longer had to travel to Africa.

Group of traders and wives celebrating being Number 1 at yearly gathering in 1982. I am in the far–left foreground, and Howard is in the last row, second from right.

24

Trial in Uganda

They would simply claim he was shot trying to escape.

My path to getting out of the business was further strewn with roadblocks when, in early summer of 1982, I received shocking news from Mike. "Claude, the police have just arrested Musoke in Kampala and we're being blamed."

"What! What the hell are you talking about?"

"We closed two large contracts with him a month ago, one for Uganda standards, and one for BB Bits. Musoke has been accused of shipping both contracts as standards, but billing the second one as BB Bits, obviously at a huge discount."

"That's absurd. We should be able to disprove that easily enough by taking samples."

"Well that's not easy."

"Hold on, let's discuss this in the private office. This trading room is just too noisy."

I motioned to Howard to join us in the inner sanctum. Mike told him the same story he had told me and then continued. He explained the difficulty in that the standards had been shipped or were about to be shipped via the Kenya railway cars, and no one was disputing the validity of that contract. The BB Bits had all been shipped by our own trucks. He went on, "We were concerned about loss of weight due to poor handling of such small beans in the bag if they went by rail. Because of our efficient setup, the trucks will meet up with a steamer in Mombasa, immediately off-load, and the BB bits will go to New York. So the only place we can draw a sample is in New York when the coffee arrives." Mike further explained that the politicians could claim we manipulated the coffees and that the sample was not the original one. The whole thing was bogus, but obviously a very powerful person in the Idi Amin camp was after Musoke, and most likely his job. Musoke was too straight, and Idi's friends probably wanted to get a person in there who would take payoffs and take care of Amin's cronies. On top of all that, the problem had been leaked to the London papers, and our name was being dragged through the mud. Mike finished, "In fact, that's how I found out. One of my London friends called me."

"Son of a bitch. Any clue where those coffees are located right now?"

"They should be arriving in Mombasa momentarily."

"Then hold the whole lot. Find our freight forwarder and cancel our freight booking. Put all of the coffee in a private bonded warehouse with a guard." I told him to get in touch with General Superintendents and have them draw sealed samples, with one set per each lot for the New York Green Coffee Arbitration Panel, instructing them not to break the seal until a formal complaint was filed; a second, similar sealed set was to be drawn for General Superintendents' main office in Switzerland, and a third sealed set was to be kept in their local Mombasa office in case of need. Furthermore, I asked to get General Superintendents to draw a regular open set for us, so we could look at the coffee. A second open set would be sent to the Board in Kampala, so the Board would know we were not going to accept this lying down.

General Superintendents is a worldwide independent Swiss organization who can be used to draw samples of any commodity or material worldwide for approval, arbitration, or court action.

Mike responded to my sample directives. "That's all well and good, that's how we can prove to the world that there was no monkey business and save our reputation, but what about poor Musoke? He's been thrown in an Uganda prison, and the survival rate there is not good. The politicians will disregard our General Superintendents' samples and simply say we paid them off and switched samples, giving them justification to literally get rid of Musoke. We need to save his life."

Howard picked up the conversation. "Let's go to court and defend Musoke." He leaned back in his chair to see our reactions.

I reacted. "Howard, that's absurd. In what court are we going to defend him? Ugandan courts are a joke. They simply rubber stamp the outcome Idi Amin wants."

Tilting his chair forward again, Howard pressed. "Maybe so, but he still depends on outside supplies, particularly from England and Kenya. If we can make enough of a stink by hiring a lawyer and getting the event in both the London and Nairobi papers, we might just hold Amin at bay and get Musoke released."

"There isn't a lawyer in Uganda who is going to defend Musoke against the government. It would be suicide," Mike said.

An idea rattled around in Howard's head, and he said: "Mike, it's a wild strategy, but it might work. The Kenyan and Ugandan laws are supposedly based on the same British principles of common law. Why don't we hire a Kenyan lawyer, and announce the fact to the Ugandan government and to the various press offices. Then we will charter a plane each time the lawyer has to go to Kampala for the case. In and out in one day, as you have done when you were on business there."

Mike agreed. "It's definitely a wild card, but the only one I see, so I'm willing to try it. I will contact Hagemeyer's office in Nairobi to see if they can locate a lawyer brave enough to undertake the case."

"Okay great," Howard said. "By the way, is there a way to contact Musoke's wife and family, and let them know we're going to try the impossible—to get him out of jail and defend him?"

"I don't know. The best person would be Zulu. He knows all the ins and outs of the tam-tam (the drum telegraph system). He would know how to get a message across the borders, without it falling into the wrong hands." Mike had grown up in Kenya, spoke Swahili, and knew his way around. He had introduced us to Zulu, an old friend who still operated in East and North Africa. Zulu was a tall Britisher with a fair complexion and lots of freckles. He had the uncanny knack of getting along with all the local people, whether African, Indian, or Arab. He had great ability with languages and spoke fluent French, fluent Swahili, Hindi, and a good smattering of Arabic. He knew how to operate in the back streets of a *souk*, an Arab market, or in the middle of the African jungle. We had done some successful East African contracts with him. Although he was a maverick, I trusted him.

"Musoke's family might be under guard."

Mike responded. "I don't think so. And besides, I'm sure his wife and children have gone back to the small village of her family for security."

"You're probably right. Get hold of Zulu and see what we can do."

A few days passed. We were all on pins and needles. Progress, however, was being made. The trucks were unloaded into a private warehouse, and General Superintendents drew all the required samples. We found a Kenyan lawyer who was willing to undertake the task of defending Musoke. The newspapers covered our actions, so the case became an international affair, no longer confined to local Ugandan politics. I suspect that the Kenyan lawyer undertook the case because of the publicity, which would enhance his career and minimize the possibility of his having an "unforeseen accident" in Uganda. The problem became a game of words between the Ugandan government, the Kenyan lawyer, and us. In the meantime, Musoke was rotting in a Ugandan cell.

We filed a formal arbitration request with the New York Green Coffee Association against the Uganda Coffee Marketing Board. We knew the problem was not with the Board, but with Amin's cronies. This action was another way of increasing the pressure. More newspapers picked up the story, and our Kenyan lawyer made a motion that Musoke be released under house arrest until all the facts could be brought to bear. Amazingly, the Uganda court agreed to release him and put him under house arrest. Zulu had found a way to contact Musoke's wife, and we ascertained that all was well with his family. Since Musoke's family was now located in their small upcountry village, the court miraculously agreed to let Musoke join them there. We now knew he would be properly fed and regain his strength.

We held a meeting in the office. I wanted to make some strategic moves. "Mike, do you think Zulu could set up a system to sneak Musoke and his family out of the country?"

Mike objected. "I think you're crazy. If we get him out of the country now, all of us will be proven guilty by default. Since we have gone this far, we need to defend him and clear the slate."

"Come on, Mike. That's not going to happen. Amin's boys are not going to get egg all over their faces. If we take that route, I bet Musoke will meet with an 'accident.' I'm convinced that the only reason the government let him out of jail and go back to his village was to let him escape, which then absolves them of any wrongdoing, and frees up his job for their own man. They can point the finger at us, but you know the International community will not believe them, especially if we go ahead with the arbitration, proving that the coffees are exactly what we bought."

"Let's assume you are right, and we try to get him out. How do we know that there isn't an ambush waiting to kill him and his family? They would simply claim he was shot while trying to escape."

"I agree that is a possibility, but remote. His village is pretty much in rebel country, and the military has control of only Kampala and the main roads. You know that Musoke is part of the rebel underground. I'm sure he knows how to get out with his entire family. What we need to do is get him a message through Zulu that we will provide for his financial security if he can make it to Kenya."

"How and why should we do that?"

"We have been talking about setting up a base in East Africa for a long while. Musoke is one of the smartest people we have come across. Why not hire him as our agent, operating out of Hagemeyer's office. He knows the business inside out. He could cover Kenya, Tanzania, Rwanda, and Burundi. He speaks a fairly decent French. He probably could even cover Zaire. Some day Uganda will cool down, or Idi Amin will be overthrown, and then he could cover Uganda as well. Needless to say, we are not going to get any coffees direct from Uganda for a while."

Howard cut in. "I think the idea is a good one, and I agree that we are in a no-win situation in pursuing the legal case any further."

"Okay, I'll contact Zulu and get a message to Musoke. I hope to God this works out."

The plan was put into motion, and, within a month, we had Musoke and his whole family safely in Nairobi. He became an outstanding agent for us and for Multitrade in East Africa. He reopened Burundi and Zaire, so once again we were doing reasonable quantities in each country. We arbitrated the coffee and won, just to prove to the world that everything had been done correctly. Eventually, Idi Amin was overthrown, and history records the rest.

25

Bad News and More Bad News

She went over to shake her gently.

Howard and I accelerated the withdrawal of our responsibilities at Saks International in 1983. The process proved to be fraught with nightmares. In May, I traveled to Europe to make a round of my contacts. My last stop was Amsterdam to check in with Multitrade. Each year since our sale to Hagemeyer, Multitrade had become increasingly independent and was not taking our advice. They were successful, but I felt their arrogance would someday be their undoing.

I returned to the Marriott one evening after a full day at Multitrade. I was planning to update Howard on what was going on, and intended the next day to confront the chairman about the lack of communication between sister companies. As I walked into the room, I noticed the message light flashing.

I called the Marriott operator. "Message from your sister, Marianne. Call urgently."

My sister and I did not communicate often with each other. I dialed Long Island.

"I'm afraid I have some bad news, Claude. Maman has died."

There was silence on the line for a while. Maman, as Mother was called, was sweet and lived in her own world.

"How did it happen?"

"Aunt Denise was going to take her out for dinner, since it was Lilian's day off. She called to confirm the time—you remember

Maman's unawareness of time. There was no response, so she went over to check. When she entered the living room, she saw Maman snoozing in her favorite chair. She went over to shake her gently. She was dead. The doctor believes she had a silent heart attack."

"Well, if you are going to go, I guess that's the best way. How are you doing?"

"Maman hasn't really been there for me, although I have spent a lot of time with her. Yet, when this happens, the physical loss is a shock."

"I know. I feel the same way. Listen, I'll catch the first plane tomorrow."

I arrived in New York the following afternoon and met Marianne at the funeral home. We drafted the announcements for the papers and made a list of people to call. Maman had always loved flowers, so we arranged for lots and lots of flowers. The funeral and cremation was to be held three days later. My mother wanted her ashes next to my father's in Brussels, Belgium, where the old family plot was located. I was amazed at the number of people who showed up for the funeral; my mother had been a recluse for the last couple of years. Half of the New York trade showed up. I was very moved.

I sat in the front row and listened to a good family friend deliver a eulogy: "Annine, as we all knew her, was the only person who never had a bad word to say about anyone. She was accepting of all peoples, and that is what made . . ." I drifted off in my own thoughts to the summer when Marc had turned sixteen. He was a rebellious teenager. He was drinking too much, getting poor grades in high school, and I was concerned he would get involved in drugs. I never found any evidence of this, but he and I were at loggerheads on just about all subjects. I did not want him to be at home alone, working through the summer. I wanted him to have a job at the seashore and stay with us. He refused, and we had reached an impasse. Maman suggested that he stay with her at the shore. She was alone except for Lilian, the housekeeper. A perfect compromise for the two of us. Marc had just gotten his driver's license, so he could help with the groceries since neither Mother nor Lilian drove. He found a job with a contractor, painting houses. Emotionally, Lilian had adopted Marc for the summer. Her own grandson, Marc's age, had died two months earlier—pushed onto the tracks of an oncoming subway train. Three weeks passed, and I went to check up on the arrangements. It was a Saturday, and Marc had the day off. As I parked in the driveway, I could hear reggae music coming out of every window and door. My tension started to rise. What kind of mess was Marc making of my mother's house? I walked in. No one heard me above the volume. As I entered the living room, I saw Marc's easel with canvas on top of the coffee table. His palette of paints rested against my mother's silver ashtray. Lilian, a wonderful large black woman, was swaying with the reggae. Marc stroked paint onto the canvas with a flourish, and Maman was sitting in her large red velvet cane chair, humming to the music. I was about to blow up in a rage when suddenly an axe came down and cut the cord. Maman was accepting Marc and all his joy in her home. The whole scene was joyous. Marc was happy. Lilian was happy, and Maman was happy. A big smile broadened my face. I went up to Marc and gave him a big hug. I got it. I accepted. I had found a son again. I had found myself. As Maman's eulogy came to an end, I knew that moment would always be my best remembrance of her.

Once back into the office momentum, I became aware that we were doing increasing quantities of Ethiopian coffees with Zulu. All the contracts were very profitable, but what made me curious was that the coffees were being shipped out of Port Said, Egypt, instead of Addis Abba. I asked Mike what was going on. He explained that due to the civil unrest in Ethiopia, Zulu had found a system to bring the coffee out through Port Said, which was a free zone, and where he had set up a major operation with an Arab freight forwarder. I asked if the ICO documentation had been checked, and was assured by our documents department that everything was in order. I let the matter go until Zulu offered us a very large quantity—3,000 tons—of Yemen coffee, also out of Port Said, for the United States basket quota, similar to my early Cameroon deal with Father. Howard, Vic, Mike, and I met in the private office. Vic and Mike informed us that Zulu was being financed by his Arab friends from East Africa, and that he was personally overseeing all operations.

The coffees would have all the necessary papers for U.S. Customs: a certificate of origin, signed by the Yemen Ministry of Agriculture, and ocean documents showing transshipment from Port Said. "That's all that's needed for the basket quota," said Mike.

At this point there was a knock on the door. The frame of our cupping man, Big Bird, filled the open door. "I've just put down twenty cups of those Yemens. I must tell you, they are some of the nicest coffees I've ever cupped." Howard and I looked at each other, each knowing what was going through the other's mind. Yemens were famous for being great coffees but we had never heard of more than 100—maybe 200—ton shipments. The offer that Zulu was making was unduly large and also unduly profitable—there was a chance that these coffees were not Yemen, which meant we could get in trouble with the ICO and consequently the United States Customs. But quality and documentation seemed correct from our end and Zulu had given us assurances that all contracts were genuine. Why should we become detectives and holier than the Pope?

We all agreed that we wanted to do the business. And, since Howard and I were leaving, we were reluctant to torpedo a very profitable deal for the new management. The coffees were shipped and landed on New York docks in the third week of October, which was late, relative to the basket opening, but in time for entry.

Two days later, I traveled with Bette and my sister to Brussels to bury my mother's ashes. It was a beautiful fall day, warm, with a light, cool breeze which fluttered the drying leaves in the cemetery trees. I contrasted the climate with the day when I had come to bury my father, when it was cold, rainy and blustery, with dark scudding clouds. His dark side was still with me; I was to deal with it later.

Some twelve people had come to pay their last respects to my mother. From the cemetery, we all went back to my aunt's for a light dinner and drinks. Other old friends, whom I hadn't seen in twenty-five years, arrived. Glass of wine in hand, I stood there looking at these old European friends. I felt so distant, so far away from the Europe I had known as a child. All through my business years, my European background had been important for language, manners, politics, and knowing who was who. I stood there realizing this life no longer mattered. I was from the other side of the ocean. I felt the chapter on my youth and my European connections ending. The burial of my mother was the final closure, yet with this closure came a new opening. Marianne and I had left our European youth behind; both our parents were dead, and that left an opening for the two of us to slowly reconnect. That process would take years, until we were once again talking and seeing each other on an ongoing basis.

Bette and I flew to London the ensuing day to relax, take in a play, and check in with the local traders. The weather in Europe was still magnificent. We hired a car and drove up to the Cotswolds for lunch. Returning to the hotel, I was picking up my key when I was given a message to call Howard at the office.

"Hi, it's been an absolutely beautiful day here. What's up?"

"We may have a potential problem. U.S. Customs has held up all basket quota entries, including ours. We had a visit from an agent, stating that certain abnormalities were being investigated."

I could not believe that this dark tornado was about to hit me just as I was leaving the business.

26

Stormy Weather

Why don't you throw Zulu to the wolves?

Back in New York I called our lawyer, Rod, and apprised him of the situation. We had large amounts of coffee being held by customs without formal detention or charges, but they were claiming that these coffees were Salvadors not Yemens. They had started an investigation, and we needed his help to counter their allegations. He felt we had a serious problem and would find a customs expert to work with Cadwalder. At his suggestion, I reached Hagemeyer's Chairman at home and informed him of the situation as I had described it to Rod.

Events began to unfold rapidly. Monday afternoon, Rod suggested Barry as our customs lawyer and representative. Tuesday, we met Barry, a tall man with gray streaks in his dark hair. His eyes sparkled with intelligence and mischief. He proved to be a great joke teller, which eased the tension at meetings. In fact, he always looked so joyful that at first I was concerned as to whether he was taking our situation seriously. He did.

He laid out the three possible degrees of culpability which U.S. Customs could claim. First degree would be simple negligence; the coffees were not Yemens, without any involvement or knowledge by us, in which case re-export of the coffees would probably be allowed. The official penalty is 20 percent of the value of the goods. Second degree would be the same as the first except Customs would try to prove we knew the coffees were not Yemens. In this case, there would be a stiff fine of up to 40 percent of the value of the coffee, and in principle the government would allow the re-export subject to the negotiated agreement. Third degree would be proving that not only did we have knowledge but we conspired to commit fraud, in the sense we helped to bring in coffee which was not authentic. Mis-labeling, if you will, but technically fraud, even though there was no monetary loss to the government or customers. He explained that there was a new head of Customs who appeared to want to raise money by cracking down on offenders of all types. Barry told us that the fine for third-degree culpability was up to 100 percent of value and destruction of the coffee.

Howard was in a frazzled state. "I don't believe this! You are talk-ing about some very serious money. I can't believe we could be in such deep soup for a simple case of potentially mismarked bags."

"Mislabeling a product to the consumer is a fraud," Barry said flatly.

As I listened to the scenario, my stomach muscles fluttered with fear. My mind created the darkest of scenarios. My entire body was full of anxiety, fearing loss of money and loss of reputation. I could not believe we were in such a mess. I wanted to get out of the busi-ness. I had planned every move of leaving the business correctly, and now, with a year to go, I was in this chaotic situation.

I decided that Barry needed further information, so I told him about 4,000 tons of Ethiopians that we had also bought and that, if Zulu pulled a fast one, these were probably Salvadors as well.

Howard interjected, "Come on now, all those documents are in order. We are familiar with those, and the paperwork is quite cor-rect."

I responded, "Howard, if Customs can show other origin in the bags, the government will not care if the documents are originals."

Rod's office, with two windows, full of light and cheerfully deco-rated, did not help our somber mood. The meeting broke up, and Howard and I walked back to our offices. I did not want to talk, and so we walked slowly in the cool November air. I wanted to prepare for battle. The lawyers would be on the front lines. However, for them, it would simply be another client, another problem to solve.

There would be no emotion involved. Certainly that is the best way to be in a fight. And poor Howard would be a shock troop, as he was the president of the company and I technically only an employee. He would be the one meeting face to face with the Customs agents. This would give me the advantage of remaining in the background, trying to analyze and see things as clearly as possible.

I had just finished some deep Taoist meditation work, and decided then and there I would have to increase my meditation practices to an hour and a half per day, even if that meant getting up at 5:00. I also decided to increase both my Taoist practices of Iron Shirt Chi Kung and Tai Chi. I wanted my body, mind, and spirit to be on the razor's edge. I reflected that the tensions between Howard and me would have to go on the back burner.

Two days later I flew to Amsterdam and met with the Chairman. I laid out for him our problem and exposures, as well as our actions to date. The Chairman agreed with what we had done, and then he informed me that he had retained separate counsel for Hagemeyer. I was not overjoyed, but had to acquiesce. He insisted that their counsel would not second-guess any of our moves. All communication either way would be done through him. My last request to him was to make Bernard available to us, so we could find out what was happening in Port Said. He agreed. I thanked him for his understanding and support.

Multitrade had changed since Howard and I had reduced our involvement. A Dutchman had been made head trader, and Bernard had taken over all source purchases, operating independently from Paris.

Before flying to New York, I spent several hours on the phone with Bernard, explaining our predicament. He agreed to get detailed information for us in Port Said, but I couldn't push for an earlier time frame than the middle of January.

Three days later, Customs detained the 4,000 tons of Ethiopian coffees, giving notice to all the roasters who had bought the coffee to return any unused portion to the New York bonded warehouse. We now had 7,000 tons held, under investigation. It was evident that the word was out on the street that we were having problems with Customs. Pandemonium held sway at SINT, with mounting financial pressure, as all coffees were on loan with Banks. In addition to the detained coffee, we had massive positions in other growths of coffee. I decided I needed to get back in the business with both hands. "Howard," I said, "we may be turning this company over in a year and we have been encouraging the new management to run positions. Right now, however, I want to batten down the hatches and cut way back. I think you need to talk to the roasters, and assure them we are fighting Customs claims and intend to come out on top. For my part, I'll talk to our banks, explain the situation, and assure them that the business is under control."

"Let's not go crazy. This will straighten itself out within a month. We can't cut way back. It will be too obvious to the market."

"I don't give a shit what the trade thinks. Just explain that we're being cautious until everything is cleared up. I'm adamant about cutting back. Our lines of credit are full up, and if called by a bank we have no room to maneuver."

"Do you really think one of our banks would call our loans?"

"Yes. Particularly Chemical Bank. Since Peter left the new person in charge is a glorified clerk, who is still wet behind the ears and would not stand up for us to his upper management."

"Okay, okay. We'll tell the boys to stop the positions and only do back-to-back business, just like brokers."

Howard talked to the trade. I spoke to the five banks. Three of them were our major banks, and the other two had approached us to do business. I thought that if we ran into trouble with one of our main banks, it would be good to have new financing available. Both new banks were European and were anxious to get into the trade. I kept my fingers crossed.

Howard's new wife delivered their first child on December 22, which was also my wedding anniversary. Joyous occasion—Happy Hanukkah—Merry Christmas.

The first working day of January 1984 was the pits. I was walking up Wall Street with Howard—two friends of thirty years, both deep in thought, under gray skies, in our pin-striped suits, Howard sporting a mustache and I, a full beard. This was not a good day—definitely not a good day. It was cold and wintry, with winds gusting up Wall Street and Broad Street. January, slushy, wet. We reached the top of Wall Street, the apex of power in the financial world, and also home to Rod's prestigious legal firm. We rode the highly polished paneled elevator to the thirtieth floor in total silence, except for the whoosh of the air being compressed in the elevator shaft and squeezed by its sides, seemingly whispering all the secrets carried by other clients to their threshold. From Rod's law offices one can peer down to one side and see the New York Federal Reserve building, and on the other, J.P. Morgan & Company. We were whisked through reception and asked to join the meeting with the top guns in this fine Wall Street firm. The subject, of course, being us, our company.

The meeting was held in the large conference room with no windows, and a long mahogany table, stacked with papers about our case, with six lawyers in attendance. This room was to become my new war room away from trading for the next four months. Each lawyer had a different perspective. Howard and I were asked every question imaginable. Rod was not present. Barry said, "All right, Claude. I understand that Zulu may have remarked Salvadors as Yemens and shipped the coffees under the basket. What I don't understand is, if he marked Salvadors as Ethiopians, where and how did he get original documents for the coffees?"

"That is the mystery question. I don't know. The Yemen documentation could be of local fabrication—that is, forgeries; we have no way of knowing. The Ethiopians are all original ICO documentation with export stamps. They are genuine; we checked them. We have Bernard, from our sister company, going to Port Said within two weeks and I hope he will get some straight answers."

"Tell me. Why don't you throw Zulu to the wolves and save your own skin?"

I explained that we had talked about the possibility, but it wasn't the way we operated. And besides, there was no way to do that. He was a British citizen, operating out of Egypt. I granted that he had circumvented the ICO, but he had not broken any British laws. As far as I knew, none of the coffee had gone to Britain. So he was clean there. As far as Egypt was concerned, it was not a signatory to the ICO, so they didn't care as long as he operated according to the rules of the free port. Of course, there was no way that he would come to the U.S. and admit he was the bad guy. Why would he take the chance of being arrested? Even if we got him here, it wouldn't accomplish Customs' purposes. He had no money. His Arab backers were the ones with the funds, and no one was going to get their hands on them. I didn't even know where to start. Customs' best move was to come after us. We had the money to pay a penalty and we were the largest importers, making us a wonderful example to the entire trade. Also, we wanted to keep Zulu neutral. If we could re-export the coffees, we wanted him to take the coffees back and reimburse us. No, there was no way out. We were it. I said to Barry, "You are going to have to help us come up with some solution."

Joanne, one of the litigators, exclaimed, "God, this is the wildest and most exotic story I have ever heard."

I continued my explanation. What concerned me was the time factor. The longer the matter dragged on, the more nervous our banks would be, and at some point our loans would be called. With 7,000 tons detained, worth about fifteen million dollars, it was not going to take too much to put us on the ropes. On top of that, our customers would all run if they believed we were on shaky ground. Time was working against us and in favor of Customs.

Every day, we met in the large conference room. Howard had taken on the task of statistics. We knew that many shipments that came into the U.S. were not from the country of origin claimed by the documents. We also knew that the government was fully aware of these situations. Howard set up a task force with Joanne, the lawyer who would defend us in court. They sent out requests based on the Freedom of Information Act (FOIA) on all matters pertaining to improper entries to Customs, the Justice Department, the State Department, and the President's Special Trade Advisor. I was not convinced that proving the government had knowledge of events would help our case. However, no harm would be done by finding out how egregious the violations of the ICO were in the U.S. As far as I was concerned, we needed to prove that we were innocent victims.

A few days later, we got word from Zulu via Bernard that U.S. Customs had sent a special investigator from Rome to Port Said. It was impossible for Bernard to go over and run his own investigation. Just what I had feared—Customs was getting the information before we did. Bernard had to wait for the coast to clear to go in and get the information.

During this time, Joanne was working up a presentation, using Howard's statistics and the documents we got back from the FOIA request. Joanne wanted to make an in-depth presentation in Washington. Howard was enthusiastic and worked closely with her to put it together. All the players were plunging into the task.

I remained aloof. I was not convinced we were on the right path. I not only needed time to think but also needed more time to feel. Things just did not feel right, but my intuition could not get clear because of all the fear and anger surrounding me. I went further into meditation and exercise. At times I would get up at 4:00 or 4:30 in the pitch dark and meditate until the birds signaled time for exercise. I was losing weight steadily, both from toning and from anxiety. In the old days, when I was worried about a position or other problem I would overeat and gain weight. Now pure fear was consuming me.

One day the fear suddenly snapped during meditation. I became an observer of the fear and the whole process. I felt totally detached and clear, like the great Samurai fighters who are prepared to die each time they face opponents. If you fear death in combat, you may die. If you do not fear death, then it does not matter if you live or die. The Samurai can bring all his years of training down to a single point deep within himself. He becomes one with his sword; as the Taoist would say, "your hand is not your hand," meaning that your hand is your inner self, your inner motion. You become an observer. That was the way I felt. I felt very clear, exhilarated. I prepared for the worst: loss of money, loss of reputation, and in my wildest nightmare incarceration. I decided that my true friends could be counted on three fingers. The rest were cocktail acquaintances. I would be alone.

Howard was also losing weight, and his hair as well as his complexion turned greyer every day. I was getting concerned about his health.

Meetings were again held in the big room, which was stale with Joanne's cigarette smoke. She smoked three packs a day. I thought extremely highly of her abilities, but at times I thought I was attending a funeral; Joanne was 5'11" and always wore black high-heeled boots with a black skirt and black cardigan over a white blouse; with her gaunt appearance and dark hair she gave the impression of a vulture waiting for a carcass. This day, Cadwalder had brought in one of their Washington lawyers to help with Joanne and Howard's presentation.

Discussion continued, everyone talking at the same time about how to make the presentation in Washington, whom to contact, what to say. I sat off to one side of the conference table and listened. The Washington lawyer expounded as to whom he knew and how important a job he had held. The talks did not make much sense to me. The time was now 4:30, and I decided to stop the circus. In fact, I was getting angry. I stated I did not want any involvement in Washington until I could think over the ramifications.

The meeting ended. Howard and I walked out, and I motioned for Joanne to join us.

As we walked down the hall, Howard turned to me. "What was all that about? Don't you want him to go to work for us in Washington?"

"I don't think so. In any event, I want the three of us to have a meeting with Rod. I'm not happy."

"That's obvious."

When we reached Rod's office, I explained to him, "I think our meeting was a fiasco. Barry is a great Customs lawyer and Joanne is a great litigator. Howard and I know how to manage a commodity business. This Washington guy, I don't know. He ran off at the mouth a lot. The problem I am personally having is that there is no legal manager over the whole case. I'm not in a position to make legal judgments, and I'm not sure about my strategic judgments in this field. We need you to overview and manage the team from a legal viewpoint."

"All right. How do you feel about it, Howard?"

"I think Claude summarized it well."

"I agree," said Joanne.

"Well then, it's done. I'll start clearing my calendar and get into the case. Anything else?"

"Yes. I'm not convinced about making a big presentation in Washington." I explained that I had learned early in my career, on an Ivory Coast deal, never to bring out my big guns immediately. If you failed, there was nothing to fall back on. I was willing to start at the local level, but I was not sure. That was one reason I wanted Rod involved. He could judge the players from a legal viewpoint. I thought the workup on the Washington presentation should continue. It would gel all the issues and clearly lay out the parameters.

Rod's face seemed to get sterner. "I have no problem with any of that. I'm just not certain that a decision can be made at the local level."

I responded: "We leave for the Boca Raton convention in ten days, and will be back on February 4. Let's aim for a major decision when we get back."

"That will be fine."

The meeting broke up, and over the next couple of days Rod caught up with all the issues.

A call came in from Chemical Bank. "Mr. Saks, we've been reviewing your company's line of credit, and presently you have on loan forty-two million out of a line of fifty. My boss, the head of the loan review board, and I would like to have an immediate meeting in light of your apparent difficulty with Customs."

At 2:30 sharp that afternoon the two bankers sat down in our conference room. The commodity officer started the conversation. "Mr. Saks, we're very concerned with your present problems with Customs. Could you bring us up to date?"

"I'm afraid there is not much to add to our discussion of a month ago. Customs has detained our coffee. Customs is investigating the origin of the coffees. We are confident that there will not be any formal charges and that the coffees will be freed."

The commodity officer's boss cut in. "Does that mean that the coffees are of proper origin and will enter the U.S.?"

"That I cannot say. The determination of the origin rests with the seller. The main point is, we have not been involved, and I'm confident there will be no formal charges and our name will be cleared."

The head of the loan department was a heavyset, ruddy-complexioned man, with a very red nose. He wore a pin-striped suit and heavy wing-tipped shoes. He gathered all his bulk in his chair, puffed up his chest, and said, "Let's cut this meeting short. Our bank no longer has any interest in continuing a credit line for your firm. As all these loans are demand loans, we want full payment of the forty-two million tomorrow morning."

The commodity officer was embarrassed and did not know what to do with his hands. He kept fidgeting with the cuff of his suit, trying to think of a statement that would defuse the bombshell.

He opened his mouth to speak, but I cut him short. "Well, that's clear and to the point. Let me point out a few things to you, sir. We are not in a position to pay down forty-two million, as you are well aware from our financial statement. We could declare bankruptcy, and in the scramble, you would be lucky to get ten cents on the dollar. All those loans are coffees being delivered to customers and will be paid off in due course. If you insist on your path of action, I assure you that you will end up with some serious lawsuits on your hands which will not enrich your reputation in the commodity trade. So I suggest that this situation be handled between gentlemen, and we find a mutually agreeable pay-down schedule."

"What's your proposal?" he grunted.

"Excuse us. I want to review things with my partner."

Howard and I stepped out. Howard exclaimed, "Goddamn, I'd like to kick that guy in the balls."

"Relax. We're going to have to pay the loans down. See why I was insistent on lowering our positions? In fact, they are not low enough."

"Claude, for God's sake, we can't move that fast in such a short period of time. We're working on it. How the hell are we going to finance the coffees which have not yet been shipped, if they don't let us put on new financing?"

"They won't let us put on new loans after we pay down the old ones. I will try and meet with The Bank of New York, our other main bank, before we go to Boca, and see if they will increase our lines. In the meantime, we're in review with two European banks.

I'll spend time with them in Boca. We should try and sell any unsold positions on a documentary basis to dealers, so we won't have to finance the paper. Unfortunately, Hagemeyer is tight on cash so we can't turn to Mama."

"I'm fucking fuming."

"Shit happens, Howard. We are in the drink, so let's swim."

We walked back into the conference room and the stone faces seemed to have grown. The energy was stultifying. We went around in circles for a bit. The best we could do was a pay-down schedule based on receipts from the roasters.

As soon as the bankers left, I called The Bank of New York and set up an appointment with their commodity group. The following morning I met with the group as well as the chairman, a friend of mine. I again explained our differences with Customs. I also explained our major loss of credit lines and how strapped we were. I expressed the hope that they could help us out. I left with a good feeling. Two days later, the Bank called and gave us a fifteen million increase in our line of credit. I thanked the chairman profusely and breathed a sigh of relief. I knew the amount was very tight, but I felt we might be able to squeeze by for the next crucial month, and then our financing needs would drop.

We left for the Boca convention that weekend. I spent all my time with bankers. Howard, Vic, and Mike covered the trade. The trade was aware of our problem, and we spent the entire convention explaining and assuring everyone that we would survive financially.

During our stay in Boca, Bernard had finally been able to get down to Port Said. He left a message at the office that he would be in New York the following week to give us a report. Upon our return, I knew the music would start again.

27

Showdown

Can you boys afford the bill?

New documents on shipments were coming in, and our increased line of credit was being fully used. Although our pay-down to Chemical Bank was proceeding in an orderly manner, our financial situation was becoming critical. Barry spent some time with Customs explaining our financial predicament. He tried to get them to commit to a course of action, either making a formal charge or releasing the coffees. Customs would not budge and was keeping the coffees in detention until their investigation was complete. Some of our roasters began to shy away from doing business with us. I did not like the Customs stance but, personally, could sympathize with their actions. I put myself in their shoes; looking at us, I would come to the same conclusions. I racked my brain for a remedy which would clearly move us from limbo to center. That remedy appeared when Bernard arrived in New York.

We sequestered ourselves in our private office with Howard, Vic, and Mike. Speaking English, Bernard proceeded to explain the situation in Port Said, breaking into French for the finer points. He laid out the entire scenario. Zulu had the backing of his Arab friends from Mombasa. Not only were the Arabs financing him, but they had also put him in contact with family and friends all over the Middle East. Through these contacts in Saudi Arabia, Zulu found out that the Saudis' favorite coffees were Ethiopians and they were willing to pay a substantial premium for the coffee. Of course, the ironic part was that Saudi Arabia was a nonmember to the ICA. The country could buy non-quota coffees from all around the world at tremendous discounts, which in some cases they did, but the preferred type was Ethiopians. The Saudis paid exorbitant prices for them. Zulu got clever. He figured that if he could buy the coffee directly from the Ethiopian Board as quota coffee, say for New York, at the same price as Saudi Arabia or cheaper, then he could switch them.

"Holy shit!" said Mike. "What a fortune he must have made."

Bernard went on. "Hold on. In the final analysis, I'm not sure how much money he made, but I'll get to that later. So he worked a switch. He buys the Ethiopians, destination New York, transshipment via Port Said, Egypt. Port Said is a free port, so he can do what he wants without officials looking at his work." He continued, explaining that at the beginning of the operation Zulu was buying good non-quota Kenyans from his Arab friends in Mombasa. His friends were not giving him such a big discount—between 10 and 20 percent. Zulu brought the Kenyans to Port Said. In the meantime, he had purchased new bags from India, again through his friends. The new bags were marked Ethiopians, non-quota for Saudi Arabia. The quota Ethiopians were re-bagged into the non-quota new bags and sold to Saudi Arabia at a small loss due to the cost of re-bagging and financing the operation. Now the Kenyan coffee which he bought was re-bagged into the old quota Ethiopian bags. These he sold to us at full market price and after the expenses made a small profit. He caught an unusual market disparity.

"So what about the Salvadors and Yemens?" asked Howard.

"Okay, so he plays around with the Kenyans for a while, but two things happen. Kenya can't keep up the non-quota supply, and, secondly, the coffees are not cheap. He looks around for a coffee which is similar in quality and inherently free of defects. He finds an eager seller in Salvador. *Voila!* You know the rest."

"Yeah, but what makes him jump into the basket, which is a different operation?" asked Vic.

"Listen, I'm not in his mind. It took a lot of drinks one night in a low-class dive, complete with belly dancer, to dig out this info. I know he did baskets to Europe in the past. I think he saw Yemen next door, and the only way he could get Salvadors was by charter, which meant a large quantity, so he put the two together. I asked him about the certificate of origin, and he said that a local Yemenite was paid a large sum to get it from the ministry. Obviously, a double-cross. He said he understood enough Arabic, and saw from the stamps that the certificate appeared correct. The problem is that the signature may be a forgery."

I did not want to ask, but I had to. "Okay, what are the gruesome details?"

Bernard gave us the rundown. U.S. Customs sent over an investigator from Rome. He probably did not get as much detail as Bernard, but certainly enough to verify that SINT did not receive Ethiopians or Yemens. The records at the switching company were abysmal. There was no way of checking the kinds of coffee that came in versus the kinds that went out. Egyptian Customs did not care about markings. It was a free port. As long as the total quantity in equaled the total quantity out, they were satisfied that no coffee went into Egypt. The Rome investigator used some scare tactics with the employees, threatening to turn them over to the Egyptian Secret Police for interrogation. Since there were no human rights considerations there, the employees, not understanding that they had broken no laws, were frightened and said almost anything the investigator wanted to hear. Bernard sighed with relief at the end of his story.

Howard picked up the ball first. "We certainly know about the coffee on the docks, but I don't think this hurts our case. Sure, Customs knows the coffees are Salvadors, and it is obvious Customs will not let us enter them. We might as well tell Zulu that he owns them. We want our money. As far as Customs is concerned, I would hold tight. We were not involved with the setup and therefore should not have to pay the price."

I could not believe my ears. I viewed the situation quite differently. "Come on, Howard. You've got to be kidding. I think this changes the whole complexion of the case. In the first degree of culpability, all Customs has to show is negligence on our part. I don't think that would be that difficult. After all, we are the largest importers. We should know better than to buy large quantities from a non-origin port. In fact, if you recall, we all questioned Zulu's ethics. When the really large quantities were offered, particularly the Yemens, we chose to close our eyes and not probe deeply. And I am as much as fault as anyone. I've traded at source all my life and I should know better." Concerning second-degree culpability, I said Customs had to prove we actually knew the coffees were Salvadors. The fact that we were the largest buyers of Salvadors for quota markets to this country did not help our case. The evidence was a bit circumstantial, but still could be argued as too much of a coincidence. "As to third-degree culpability," I said, "I don't think Customs has a leg to stand on, but they can threaten verbally to scare us and force us to the table. And that is exactly what I recommend we do. We need to change our *modus operandi* from aggressive to defensive. We should get Barry to see if the government might be willing to settle. And, by the way, I also disagree on the approach to Zulu. You can't just jam these coffees back to him. He doesn't have the money, and if you think his Arab backers are ever going to reimburse us, you're dreaming. I agree that we should put him on notice. Let him start a dialogue with his Arab friends about what we can recoup. I think we need to concentrate on reselling the coffees ourselves. If we can collect 50 percent of our cost, we should consider ourselves lucky."

Howard stared at me and said, "Don't get so intense. We're all in this mess together. Let's see what makes most sense. On Zulu I agree. Let's table that problem for down the road. We still need to make a case to Washington. Trying to work out something with Customs is not good enough."

I was adamant. "I'm not a lawyer, but I sense that the first presentation should be made to customs, no politics."

We agreed to discuss my approach. We set up a meeting at Rod's for the following afternoon, and the gathering broke up.

All the players were gathered in the long, stale, windowless conference room, with the stacks of documents at one end of the table. Howard and I gave them a blow-by-blow description of Bernard's report. The faces around the table were glum. I presented my view to change the approach. "So far we haven't been willing to give an inch. I think it's time to reverse strategy and indicate we're prepared to come to the table. We need to find out if Customs is prepared to talk as well. Barry, that's your bailiwick."

"I certainly will give it a try, but they have not indicated any inclination to do so."

I continued. "If they're not, our course of action is clear. But let's give it a shot. Our banks and some customers are running out on us. We just don't have the staying power—both from business and our personal health and sanity."

Rod sat back and listened to the developments. He then summarized the situation and detailed the approaches for each lawyer.

It took until mid-March to get feedback from Customs. Our conference room group reconvened. I had been there for so many different meetings I began to feel a part of the decor. Barry reported on Customs' concerns and attitudes over the many meetings he had with them. He finally summarized it by saying, "They will consider a settlement of $3,300,000 provided coffees are reexported to non-quota countries and other points to be negotiated."

Howard was beside himself. "That's an outrageous sum. We're better off going to court."

"Slow down, Howard," I interjected. "Let's analyze the cost of going to court. Apart from the potential problem of customers and banks abandoning us, any rough clues?"

Rod responded, "Over and above the sums you have already spent, you will have to figure a minimum of a million. That's assuming things move quickly, say six to nine months. It could be as much as two million, and when all is said and done you have no guarantee of winning. You could still get stuck with first-degree culpability, which is simple negligence. On top of that, you have to figure your financial costs as far as customers lost and banks pulling out. You are under extreme financial pressure now. It won't improve if you decide to fight."

Barry added, "The three point three million is based on a calculation of simple negligence."

"Seems to me, Howard, we don't have much choice. Besides, I must tell you I could not keep going with all this anxiety for another year or more. We would be under continual pressure and unable to do business. We need a clear slate for when we leave the company in eight months. Barry, how far down could we negotiate?"

"I don't think they will budge, but I'm willing to try. Can you boys afford the bill?"

I responded, "It's like the story about when your child is sick. You are prepared to pay any amount to get him well. Once he's cured, though, you think the doctor's bill is too high. This will certainly wipe out our year's profit and put a crimp in our capital. But we can survive and continue in business."

"Then I think you should not push too hard on the money and maybe negotiate on the other points that are bound to come up."

Howard came around and said, "I agree. Joanne, any response?"

"I must say that I still think we should make a political presentation in Washington. I think we just have to wait and see if Customs presses charges, and then defend as best we can. I think I can make a case in court."

It took three hours of talks to convince Joanne that even though we thought highly of her skills, we did not want to go to court, but rather wanted to pay the settlement and go back to trading.

Rod and Barry added their own legal points to the discussion. At 7:00 that evening, the meeting finally broke up.

The next week I was on pins and needles while Barry talked to Customs. I was down to 175 pounds, the slimmest I had been since I reached my full height. I dug deeper into my meditations, or should I say prayers, to the divine powers to get us out of this mess. I continued exercising. I was so attuned to every moment of my life that I thought I was going to burn up every ounce of my energy.

Rod called a meeting. Barry reported that Customs would not budge on the figure but would entertain the idea of a negotiated contract on the other points.

The key to the deal was that we pay a settlement, not a fine, and that we not be officially charged.

Again we returned to our office to wait for answers from Barry. Howard became involved with Joanne and Barry ironing out the details of the agreement with Customs. Howard was terrific at reading contracts for detail wording. That has never been my forte. My strength has always been the broad concepts. So Howard spent more time with the lawyers, while Barry went back and forth between Customs and his offices with the various proposals and changes. Finally, a document was produced with which Customs agreed and with which we felt we could live. In the midst of this a ray of light appeared. We received calls from both European banks approving five and twelve million dollar lines of credit. We could breathe more easily.

We paid the piper. Howard went up to Customs with the certified check, and the agreement was signed. By the time we finished paying all our lawyers' bills, we were out of pocket over four million dollars, not counting our personal pound of flesh.

Howard was very depressed. He walked slowly, like a very old man, with his head hung low. He confided to me that he felt he would never recover, that he had lost part of himself in that big conference room. I tried to explain to him my view that all humanity had problems, whether a heart attack or legal problems or starvation. The issue was not the problem but rather how we learned, transformed, and grew out of it.

I wanted so desperately to be out of the business, yet this dark cloud had appeared. I had to absorb it and use its energy as a lesson in being more conscious, trusting more deeply my inner intuition.

We had a lucky break with the coffee. Bernard had developed a good relationship with some of the Iron Curtain countries. They were in the market for large quantities. Although the regular quota market had come down, the non-quota market had firmed up, due to lack of supply. We were able to sell all the coffees at a minimal loss and claimed the difference back to Zulu. He eventually made good on the money.

Throughout this episode, Hagemeyer held firm, and backed our every decision.

28

Unraveling

You're home!

Howard and I were leaving the company in just six months' time, and we were going to finish the year with a major loss. The only fortunate outcome was that we had lowered the position drastically and gone short. The market had been coming down steadily, so on the basis of our trading we were starting to recoup. How to make up the remaining losses? I could not think. I needed some recuperation time.

I took a few days off and thanked all my guardian angels. Even though Howard and I had been growing apart over the last few years, I was most appreciative of his tough-as-a-bulldog stance throughout the entire episode. In our defeat, we came out with different attitudes. I looked at the experience as a major awakening to my inner depths. I vowed that the spiritual path was to become the most important part of my life. Howard, on the other hand, appeared to me very depressed and embittered by the experience.

Re-centering myself, I put my mind to work to try and recoup our losses. In October 1984, two months before I was to leave, an idea came to me. The only way to recoup our losses would involve a large gamble. I wanted the new management's agreement, as well as that of the Chairman of Hagemeyer. Vic, Mike, Howard, and I held a conference in our private office and called the Chairman on the speaker phone.

I laid out a scenario whereby we would force the market up, squeeze the January London robusta contract. The port of Abidjan in the Ivory Coast was not shipping due to labor difficulties. Without the Ivory Coast coffees coming to the London terminal market, I felt a successful squeeze could be orchestrated. By forcing the shorts to pay large premiums to get out, we could show a large paper profit and thereby wipe out most of our losses and all of us would accomplish our goals. Howard and I wanted to collect our final percentages and bonuses based on the performance of SINT. Mike and Vic as well as the other employees wanted to collect bonuses, and Hagemeyer wanted to show positive results for the year for their shareholders. We needed to build an option strategy, escape, to collapse the back months and the entire market if our squeeze did not work. The coffee world, and commodities in general, are gladiator pits where there are no holds barred with no quarter asked or given. My spiritual training had taught me that the life force was everywhere, even in the pits of combat. All the short speculators were trying to force the market down to make a profit; we would take the opposite view, using our knowledge of the Abidjan problem and our strength to force the issue. The key was to have an open heart and clarity of action, even if it included losses, thereby engaging the energy fully. I concluded, "This operation is definitely risky, but the market is offering us an opportunity we must grab. Any comments, gentleman?" This was to be my last grandstand play in the business.

There was a total silence. Everyone was stunned at the magnitude of the idea.

The Chairman piped up on the intercom. "Vic and Mike, you boys are going to be in charge as of January, so you must feel comfortable with this gamble!"

Slowly, one by one, each person came around to the gamble. The plan worked perfectly. We covered most of our losses and ended the year with a minimal profit.

We were all happy. As of January 1, on an as-needed basis, Howard and I were consultants for another three years at a substantially reduced compensation. It was the new management's option to cancel our contract with thirty days' notice.

The company had been tendered more coffee than we expected, so we switched to our fall-back plan of collapsing the market into a

Howard and the Reichmeister, Tijss, at our retirement party, January 1985.

free fall of prices. SINT then sold the hell out of the futures position, including January, to retender the coffee. The trade was paralyzed for three days before they understood what was happening. Then a problem developed. Multitrade convinced Vic and Mike that Multitrade could sell all the better coffees tendered at a major premium to the roasters in Europe, even though huge quantities had been tendered to us, and the port of Abidjan had been cleaned up.

Howard strongly disagreed. "Multitrade is still wet behind the ears. The Ivory Coast ships are going to arrive full of coffee. Not only will the premiums disappear, but the coffees will probably go to a discount to the Board. There is too much coffee around. It all must be retendered." Retendering meant giving back to the futures market the coffee we had received.

With Bette, at our retirement party in January 1985.

Vic made the stand that it was his decision.

"Look, Howard, I agree with Multitrade. It is my opinion that we can sell most of the coffees at a tremendous premium. The ones we can't, we will retender to March."

I cut in, "Maybe so, but the coffees you retender to March are at a tremendous discount. Why take a chance? If the scheme does not work, you will have a loss. Retender all the coffee to January now and make your money on the collapsing March and May positions."

"Claude, we went along with your big gamble and it's worked so far. I'm saying I want to push it a little further and maximize our position."

"Vic, you are president now and it's your decision."

We could not sway Vic and Mike, and we could no longer over-rule them. We were only consultants without power.

The poorer coffees were all retendered. The back months did collapse. And sure enough, the premium on the high quality coffees disappeared. January was over and SINT had to carry 5,000 tons of unsold coffee to March for delivery. Losses ensued. We were advised that our consulting contracts were terminated. As of March 1985, Howard and I were out of the company we had created and so dearly nurtured to preeminence in the coffee world.

This ignominious dismissal was devastating to me. Certainly, I had wanted to get out of the business, but under different circumstances. My emotions were all mixed up. It did not matter that my view was correct and that SINT ended up losing great sums. My heart was broken. I felt personally beaten, and once again I had to delve deep into my psyche and meditation to heal my heart. The transition would take time and involve a further exploration of the dark side.

Howard and I now operated out of an office in New Jersey and had our funds consolidated into a holding company, which was an outgrowth of the sale of SINT. Howard was still very depressed but anxious to get into a new business to divert his feelings and make money. He decided that real estate would be his endeavor and that he would apply the same concepts as we had done in coffee, buying the low end of the market and upgrading to make great sums. He proposed that we do it together.

I was reluctant, as I was no longer interested in the politic and people game, and I still felt very uncomfortable about his motives. I had greatly disliked his bravado in trying to take over SINT as the big macho man after my heart attack and before the proverbial shit hit the fan. I felt he envied me because I was now worth more than he was, due to his costly divorce. I decided I would do one real estate deal with him to test the waters. We bought a complex of rundown buildings in Montclair and refurbished them. From that experience, I clearly understood that I no longer wanted to wheel and deal and no longer wanted to be partners with Howard in business. I was not clear what I did want to do and was in no rush.

Howard's and my funds were stuck together, a situation which disturbed me, as I did not like the atmosphere in the office. I felt

Howard become more haughty and unpleasant after my decision not to participate with him in real estate. He would come up with what I considered very risky deals in the rundown sections of Newark, New Jersey. He bounced the concepts off me to get my input and then, as if to prove to me that he knew better, went ahead with the deal over my objections. Several of them turned sour, and in a strange way I was pleased to have my intuition validated, although I felt sorry for Howard, who got himself embroiled with lawsuits and arguments in every direction.

As I was stuck in the office, I started trading currencies, which had always been my favorite game. Unfortunately, I was very successful, and became arrogant to the point of going on a sailing vacation with a massive yen-British pound straddle open position. Needless to say, while I was gone the market went against me, and I gave back 70 percent of the profits. I was still ahead, but unsure what direction to take.

Through these reverses, I finally understood with my mind what my higher self had been telegraphing all along. I had made enough money. I was ready to move from trader warrior to spiritual warrior. I would now devote my time to my spiritual path. My ultimate clue came with my last business deal, which brought about a new consciousness, a deal which, in later years, was to make me wonder whether my seventeen years in the coffee world were only a precursor to my true life's journey.

In late fall of 1987, I received a call from an old coffee friend who asked me to help him negotiate a deal in India. He offered an attractive retainer which I accepted.

The Universe had other plans for me than a business deal; it wanted to show me, in no uncertain terms, that the spiritual realm of the most high God existed. Upon my late-night arrival in Bombay I had an enlightening experience while meditating in my hotel room. I felt my entire body invaded by golden warm light that pervaded unconditional love through my entire being. I was in total ecstasy, sobbing and smiling all at the same time; I wanted to surrender and remain in this state for the rest of my existence. My mind vaguely recalled Master Chia's instruction should this ever happen: "Marry the light, the energy, make love to it." I could feel my sexual energy rise and fill my body as these golden energies intermingled with my own energy. My body was vibrating at such a high pitch that I felt my molecules move and was afraid I would explode. When I felt I could contain it no further, I saw the figure of an avatar, Sai Seria Baba, appear in the halo and welcome me to India. Eventually—either a few minutes or hours elapsed—all the energy collapsed and I straggled to bed.

For the next few days, everything was surreal and all business negotiations, to my surprise, proceeded smoothly. After business was completed, I went to Sai Baba's ashram and was personally picked by him out of a crowd of more than 300 people. My heart center was opened and I felt warm waves of love enter my being. I was to learn later that Sai Baba is famous for saying there is only one religion—love. This experience in India changed my life radically. I came to understand that my success in business had taught me to follow my intuition, engage the energy at all times, and that eventually I would use my financial success to promulgate the word of Spirit.

After my return from India, the petty irritations of the office with Howard and my trading seemed inconsequential. I decided I needed a new direction and went less and less often to the office.

It was during this time that I had my first reconnection and resolution with my father. I had been in a deep meditation and sensed my father's presence. As I came out of my inner being I had an urge to write him a letter. I wrote to him my deepest feelings, including my great sadness and grief that we were unable to be partners in life, partners on the business warrior's path, partners in joy. I expressed my thanks for all the lessons he taught me, the wisdom he had given me, the deep love he had kept in his heart, all of which I could now receive and accept. I signed the letter, "With deepest love, your son, Claude." I sat in my big club chair and tears streamed down my face. I remained quiet.

The page of my notebook turned. My hand moved. The writing on the paper was in French, and in my father's script. He expressed in the most tender of terms his love for me and his regret that we had not been able to be open and close. After two pages of emotional outpouring, my hand stopped writing. My entire body shook and sobbed. I released and accepted my father in that moment, as he was—not more, not less.

Claire was off to college and so Bette and I spent more time together and began to rediscover each other and how we had changed over the years. We began traveling around the country together to find where someday we might want to retire. In the process of trying to find a place and trying to find myself I started to get the urge to write. In June 1989, I decided to travel to Taos, New Mexico, to take a writing seminar with Natalie Goldberg. I had read her book *Writing Down the Bones*, which Bette had given me, and decided I wanted to explore the possibility of expressing myself on paper, to express spirit.

After the seminar, I visited Santa Fe for the weekend and felt as if a huge voice from the mountain screamed out, "You're home!" When I got back to Montclair I told Bette that we should retire in New Mexico, that I loved the place. She had traveled there five years earlier with Claire to go skiing and I knew she loved it as well. Bette had started her Master's degree in social work at Rutgers University and did not want to move until she had completed the course work, but I was chomping at the bit to leave Montclair. I could not stand going to the office and was spending a great amount of time at our seashore house, on Long Island, writing and doing meditations.

Howard kept expanding his real estate business and leveraging every deal to the maximum. I was getting anxious financially, as the borrowing was up to his limit and might impinge on my half of the company. Once, when I was in the office, I asked him, "Howard, I don't understand what you are doing. You ask my opinion about a deal, but when I give you the negatives you go ahead and do it anyway. You are leveraging so much that I feel at times that you are trying to prove to me that you can make huge money on your own, and in the process you are putting my funds at risk."

He was leaning back in his chair with his feet up on the lower drawer of his desk. His eye was twitching, indicating discomfiture.

He said I was a difficult person to compete with. At that point, his phone rang and without a second thought he picked it up and cut me off. He stayed on the phone for an hour, and I waited because I wanted to pursue the conversation. I did not understand how we were competing; he was in real estate and I was writing while still doing some limited trading. After he hung up I tried to re-initiate the talk but he dismissed me brusquely and walked out of the office.

I was fuming. I felt again at the receiving end of displeasure—echoes of the way my father had treated me all those many years. That was it. I proceeded to implement our legal separation and get my money out of our holding company. We had a document on how to dissociate but it still took my most delicate negotiation to obtain what I wanted. Three months passed before the lawyers and accountants finalized our agreement.

I talked to Bette and told her I wanted to move to New Mexico, and that I could no longer stand the office and saw nothing keeping us in New Jersey. Bette researched the possibility of completing her MSW in New Mexico, and found Highlands University willing to accept her credits from Rutgers. We put our house on the market. Once again, my step was light, and I moved forward with great hope and joy.

On a beautiful June morning in 1990, Howard and I met in our office with the Cadwalder lawyers and signed all the documents closing our association. I was saddened to see a friendship and relationship of over thirty-four years come to an abrupt end. The treasurer of the company, who had worked with me since 1978, also quit the company and has since started her own business of financial management for individuals. Bette and I had sold our house and the moving men had picked up all our furnishings the day before. After my closure with Howard, I picked up Bette and rushed to New York to sign the closing papers on our house. In one fell swoop I was out of Montclair and business dealings with Howard.

Real life is not like the movies, where everyone lives happily ever after. Rather, life is always a combination of the light and dark sides. Joy comes from the ability to embrace both, and particularly to grow from the trials. The next five years were a period of great spiritual growth, at the end of which I wrote *Inescapable Journey*, my previously published book. After the completion of that book I went to recharge at the seashore where I seem to drink deeply from the well of understanding. It was during that summer of 1995 that I was able to finally resolve my issues with my father, and with Howard in the process.

EPILOGUE

Dagaz

*The rune of breakthrough and complete
transformation in attitude.*

In the spring of 1992, I met Michael Morgan through the introduction of some Taoist friends. I did some spiritual initiations with
him in Egypt. The story of those initiations and breakthroughs has
been related in my first book, *Inescapable Journey: A Spiritual Adventure*. My story here goes beyond those adventures, yet backtracks in
its path to my father. Michael Morgan is the channel for Yokar, a
spirit from the Most High Realm. In early summer of 1995 Michael
Morgan visited me in New Mexico and gave some teachings on the
methods of spiritual healing and psychic development. At the time
I had asthma, which I had not experienced since the days with my
father. I asked Michael if I could have a private session with Yokar.
It was a beautiful sunny day, and as we sat outside on my terrace,
Michael set up his recording equipment and went into trance. His
body collapsed in his chair as his spirit left and Yokar came in.
Michael's body trembled and he snorted a few times as Yokar man-
ifested. With his eyes closed, Michael's head moved up and down
and side to side; I knew Yokar was scanning my energy. Then he
spoke: "Greetings to you from the Most High."

"Greetings to you, Yokar. I have a few questions."

"Proceed."

"I'm having tremendous asthma attacks—in fact, one night Bette had to rush me to the emergency room of the hospital to obtain relief. What is going on?"

"It is a question of worthiness."

"Yokar, that is a simple answer, but why? And how do I resolve it?"

Yokar proceeded to tell me that I still had not resolved my relationship with my father. I had had a heart attack in self-hatred. I had beaten my father at his own game. Subconsciously I could not accept a son beating his father, and the self-hatred had stopped the life force from flowing through me and induced a stoppage of my heart. Yokar explained that my father had thrown down a gauntlet, and that I had no choice except to fight or cower into submission. In either case, it was a no-win situation, and in either case an issue I would have to deal with in later life. The third choice—of walking away, on my own path—would still have left me unresolved about my self-worth vis-à-vis my father's bullying me at my critical stage in college.

Yokar continued. "A father should never give a son such an ultimatum. However, this was the case, and you chose to fight. So you really need to work with the old, reptilian part of your brain, the limbic, to get in touch with and resolve that energy."

"What do you mean, psychotherapy? I did enough of that after my heart attack."

"No. Your work with Dr. Morano was good. But psychotherapy can only go so far in the brain. It cannot reach the limbic, which is beyond reasoning because it is an implanted pattern. The limbic must be accessed through reliving the experience in order to clear it."

"Please explain, Yokar."

Yokar detailed my work, referring to the class on psychic ability that Michael had just given in Santa Fe. What Yokar had taught through Michael was an advanced alchemical teaching which went beyond what I had learned from Master Chia in the Taoist Kan and Li practices. The various Kan and Li energy meditations were designed to raise our vibration by reversing the fire and water elements in the body. Yokar's work went further by teaching us how to pull water out of fire, and fire out of water.

Yokar explained. "You must do these exercises with a concentration of the limbic. Bring your consciousness to the back part of your brain three fingers above your neck connection. When complete, sit down and meditate. In your meditation, relive your experience when you were nineteen, in college, and your father confronted you. When you are finished, you can then open up your aura." Yokar had given instructions on how to seal the aura so as to keep all the energy at its apex, without diffusion, then at the end of the exercises to open the aura. One way was to clap the hands in front of the throat, then sweep the hands in a downward motion. The other was the sign of the cross. I found it interesting that anyone entering a church and making the sign of the cross was opening their aura fully.

I asked Yokar: "Why back to nineteen and college, and what do I do with it?"

"That incident at St. Lawrence, at nineteen, is when your father confronted you about you painting and artistic and creative endeavors. It changed your life, your path. What you must do in reliving the moment is to become your father. Do not try to be yourself as victim or another preconceived idea. Be your father fully with his mind, appearance, mannerism, and agenda when he came to see you."

"But then what, Yokar? What comes out and what do I do with it?"

"I do not want to lead you in any way as to what you might find or discover. Just be fully connected to the energy of that situation. We will monitor you and you can call Michael for guidance should you need it. We will be available."

I was intrigued as to where this might lead. Bette and I had rented a small beach house for August and part of September, as we had sold ours at the end of Long Island, where back in 1980 I had first opened my father's diaries about his war experience. I told Yokar, and asked if the water environment might be conducive to these exercises and meditations.

Yokar responded. "Yes, definitely. Water is very female in nature and always good for receiving. You must be open to receive whatever comes through. We feel Michael's body heating up, so we must leave."

"O.K., thank you, Yokar."

"You are welcome. Blessings of the Most High to you—and good journey, my friend."

"Thank you, Yokar." And he was gone.

Michael's body collapsed as Yokar's spirit left. After a few moments Michael came to, struggling as he opened his eyes to the strong New Mexico light.

Three weeks later, Bette and I were on the beach in Amagansett, Long Island. The house we rented was across the street from my sister, Marianne.

Just before we left, my intuition had told me to pull a rune from a carved piece of a reading that had been made for me, two years back, by my friend Steven Nickeson. Steven was very adept at reading the Viking runes—in fact, he looked like an old Viking—and had interpreted a throw of the runes I had made. After the reading, as a gift, he had carved each symbol I had picked into a cut piece of the heart of a piñon branch. He gave me the pieces in a beautifully decorated silk bag. The rune I pulled out of the bag for my summer trip was Dagaz. This rune is the symbol and energy of breakthrough and complete transformation in attitude. I wondered how this energy would play out.

The first breakthrough was a reconnection with my sister. Marianne and I went for long walks on the beach where we could talk about our parents, our separate paths, and how we now came together each having worked through our various issues. The reconnection was spread over a month of walks, tennis, and sailing, giving us a fun background to process our youth and now meet once again as adults.

I did Yokar's psychic practices three to four times a week.

In the meditations, I placed myself totally as my father, trying to figure out how to control a nineteen-year-old rebellious college student. As my father, I wanted my son to become an engineer and be serious about business. I wanted his grades to improve and for him to quit this nonsensical art which was diverting him from a true calling in real life. He probably had a girlfriend who was encouraging him in these artistic endeavors and influenced him away from the family traditions of commerce. As head of the Saks clan, I would make him toe the line—or else I would disinherit him and cut off all contact. He would be no son of mine.

I became so totally my father that I found myself scratching my abdomen where his open ulcer drain was located, and my lips stretched across my teeth in displeasure as he had so often done. Suddenly, during the third meditation playing my father's role, I broke out of my sitting position in a total fury, ready to kill him. Had he been alive, I would have pulverized him physically. I was so upset I was up all night. First thing in the morning, I called Michael Morgan and explained what happened.

"Is Yokar around?" I asked.

"Yes, but I can't give you a session—I'm too busy. If you have one or two questions, I can ask him internally."

"Okay, what do I do now?" I knew Yokar had been monitoring the situation. There was a pause.

"Yokar says, 'Good—you have fully connected with the energy. Stay with it.' And that's all he'll say."

"Great, Michael. I want to kill the son of a bitch."

"I understand—Yokar put me through some similar exercises. Good luck! I've got to go!"

I went back to the meditation practices and eventually something miraculous happened. I became a witness. As this happened, I lost any and all emotionality involved with the situation. My meditation was proceeding like an old movie I had seen many times, with the actors coming on stage with their cued lines at the appropriate moments. I sat in awe at the whole scene and then understood that had I not confronted my father my tremendous energy might never have been unleashed. Because of my father setting the stage, I came to understand energy in some of its most basic forms—money and power. I learned to respect these energies and eventually through all my spiritual work came to understand that these energies were only variations of the life force—the purest form emanating from the Most High realm. I understood that with making money and obtaining power in this Earthly reality came the need to accept and take responsibility for all the ramifications. I realized that had I pursued the artistic life I might not have had the challenge, determination, and wherewithal to engage the life force energies and the path of Spirit. I felt, in a convoluted way, thankful to my father for his ultimatum those many years ago. I called Michael again and related my experiences. "So Michael, am I complete now?"

"No, no—now comes the really tough part that Yokar also put me through. You need to come to love your father unconditionally."

"What! How can I do that? Even if I tried I'm not sure I would succeed. My monkey mind would conjure the thought that indeed I loved him unconditionally, but it may not be true in my deep self."

"Exactly. You need to experience that love to the fullest in every molecule of your body."

"Hell, Michael, how do I do that?"

"You need to picture clearly in your meditation that you're willing to give up your life for your father, which is the ultimate sacrifice. I accomplished it by understanding that I had by far outgrown my own father spiritually and I could feel enough love for him that I could give up my life to give him the opportunity to grow and move toward the Most High Realm."

"Jesus! Michael, that's a hell of a task. I don't know if I can do it!"

"Yes, you can. Just do it. Later." And he hung up the phone.

Once again I started meditating in the living room of the beach house late at night. It was quiet and I could see the stars outside and the billowy clouds moving under them as the southwest breeze came in through the sliding doors. I closed my eyes and pictured a scene that happened when I was in my early twenties. My father and I went to a garage where we were to pick up his car. I got in the passenger's side and closed the door, waiting for him to pay the bill. The next thing I knew he was in an altercation with the garage attendant about a scratch on the fender. The yelling reached a high pitch and it looked like the attendant was about to punch my father out. My father was tall, but with his ulcer and vulnerability a child could have pushed him over. I got out of the car and placed myself between my father and the attendant. In the actual scene, everyone calmed down and a resolution was reached about the scratch. In my meditation, however, I accentuated the scene. In this version, the attendant reached for a tire iron and beat me to death as I protected my father. I could picture the scene but I could not accept the outcome. Slowly, after several tries, I came to feel that love for my father more deeply. In the process, I hit a brick wall. What was, or is, the difference between loving my father unconditionally and anyone else walking the planet? I called Michael Morgan again.

He chuckled softly at me. "Now you get it. You now understand deep in your cellular structure that there is no difference. We are all connected. We are connected to everything."

I responded. "As the Native Americans and the Taoists say, 'All my relations.' But Michael, there are several people out there who are not my favorite human beings. Also, doesn't this contradict Yokar's teaching, 'Engage the energy'?"

"Listen, Claude, if you can complete your meditation about unconditional love for your father, who was not a savory person, what's the difference with everyone else on their journey? As far as 'Engage the energy' goes, this does not contradict what we are talking about. In the real case of the garage attendant you engaged the energy—you brought your energy up to the attendant's level and therefore neutralized the situation; it was a standoff. But in the process you were defending your father. Why? Love, my friend. Deep down, it was love."

"Okay, I hear you. This is going to take some work."

"As Yokar says, once you agree to walk the path of Spirit there is no turning back. And the work is hard. Have a good time! Bye!"

I went back to my psychic work and meditation. I came to realize that one of my standard meditations, the Tibetan Buddhist Chenrizig practice, a meditation of compassion, was related to what Yokar was trying to get me to feel at a deep cellular level. Briefly, the Chenrizig meditation involves sending compassion to all sentient beings through a combination of visualizations and energy work. When I do the meditation I always begin by sending compassion to a particular police trooper in an airport where I once was. At the time, I had phlebitis in my right leg. I was in much pain and concerned about connecting to my next flight. I leaned heavily on Bette. We were trying to decide whether to walk back two gates from our landing gate to the train shuttle or take a short cut, out of the security area, through the main airport, to our next gate, which would be shorter and less painful. We started to walk out of the security area when I realized my leg was in too much pain. We turned around to walk back when this tall stern-faced officer in a beige-grey uniform with a black stripe on the side told me we had crossed the security line. We had literally gone over it by three feet, and he was watching us as I struggled to walk. I responded, "Officer, I have a bad leg, and you saw us. We only just crossed the line. I need to go back and catch the shuttle."

"I'm sorry, but those are the regulations. You will have to go around through the security check."

"Come on, we haven't been anywhere. You watched us."

He drew himself up to his full height and put his hand on his night stick. He knitted his brows and his dark eyes pierced into me. Even his dark hair and shaving shadow seemed menacing. "Are you about to argue with me, sir?"

As he said this, a picture of a Nazi SS storm trooper flashed through my mind. My martial arts training swirled in my mind— deflect the blow. I smiled at him. "No, officer, I wouldn't argue with you. It's a no-win situation." And I turned my back and hobbled along on Bette's shoulder.

I always use this situation in my compassion meditation, but now I had to go one step further. Could I exercise unconditional love toward this policeman and everything he represented in his demeanor? I was also very cognizant of Yokar's teachings and my own martial arts experience to engage the energy to the appropriate level to neutralize the situation.

I went back, alternately meditating on dying for my father, the airport officer, and Howard, who showed up in the meditations. I realized Howard had been a variation on the theme, a mirror to me about my own self-worth. I needed to walk my own path, which diverged from his real estate dealings; in my meditations I smiled and sent him blessings on his journey. I felt complete with Howard but three weeks elapsed before I could truly feel at the cellular level that I was fully engaging the energy. If the outcome meant my dying for the other person's growth then I could yield. I remember asking Marc once how he could love all the different personalities in the ashram. He replied, "I love them all, Dad, but it doesn't mean I like them all." I was jubilant at having reached the unconditional love place in my being.

In the process of meditating on unconditional love, I revisited my father's deathbed at New York Hospital. I could approach the scene, while he pleaded for his mother, with open heart. I felt tears well up and could not only express my love for him but, perhaps more importantly, verbalize my thanks to him for everything he had taught me. I realized I had carefully chosen my incarnation and that Father had provided the perfect scenario for me to develop and express my inner strengths—for me to become fully who I was. In my meditation I bowed to him in respect and prayed for his spirit to have a good journey in rejoining the Most High Realm.

Again I called Michael to report. I could feel his smile over the phone. "Good work. Now work on your worthiness issue to speak out and teach on behalf of Spirit so as to totally clear your asthma."

"Oh God, Michael, will this ever end?"

"No, it doesn't, because your vibration keeps moving up and you need to adjust. Keep up the good work."

The story is never-ending. I decided that the remaining two weeks at the seashore would be dedicated to sailing, the beach, and totally hedonistic endeavors. I kept my meditations to a minimum.

The last day was a beautiful, sun-filled, wind-blown experience with large kicking waves and spume blowing high in the air. I stood on the empty September beach arm-in-arm with Bette in total awe at God's creations and power of destruction. The light and the dark. Tears flowed down my cheeks as I felt in communion with the planet and the entire universe. As we walked back to the beach house my hand reached into my pocket and I pulled out the carved rune that had been with me all this time. The Viking rune Dagaz—the rune of breakthrough. I smiled down at it as we walked and realized the appropriateness of the draw.

The next morning at 6:00 A.M. we flew out of the Islip airport. As the plane circled north and west around New York City, I peered out the window down onto Manhattan. All those years down there in the gladiator pits of the commodity world with its grand self-importance. And for what? From this perspective, Manhattan looked like toy blocks on a spit of rock jutting out in the middle of water and land. One earthquake or tidal wave and what statement would man have made, in retrospect, in the history of Mother Earth?

Glossary of Commodities Terms

arabica coffee: better quality coffee, usually with some acidity.

afloat: coffees that have been shipped and are on a vessel.

back months: future months beyond the closest two trading positions on a futures market.

bull market: market moving up, indicating more buyers than sellers.

certification: approval of coffee that has been submitted for delivery to futures market.

commodities: something of value traded for future deliveries.

forward: commodities traded for delivery in the future (months).

futures: commodity markets traded in coffee (commodities) on an exchange market in forward months (i.e. May-July-September).

futures market: where futures are traded.

growths: different crops or types of coffee.

hedged (position): owning a physical commodity and selling the futures market to minimize fluctuation and lock in a differential (gain or loss); the reverse can also be performed.

ICA: International Coffee Agreement.

ICO: International Coffee Organization.

long (position): owning a commodity in the hope of selling at a higher profit; i.e., to go long: to purchase something to resell at higher value.

margin call: a call for more collateral by a broker to protect from loss on a contract.

ONC: Office National du Café.

open interest (position): contracts outstanding, not yet fulfilled, either long or short on a futures market.

position: a view or placement in a market (see long; short; hedged).

privilege: a giving of allowance to a buyer in terms of time and money (i.e., 30-day privilege in warehouse), meaning the sellers absorb costs of financing, insurance, etc.

quota: limit of export by member countries of coffee under the ICA.

> **basket quota:** limit of import by member countries under the ICA for small producing countries who are not members of ICA.

robusta: a lower grade coffee with little or no acidity, used partially as a filler. Also used in instants and vending machines.

short (position): having sold a commodity in the hope to buy it back cheaper in the future.

> **go short (sell short):** selling a commodity without owning it, in the hope of buying it at a lower price.

> **go short markets:** sell the futures short.

SINT: Saks International, Inc.

squeeze: a financial pressure caused by shortages; the act of causing the shortage, forcing the prices up.

tender: to deliver a commodity to the futures market.

> **retender:** to redeliver a commodity to the futures market when originally tendered to you.

terminal market: term synonymous with futures market, used more often in England.

$\mathscr{H}$EARTSFIRE $\mathscr{B}$OOKS

When we follow spirit, we are transformed by the fire of the heart, the fire of life. *Heartsfire Books* publishes the stories of people who are following spirit whether in their personal or professional lives. These stories often include methods that can be used to connect to or develop spirit from within. They encourage all of us to be in touch with our inner selves and to become more aware of the world beyond. *Heartsfire Books* publishes the message of spirit, the message of the heart. We hope our titles challenge you to go beyond yourself.

If you have a manuscript that you feel is suitable for *Heartsfire Books*, we would love to hear from you. Send a query letter and three or four sample chapters to:

Acquisitions Editor
Heartsfire Books
500 N. Guadalupe Street, Suite G-465
Santa Fe, NM 87501

Titles in Print:

Inescapable Journey:
A Spiritual Adventure
by Claude Saks

The Emerald Covenant:
Spiritual Rites of Passage
by Michael E. Morgan

The Search for David:
A Cosmic Journey of Love
by George Schwimmer

Strong Brew:
One Man's Prelude to Change
by Claude Saks

Forthcoming Titles:

Gifts from Spirit:
A Sceptic's Path
by Dennis Augustine
(April 1997)

Message from the Sparrows:
Engaging Consciousness
by Taylor Morris (May 1997)